Earl Morris & Southwestern Archaeology

MAHOOD

Earl Morris & Southwestern Archaeology

FLORENCE C. LISTER & ROBERT H. LISTER

UNIVERSITY OF NEW MEXICO PRESS Albuquerque

 Manufactured in the United States of America. Library of Congress Catalog Card Number 68-19737. International Standard Book Number 0-8263-0455-9.
Second paperbound printing 1981

The authors and publisher gratefully acknowledge the cooperation of the following institutions for granting permission to use photographs from their publications: The American Museum of Natural History (from Anthropological Papers, No. 26, pt. 2); Carnegie Institution of Washington, D.C., (*Anthropological Studies in the La Plata District Southwestern Colorado and Northwestern New Mexico,* by Earl H. Morris, Institution Publication No. 519); and the Smithsonian Institution (*Annual Report of the Bureau of American Ethnology,* 1919).

To those
who plowed the first furrow and
dug the first trench

Robert Frost

A MISSIVE MISSILE

Someone in ancient Mas d'azil
Once took a little pebble wheel
And dotted it with red for me,
And sent it to me years and years—
A million years to be precise—
Across the barrier of ice.
Two round dots and a ripple streak,
So vivid as to seem to speak.
But what imperfectly appears
Is whether the two dots were tears,
Two tear drops, one for either eye,
And the wave line a shaken sigh.
But no, the color used is red.
Not tears but drops of blood instead.
The line must be a jagged blade.
The sender must have had to die,
And wanted some one now to know
His death was sacrificial-votive.
So almost clear and yet obscure.
If only anyone were sure
A motive then was still a motive.
O you who bring this to my hand,
You are no common messenger
(Your badge of office is a spade).
It grieves me to have had you stand
So long for nothing. No reply—
There is no answer, I'm afraid,

Across the icy barrier
For my obscure petitioner.
Suppose his ghost is standing by
Importunate to give the hint
And be successfully conveyed.
How anyone can fail to see
Where perfectly in form and tint
The metaphor, the symbol lies!
Why will I not analogize?
(I do too much in some men's eyes.)
Oh slow uncomprehending me,
Enough to make a spirit moan
Or rustle in a bush or tree.
I have the ochre-written flint,
The two dots and the ripple line.
The meaning of it is unknown,
Or else I fear entirely mine,
All modern, nothing ancient in't,
Unsatisfying to us each.
Far as we aim our signs to reach,
Far as we often make them reach,
Across the soul-from-soul abyss,
There is an aeon-limit set
Beyond which we are doomed to miss.
Two souls may be too widely met.
That sad-with-distance river beach
With mortal longing may beseech;
It cannot speak as far as this.

POEM COMPOSED ON RECEIPT OF AN ANASAZI ARROWHEAD FROM THE LA PLATA DISTRICT, SOUTHERN COLORADO, A GIFT FROM EARL H. MORRIS

Contents

ABORIGINAL CULTURAL CHRONOLOGIES, SAN JUAN DRAINAGE

1920 Chronology	*Morris' Chronology, 1920-27*	*Pecos Classification, 1927*	*Roberts' Classification, 1935*	*Date*, A.D.
Late Black-on-white pottery stage, or Cliff Dweller	Full Pueblo (open sites) Cliff Dweller (cave sites)	Pueblo III	Great Pueblo	1300 1200 1100
Early Black-on-white pottery stage, or Pre Pueblos	Late Pre Pueblo	Pueblo II	Developmental Pueblo	1000 900
	Early Pre Pueblo or Slab House	Pueblo I		800 700
Basket Makers	Post Basket Maker	Basket Maker III	Modified Basket Maker	600 500
	Basket Makers	Basket Maker II	Basket Maker	400 300 200 100
		Basket Maker I		

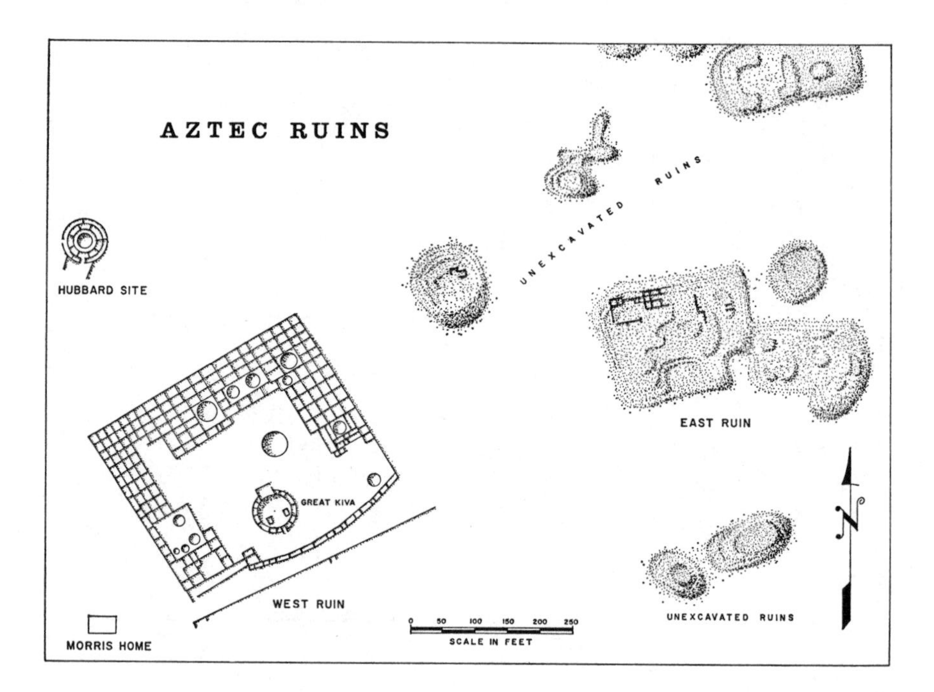
AZTEC RUINS
UNEXCAVATED RUINS
HUBBARD SITE
GREAT KIVA
EAST RUIN
WEST RUIN
MORRIS HOME
0 50 100 150 200 250
SCALE IN FEET
UNEXCAVATED RUINS

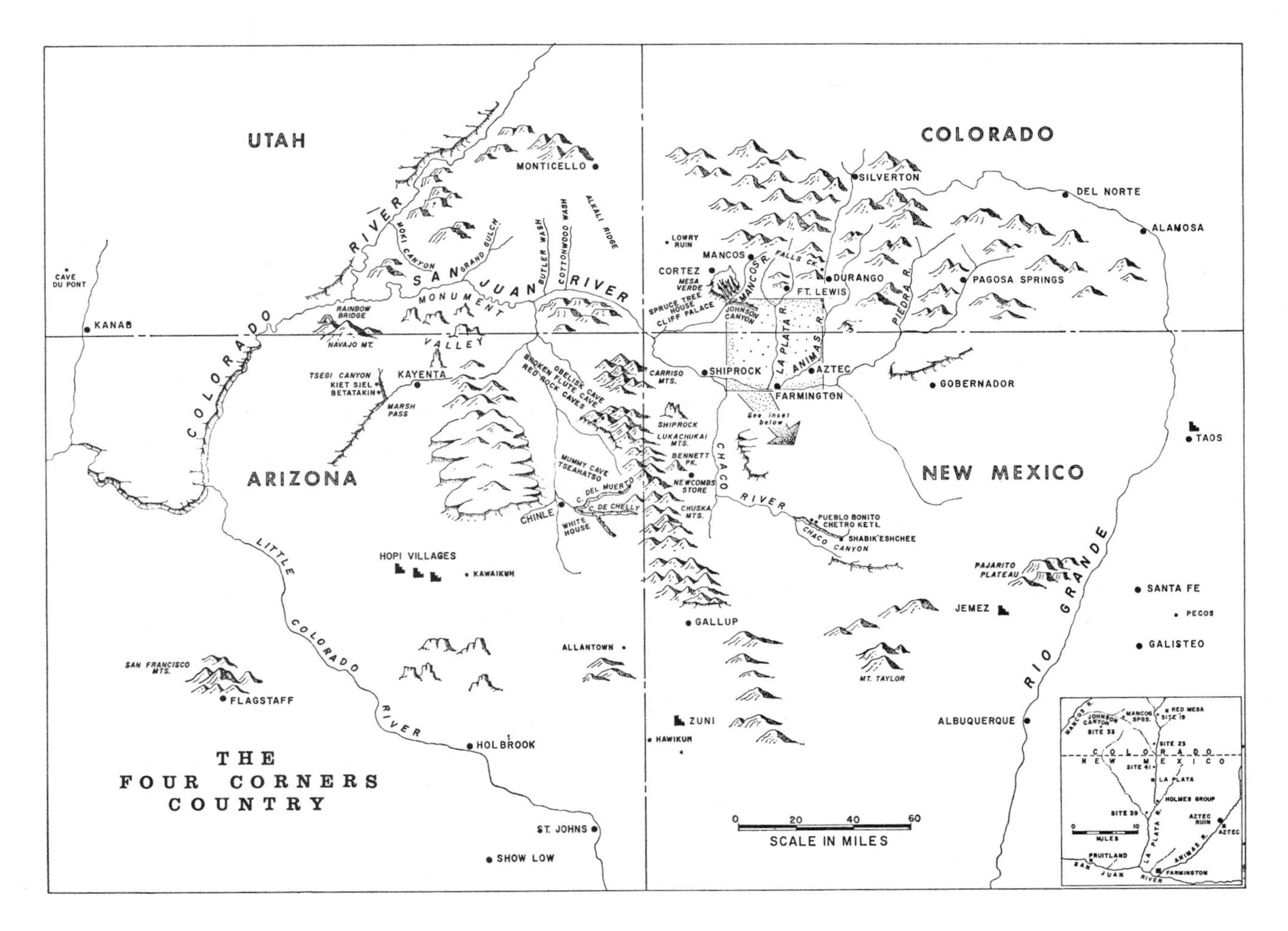

THE FOUR CORNERS COUNTRY

Foreword

By unique coincidence the life of Earl Halstead Morris so closely meshed with the flowering of scientific interest in the archaeology of the San Juan Drainage of New Mexico, Colorado, Utah, and Arizona, that in telling of the former the latter naturally follows. This book proposes to give a picture of a man and at the same time to trace the physical and intellectual discoveries which led to a large segment of American archaeological thought being focused upon the Southwest.

The pattern of the book conveniently falls into three basic sections, each one woven about a broad scholarly problem upon which Earl was one of many persons engaged. They progress, as did Southwestern archaeological research in general, from late periods of aboriginal life just prior to the Spanish Conquest backward in time to the dawn of the Christian Era. Few busy lives—and Earl's least of all—lend themselves to strict chronological treatment. Therefore, there has unavoidably been a certain amount of retracing of steps as Earl's story and the problems of regional archaeology unfold.

It should be stated at the outset that no treatment is given the Middle American work carried on for five seasons by Morris. Although he acquired considerable fame from those endeavors, their retelling would present as much of a distraction in this account as they did in Earl's life. Furthermore, both Earl and his wife, Ann, wrote popular books about that work.

Because this manuscript in part deals with the growth of ideas about Southwestern aboriginal cultures, portions of it are of a technical nature. For the professional reader it is hoped that the discussions will serve as a synthesis and, through the inclusion of unpublished Morris notes, a source of new data. For the nonprofessional reader these sections should at least serve as a reminder that all archaeology is not donning a pith helmet, mounting a glamorous expedition, and marching off into the bush. The old terminology has been employed in describing early work, and names such as Basket Maker are written in the old style rather than being compounded as they are used today. Research occurring after 1927, when terms were formalized into the so-called Pecos Classification, has been fitted into that taxonomic framework. The chart (see p. xi) is designed to show the relative relationship of distinct names for identical cultures and to lessen confusion for the person who is not an archaeological specialist.

Our greatest helper was unquestionably Earl himself who carefully kept a file of his voluminous professional correspondence from the period of his college days until his death, or more than forty years. The contents of such letters and the notations contained in field journals and notebooks, heretofore unpublished, have been used extensively to document this text. His printed writings have been drawn upon to illustrate his professional ideology and progress.

The period of Earl's youth has been sketched from information freely supplied by a number of friends of those days. To John B. Arrington of Farmington, New Mexico, who because of blindness had a Navajo boy write in his behalf; Sam Bousman of Santa Cruz, California; Dudley Ewing of Durango, Colorado, and Santa Barbara, California; Mrs. Lucille Hoppe of St. Petersburg, Florida; Mrs. Edna Jackson of Clearwater, Florida; and Mrs. Maybelle Mensinger of Montrose, California, we are indebted for background material about the Morris family and the role Earl played in his community. Others kindly wrote of the circumstances of Scott Morris's death and the condition of the ruins at Aztec before excavation was begun. Among these we thank A. G. Johnson, Harry McWilliams, and Luther Hampton, all residents of Aztec, New Mexico. A special acknowledgment is due a college friend, Dr. Robert L. Stearns, distinguished law professor, past president of the University of Colorado, and until recently Head of the Boettcher Foundation in Denver, Colorado.

Response to our inquiries came from a number of those men who shared field experiences with Earl. E. M. Weyer, Jr., former editor of *Natural History* and later Director of the School of American Research, told of his escape from a near fatal plunge in Canyon del Muerto. Dwight W. Morrow, Jr., of New Hope, Pennsylvania, son of an illustrious American diplomat and brother-in-law of Charles A. Lindbergh, described his outings on the La Plata and at Red Rocks. Willard

Fraser of Billings, Montana, son-in-law of the New England poet, Robert Frost, and now engaged in business and politics, recalled many trips with the Morrises, both along the La Plata and on the Navajo Reservation. Of the company of diggers, however, our greatest thanks are extended to Oscar Tatman, of Benicia, California, who at the age of seventy-seven years, sent us a dozen sheets in precise longhand telling of some of the adventures he had in forty years of friendship and association with Earl. Mrs. Elberta Smith of Boulder, Colorado, recently deceased, who knew Earl at the University of Colorado Museum, and Mrs. Kisa Noguchi Sasaki, who as an art student at the University of Colorado, made many of the infinitely complex basketry and sandal drawings for reports on those subjects, gave us their appraisal of Earl as a man and fellow worker.

The list of professional colleagues who shared in the development of Southwestern archaeology, and who were most generous of their time in speaking to us of Earl is long. Among them were J. O. Brew, Director of Peabody Museum, Harvard University; Mrs. Harriet Cosgrove, retired, former associate of Peabody Museum, Harvard University; Emil Haury, Department of Anthropology, University of Arizona; Neil M. Judd, retired, former Curator of American Archaeology, United States National Museum; Jesse L. Nusbaum, retired, formerly Senior Archeologist, National Park Service; Frank H. H. Roberts, Jr., former Head of the Bureau of American Ethnology, Smithsonian Institution, Washington, D.C., now deceased; Karl Ruppert, deceased, formerly archaeologist for the Carnegie Institution; Anna O. Shepard, ceramic technologist for the Carnegie Institution and geologist for the United States Geological Survey; Robert E. Smith, formerly archaeologist for the Carnegie Institution, now resident of Marblehead, Massachusetts.

Of professional associates we must single out three—Robert F. Burgh, deceased, formerly of the Peabody Museum West of the Pecos, Tucson, Arizona, who worked closely with Earl during many of his darkest hours; Nels C. Nelson who, nearly blind at eighty-five, recalled his tutelage of the young Morris; and that remarkable man of American archaeology, A. V. Kidder, deceased, who graciously devoted a half-day to reminiscences of Earl. To two others of this professional category we are particularly grateful. To Joe Ben Wheat, Curator of Anthropology of the University of Colorado Museum, and to Hugo G. Rodeck, the Museum's Director, we say, "Mil gracias" for encouragement and aid and for permitting free access to the collection of Morris papers, photographs, and artifacts at the museum.

We also wish to acknowledge the cooperation of the National Park

Service who spell "archaeology" without its middle a. Among those who gave us help were Paul Berger, Superintendent of Canyon de Chelly National Monument; Dick Draper, a Navajo college student who guided us and a power wagon up the Canyon del Muerto; Johnwill Faris, formerly of Aztec National Monument and now Superintendent of White Sands National Monument, Alamogordo, New Mexico; Paul R. Franke, retired, formerly of Mesa Verde National Park; Homer Hastings, formerly of Aztec National Monument, now Superintendent of Fort Union National Monument, Watrous, New Mexico; James A. Lancaster, Archeologist, formerly attached to the Wetherill Mesa Project and now associate of the University of Colorado Mesa Verde Research Center; Mrs. Jean Pinkley, formerly Chief Archeologist, Mesa Verde National Park, now at Pecos Pueblo National Monument; Roland Richert, Archeologist, now at the Southwest Archeological Center, Globe, Arizona; Homer A. Robinson, Supervisory Park Ranger, Canyon de Chelly National Monument; Charlie R. Steen, Regional Archeologist, Santa Fe, New Mexico; R. Gordon Vivian, deceased, formerly head of stabilization and excavation of Southwestern Monuments and Director of the Southwest Archeological Center housed in Gila Pueblo, Globe, Arizona; Jack J. Wade, Chief Park Ranger, Mesa Verde National Park; and Don Watson, formerly Chief Archeologist, Mesa Verde National Park and now operator of a trading post at Cortez, Colorado.

Acknowledgments are made of assistance from several persons who made data available prior to its publication. These are Edward Dittert of the Navajo Reservoir Project, Museum of New Mexico, and Jesse D. Jennings and Floyd Sharrock of the Upper Colorado River Basin Archeological Salvage Project, University of Utah.

Thanks are also due the Committee on Research and Creative Work, of the University of Colorado, for modest grants to aid in preparation of this manuscript.

Above all else, we wish to thank Earl's widow, Lucile Bowman Morris, and his daughters, Elizabeth Ann Morris Gell and Sarah Lane Morris, for their wholehearted cooperation and interest in this project. We hope the results here presented will not disappoint them.

I.

To Set the Stage

No corner of North America has as many spectacular archaeological remains as the relatively arid basin of the San Juan Drainage of southern Colorado and northern New Mexico and Arizona. Yet many of these finds have been known for less than one hundred years. Only as white settlers began moving into the perimeters of this area in the last several decades of the nineteenth century and the first of the twentieth, were many of these major antiquities encountered for the first time.

However, rumors of their existence across the broad sweep of land from the Rio Grande to the San Juan had been current since 1776 when Escalante's party blazed a route from Santa Fe west to the Colorado River. This entrada was followed during the next century by trappers, prospectors, geologists, Mormon scouts, army officers, and travelers, all of whom reported seeing old settlements. The many ruins of bleak Chaco Canyon south of the San Juan, which was called by some the River of the Village Indians, were known and had been mapped by the time the United States acquired New Mexico in 1848. They were thought to represent the most northerly remains of groups ancestral to Indians residing in the neat Pueblo towns along the Rio Grande.

The Hayden Survey of 1874-77, an all-encompassing government reconnaissance of the region of the San Juan mining discoveries, marked the beginning of true archaeological knowledge of the new

Colorado empire. Among its members was W. H. Holmes, of the United States National Museum. He was assigned the task of recording the antiquities of the area covered by the survey; he visited a large number of ruins from the Dolores and McElmo rivers south to the Mancos and La Plata rivers. A few years later he published the first study of Southwestern pottery, little realizing the flood of such publications which would follow. A fellow member of the Hayden Survey was the famous early-day photographer, W. H. Jackson, who not only captured on cumbersome glass plates the fascination of the northern San Juan country but traveled south to both Chaco Canyon, New Mexico, and the Chinle Valley in northeastern Arizona. South of the San Juan area two brothers, Victor and Cosmos Mindeleff, made the first architectural studies of the pueblo ruins for the Bureau of American Ethnology.

At the same time, interest in the living Indians was being awakened in the East. Adolph Bandelier had begun his journeys through the region to popularize America's first citizens. The Hemenway Southwestern Archaeological Expedition, under the lavish patronage of Mrs. Hemenway, worked in Arizona. At the Hopi towns in north-central Arizona was Jesse Walter Fewkes, later a key figure in the archaeology of the San Juan.

Perhaps the most exciting archaeological adventure of the early era, and one which was to precipitate a concentrated search for antiquities, took place in the northern reaches of the region when Richard Wetherill and a friend (and later brother-in-law), Charlie Mason, in searching for stray cattle happened upon several of the largest cliff dwellings of the Mesa Verde. For several subsequent seasons they and four Wetherill brothers camped in the caves of the region, digging in the ruins during the day. In an effort to recover relics, they thoroughly turned the dirt deposits in all rooms of the old structures nestled in natural arches on the cliff faces. The amount of materials thus obtained was staggering. It seemed that the men of old, perhaps several thousand strong, had tidied up their quarters, sealed some of the doorways with masonry, and had walked away fully expecting to return one day to resume a temporarily interrupted routine. They did not bother to carry many of their possessions with them. There were baskets, stacked one inside another, on masonry benches around the rooms; pots left beside a hearth; articles of clothing still hanging on pegs; mealing bins cleaned and ready for use; caches of corn and other foodstuffs. And beneath the floors or laid out in certain rooms were the dead, wrapped in mouldy feather robes and time-stiffened sheaths of woven matting, and accompanied by funerary offerings of pottery, basketry, and stonework of splendid workmanship. This was a diversified and advanced culture which the Wetherills had found. To their credit, although they are accused of dynamiting walls and of acts of thoughtless destruction, they did observe facets of the culture and they did keep records of the source of articles recovered.

In 1888 and 1889 the first Wetherill collection was exhibited in Denver, and the world beyond the San Juans learned of the spectacular past there; in the next few years Mesa Verde was so stripped of her treasures that the modern-day museum at the park is forced to round out its displays with many artifacts loaned by private citizens. At least five collections, containing hundreds of individual specimens, were taken by the early explorers, one of those now being on display in Finland. It was gathered by Baron Gustav Nordenskiöld, a young Swedish nobleman, who with the aid of the Wetherills, excavated on Mesa Verde in 1891. His book describing the ruins and their contents has remained a classic account.

Additional prehistoric finds were made continually in the northern San Juan country as farmers, bent on clearing the land which spread between the Dolores and the Piedra, were annoyed at the rocky mounds of former house sites encountered in their fields, making such sections unusable for cultivation. On the flanks of these mounds, furrows exposed potsherds, stone tools, sometimes human bones. Whenever men gathered, talk inevitably turned to relic hunting. The virus of "potting" has plagued the north country ever since.

Many of the ruins situated on open lands north of the San Juan River seemed to be of small size, five to twenty-five rooms, perhaps housing no more than an extended family or two. Others were considerably larger, the most conspicuous of these being one in the Animas Valley some fourteen miles upstream from its confluence with the San Juan, first noted by the settlers who had begun drifting into the area from Animas City about 1876. These people drove their wagons to widely separated points over the valley bottom which extended about a mile on either side of the fast flowing Animas River. Their community they named Wallace. They found ruins and relics throughout the valley, sometimes in the open, sometimes exposed by rain or shifts in the channel of the river. Some ancient mounds were leveled with plows and scrapers. Others were deliberately sluiced into the river bed by streams of water. Farmers crushed thousand-year-old pots upon their plow shares. On Sundays, for a family outing, groups picnicked at the large ruin, which loomed its impressive bulk along the western terrace, and gathered shaped stones to be used in their own construction projects.

The settlers saw the ruin amidst its piles of debris as an E-shaped compound of hundreds of rooms, three or four stories in height in a few portions, with roofs fallen in and crumbled walls. A group of schoolboys and their teacher searched the ruin, where they found several skeletons flexed and tied in matting.

This find so excited the men of the valley that a number of them returned to the site, where they descended to the ruin's ground floor via the schoolboys' shaft, entered the second chamber, and from there drove openings into adjacent rooms. In one, thirteen skeletons were uncovered, along with bits of matting and cotton cloth, frayed sandals, beads and ornaments, stone axes and skinning knives.

The curiosity about the ruins seemed satisfied by this venture and no further vandalism was done, other than the occasional carving of initials or the removal of stones for chimneys and foundations. In 1889 the land on which the mounds were located was patented by John R. Koontz, operator of the valley's first bar and trading post, who called his backyard site the Aztec Ruins. Shortly thereafter the post office established in the valley changed its name from Wallace to Aztec.

It was obvious to everyone that at a date before the arrival of the miners and the ranchers this area of the San Juan had been a region of extensive occupation by people of undetermined relationship and time. Popular misconception linked the local Indians with the Aztecs and gave them an age of thousands of years. So the Animas village was Aztec Ruins. The wide valley at the western skirt of Mesa Verde became Montezuma Valley. Its newly plotted town was called Cortez. A cluster of ruins southward by Sleeping Ute Mountain (now Yucca House National Monument) was named Aztec Springs.

Most of the settlers in the San Juan country thought Indian artifacts were interesting but scarcely worth the effort needed to obtain them. Cliff dwellings where articles were lightly covered by powdery dust were uncommon away from the abrupt escarpments of Mesa Verde, and the stony mounds were not so productive. But word spread that the Wetherills were reaping substantial returns for their specimens. In an economic slump leading up to the Silver Panic of 1893, when the United States adopted the gold standard, it was inevitable that the antiquities would be regarded as yet another natural resource to be exploited.

At this time Scott N. Morris, a restless young man who had drifted west from the Pennsylvania oil fields, arrived in the San Juan Basin, prepared to try to make a living for his wife and baby by operating a fleet of freight wagons. He was intrigued by these stories of discoveries of Indian relics and quickly took to pothunting. His son, Earl, then a two-year-old toddler who had been born at the New Mexico village of Chama, later wrote of his father's new enterprise.

On the way down [to Farmington], my father paused in Durango, Colorado, to lay in supplies for the winter. He had picked up a good deal of information about the Farmington country and knew that there were many ruins scattered along the valley. In talking with a group of men in Kruche's Shoe Store in Durango, he said that he intended to do some digging during the winter. A gentleman stepped up and presented his card, saying, 'I would like to have the first chance to purchase any relics that you find this winter.' It was Gilbert McClurg of Colorado Springs. Both he and his wife, Virginia McClurg, were well known lecturers at that time.

Arrived in Farmington, Father found great difficulty in securing a house in which to live. There were only about half a dozen buildings in the town then, and although the ranchers had roofs of sorts over their own heads, they had none to spare. Finally Father located an ex-slave, Albert Wooton by name, who was a rancher on what was known as the Kehoe place, although owned by S. R. Blake. Uncle Albert, as we called him, whitewashed his chicken coop, moved into it himself, and let us have his adobe house. This house was situated near the brink of the mesa about a mile southwest of the center of the town of Farmington, overlooking the swampy river valley of the Animas to the east. On the very edge of the declivity, within a stone's throw of the house, was a good-sized mound marking the remains of a small cobblestone pueblo.

The Coolidge Canal, which irrigates the Kirtland-Fruitland district, was under construction. Father got his teams on the job under a foreman so that his own time was largely free. He had talked a good deal with the local settlers about his intention to do some digging, and they all regarded it as a foolish notion because they said no one had found any unbroken pottery in that part of the country. The reason would seem to have been that none of them had dug in a definite search for pottery, and what they had turned up in breaking land for cultivation naturally had been shattered by the plow.

Father started a drift through the mound in the door yard. According to my mother's account, many times repeated to me, he worked six days without finding anything more than a few stone tools. Then, just at sundown one afternoon, he broke through a wall, and on the other side, no more than a span beneath the surface, he struck a small stone slab covering the mouth of what I now know to have been a Mesa Verde mug. When darkness fell, he went on by lantern light and before morning had taken out forty pottery vessels, many of them unbroken. He had gotten into a burial room where the bodies lay, at least in places, three deep.

This find stimulated others to begin digging. Conspicuous among these were the Brown brothers, who lived on the road to Durango, about a mile and a half east of Farmington.

By spring Father had exhumed quite a collection himself, had secured what the Brown brothers had dug up, and had traded horse gear for what a group of cowboys who had wintered at Navajo or Cottonwood Springs had scratched out during their spare time. He also acquired, either by trade or purchase, the specimens found by one De Luche, a settler in the Fruitland valley. On the way back to the mines Father displayed his collection in Durango and wired Mr. McClurg that it was subject to his inspection. At the same time McLloyd and Graham [Charles McLloyd and Howard Graham of Durango, Colorado] had brought in their first collection from the Grand Gulch country. They were rather contemptuous of Father's display because it contained only pottery and objects of bone and stone whereas their own consisted of perishable materials, including a considerable collection of "mummies." They were somewhat astonished when McClurg, who came posthaste, purchased my father's collection in preference to their own. My mother told me that there were one hundred sixty pieces of unbroken pottery in this collection. It eventually became the property of the Taylor Museum in Colorado Springs. I have seen what remains of it there, but feel certain that before the collection reached the Museum a considerable part of it had been otherwise disposed of.

The winter of 1892 saw Father again in Farmington. This time we lived in a little log cabin on the edge of a hill about two miles east of town, on what was then known as the Roger's ranch. This adjoined the homestead of the Brown brothers on the east. Later it passed into the hands of Shidler, then into those of Weightman, and finally became the property of Phil Schenk, one of the large apple producers of the Farming district at the present time. There was a good sized ruin where Schenk's dwelling and store houses now [1942] stand, and there were other mounds all up and down the terrace. Father spent a fair part of the winter digging in these, and as a result of his own activities, as well as trade and purchase, he amassed during the winter a collection which he sold to the Carnegie Library Association of Pittsburgh. I have never looked up this collection, so do not know where it is housed. It must have been that this collection was not sold immediately. Where it may have been kept until the following winter, I have no idea, but I know from my own memory that we had it in the house on the mesa edge, overlooking Farmington from the north, which Father bought from June Roberts in the fall of 1893.[1]

In a speech made shortly before his death, Earl told of his own introduction to archaeology which had occurred during that interval.

"The winter of 1892 saw us again in Farmington, and my father busy gathering a second collection. Again there was a ruin close to the log cabin we lived in. One morning in March of 1893, Father handed me a worn-out pick, the handle of which he had shortened to my length, and said, 'Go dig in that hole where I worked yesterday, and you will be out of my way.' At the first stroke of the pick into the wall of the pit, there rolled down a roundish, gray object that looked like a cobblestone, but when I turned it over, it proved to be the bowl of a black-and-white dipper. I ran to show it to my mother. She grabbed the kitchen butcher knife and hastened to the pit to uncover the skeleton with which the dipper had been buried. Thus, at three and a half years of age there had happened the clinching event that was to make of me an ardent pot hunter, who later on was to acquire the more creditable, and I hope earned, classification as an archaeologist."[2]

It was in this same winter that Scott Morris became the first to run an exploratory trench into the great hill of occupational debris which lay at the gates of Pueblo Bonito in Chaco Canyon, and, at the same time, he became the first to puzzle over the location of Chaco's dead.

To continue with Earl's account of his father's activities:

> In early winter of that year [1893] a Mr. Hill, then owner of mines near Silverton, and his nephew, an architect named Orth, came down and accompanied my father on a trip to Chaco Canyon. It was quite a trek in those days, some seventy five miles across country where the only roads were Indian horse trails—Navajo had few wagons at that time. The trip was made in four-horse freight wagons. Owing to the scarcity of feed and the necessity of melting snow at most of their stops to water the stock, no great amount of digging was done. However, my father and his teamsters cut the first drift through the great refuse piles of Pueblo Bonito on the expectation that they would contain burials as did the trash mounds of the small ruins with which Father was familiar. They brought back only a few specimens, but Mr. Orth secured excellent photographs of most of the large ruins along the Chaco and made a map

of their locations. I know that the 1892 collection was retained until after the trip to the Chaco, because among the photographs of it there is a section of a pole-and-plank ceiling which was taken from one of the Chaco pueblos. I presume it was in the spring of 1894 that this collection was sent to Pittsburgh.

For nearly a decade after 1894 my father had little opportunity to dig. We were gone from the country most of the time, he following whatever work he could find for his teams—the construction of the Trout Lake Dam, between Telluride and Rico; lumbering and tie cutting in the Cloudcroft country of southern New Mexico; railroad construction of the line that was building from El Paso to White Oaks; and railroad building in the Cherokee and Osage districts of Indian territory. Finally, in 1903, Father having sold his grading outfit, we returned to Farmington, and he repurchased our previous home, which had been lost under a mortgage foreclosure.[3]

In Scott's absence the Wetherills had chalked up several more, important archaeological discoveries. From caves in the ravines of Butler Wash and Grand Gulch, Utah, west of Blanding, they had secured evidence of a culture underlying that of the sixty centimeters of Cliff Dweller refuse. In ninety jug-shaped pits sunk into hardpan they had obtained many naturally mummified bodies whose mouths contained a handful of stone beads and whose heads were long and undeformed, quite different from the Cliff Dwellers whose heads were round and artificially flattened on the occiput. Because of the presence of numerous finely woven burden-baskets, panniers, and bags, and the absence of fired pottery, Richard called them the Basket Makers. Little significance was attached to these recoveries by the scientific world although there was interest in the perishable materials and mummies which had survived because of an arid atmosphere.

Long arduous pack trips south of the San Juan, past the ruddy formations of Monument Valley and into the remote canyon of the Tsegi, had led to the discovery of Kiet Siel, destined to become known as Arizona's largest cliff dwelling, and numerous other ruins sprinkled across the desert.

Even more important, insofar as Earl's own career would be concerned, was the ambitious excavation program undertaken at Pueblo Bonito in Chaco Canyon. Richard Wetherill had gone there in 1896 for a short period of digging, during which time he became impressed with the beauty of the site and its promise of artifact rewards. He influenced the Hyde brothers, sponsors of his Grand Gulch work, to turn their attentions to this new area. The Hyde Exploring Expedition, with Richard Wetherill and George Pepper, of the American Museum of Natural History, directing the work, devoted four seasons, from 1897 to 1900, to further digging in the silent city of Pueblo Bonito. With the aid of a hundred Navajos, almost half of the great city was cleared, one hundred ninety-eight rooms in all. Wonderful finds were made of caches of pottery, turquoise mosaics, macaw skeletons, matting, arrow-shafts, bone awls, shell beads, steatite and pottery pipes, cloissoné work on sandstone, grinding stones, and many other examples of a high level of culture. Knowledge of the details of the superior architecture of the Chaco ruins was obtained, but there were no attempts made at deciphering its course of development. Chaco burial grounds still remained unfound with only twenty skeletons exhumed. Beginnings were made at related geologic, geographic, and ethnographic studies, now standard procedures with any archaeological operation of this magnitude but in the last century something revolutionary.

After the Morrises returned to Farmington, Scott and Earl resumed their old pastime of digging in the ruins. For hours father and son would explore with their shovels, removing arrowheads, stone axes, and occasionally pieces of black-and-white pottery. For Earl there was no thrill to equal that of reclaiming pots left behind to enhance a burial offering or perhaps to house a cache of corn. He was happy in the warm companionship of his father and the excitement of discovery. And through practice and a deliberate effort at imitating his father he became a master at the art of shoveling. As a matured archaeologist he once wrote:

> Pick and shovel are the tools of a lowly and misunderstood profession. Casually it would seem that any lump of animate matter with sufficient intelligence to guide food and drink to his lips could wield them with all the effectiveness lying within the possibilities of such gross implements. Never was a notion more erroneous. There are almost as many different kinds of picks and shovels as there are of artists' brushes, and each one is shaped for a definite and specific skill. Sufficient mental alertness quickly to recognize the object which his pick point or shovel blade has laid bare, an ability to evaluate the mechanical relationship between the components of the mass to be moved, and good co-ordination between eye and hand, are, far more than size or strength, the essentials to the making of a master craftsman in the art of digging ditch or driving tunnel. And if ever the touch of the master is needed, it is in archaeological excavation.[4]

Tragedy engulfed the Morris family in December 1904, when Scott was shot and killed in an argument with a business associate. Because of this unfortunate affair, Earl's mother became a recluse, and Earl was destined to remain bitter and introspective for the rest of his life. His principal emotional, as well as physical, outlet was his archaeological hobby. Alone, on foot, he visited and revisited nearly all the ruins in the vicinity. Out by himself, hard at work with his shovel, Earl was happy. The tougher the digging, the better he liked it.

Four years later Earl was top student in the second class to graduate from the Farmington High School. In the fall of 1908 he entered the University of Colorado in Boulder, where he majored in psychology. However, his deep-rooted interest in archaeology prompted him to make himself known to Junius Henderson, curator of the University Museum, who became a personal friend and adviser. Largely from this fortuitous association Earl gradually ceased being just a collector of pots and a digger of trenches and became a scientist. For the first time, his San Juan Indians began to take on the attributes of modern Pueblos as he progressed toward their placement in a cultural continuum from some unknown past right up to the current year. With great excitement he was approaching the realization that the long and complex history of a people had unfolded in his home territory and that he might be the one to show to the world many of the fragments of that human mosaic. By coincidence several more mature scholars were preparing the way.

One of these was Edgar L. Hewett whom Earl met on a train in 1911. No man was more influential in forcing a shift from past antiquarianism to scientific study of the Southwest's prehistoric inhabitants than was Hewett, and by all accounts he outdistanced all students of the area, past and present, in creating clamor and controversy. He was a determined man who in his thirties fell in love with New Mexico where he had come in 1893 to head a new normal school at Las Vegas. The archaeology of the past and the Pueblos of the present appealed to him, and he embraced them both with customary ardor. At once he began to offer courses in what was a relatively new science, anthropology, the study of man. As early as 1896 he was conducting sketchy excavations on the Pajarito Plateau adjacent to the northern Rio Grande valley, which, if done in the rose glow of "Lo, the vanishing American" sentimentalism, were at least the beginnings of scientific approach. After 1907, when he had established the Archaeological Institute of America with its School of American Research in Santa

Fe, he also began the first Southwestern archaeological field school at Puye. It was there that Earl and another Colorado youth, Jesse L. Nusbaum, received their early field training.

The vanishing ruins disturbed Hewett too, for everywhere in the Southwest pothunting continued at an alarming rate. Largely because of his loud protests the Hyde Exploring Expedition had been compelled to end its excavations in Chaco Canyon. It has been said that he more than any other individual was responsible for stirring up interest in high-level governmental circles to bring about the Lacey Law, which was passed in 1906, for the preservation of American antiquities. The statute did not mean then, nor now, the complete cessation of potting, but it did make it a federal offense to dig without proper authorization upon public land. Through Hewett's assiduous efforts many of the national monuments in the Southwest were born. Mesa Verde in 1906 and Chaco Canyon in 1907 were among those set aside for posterity.

A second figure of importance in the newly developing study of Southwestern archaeology was Jesse W. Fewkes of the Bureau of American Ethnology whom Earl met but for whom he never worked. In both appearance and thought Fewkes was an anachronism by this time. Looking distinguished with a clipped white beard and broad forehead, clad in a belted coat and knee britches, he bounced from one bit of research to another with the enthusiasm of a child, which totally belied his sixty-five years. Intellectually, he belonged to the school of romanticists who had first popularized the Southwestern Indians and attempted to interpret aboriginal history through legendary evidence. Indeed this drive to make the mystical red man known to the literate public had become a mission with Fewkes on his first trip to the Southwest in 1888. Season after season saw him at the pueblo of Zuñi, in New Mexico, or at the Hopi towns of northern Arizona where he enjoyed observing and writing about the ritualistic lifeway of the Indians.

After passage of the antiquities act in 1906, Fewkes's official duties in the government bureau gave him a responsibility to work among ruins on public domain and prompted his entry into more active archaeology. In 1908 he arrived at Cliff Palace and Spruce Tree House to clear away the debris left from both the prehistoric occupation and the work of the Wetherill parties, and to a degree, to convert those ruins into exhibits of America's Indian inheritance, though little did he realize that eventually, in a single year, four hundred thousand persons would pass along the rimrock to marvel at their beauty. Through the next dozen years he supervised excavations at Far View House,

Square Tower House, Earth Lodge A, New Fire Temple, Painted Kiva House, Pipe Shrine House, and One Clan House and instigated some measures for their preservation. Continuing his educational work and following a routine first employed by the Hewett field schools, he inaugurated evening campfire talks as a means of popularizing the American Indian. Further, he somehow found time and energy to turn out several hundred publications dealing with that subject.

Despite all this outlay of effort, younger men like Earl coming up through the ranks thought Fewkes's archaeological work ineffectual, superficial, and even destructive. Notes upon his excavations were inadequate at the time and are now lost forever, so that little knowledge can be ascertained from a study of specimens recovered. Conditions noted during the process of digging were not recorded, maps were not accurately drawn, terminology was needlessly complex and unstandardized, and many felt that data were hopelessly scrambled.

Meanwhile on the western fringes of the immensity called the Southwest a third scholar was initiating archaeological research. Byron Cummings, a gentle kindly man who lacked the drive of Hewett, in 1906 had begun to take exploration trips to ruins of southeastern Utah and had interested the legislature of that state in its archaeological remains. Cummings was dean of the college of arts and sciences at the University of Utah; an athletic field on that campus still bears his name. In 1908 under his leadership, survey and excavation of an area south of Monticello, Utah, known as Alkali Ridge, was undertaken with A. V. Kidder, a Harvard graduate student, as foreman and Neil M. Judd, of the University of Utah, as student assistant. The following summer he moved his operations south of the San Juan into the Kayenta country where several years previously John Wetherill had become a trader to the Navajo. That season Cummings, again accompanied by Judd, became the first white man to see the Rainbow Bridge, although W. B. Douglass of the General Land Office who was also in the party claimed the honor. The Cummings group was the first to enter the cliff dwelling called Betatakin. It visited Inscription House in Navajo Canyon for the first time in the historic period.

For a number of additional field trips "the Dean," as Cummings later was known, worked through the barren headlands of that weird land, noting ruins, collecting artifacts, and doing some limited digging. Unfortunately, Cummings never published in detail upon his work. Yet his influence was to be strongly felt in a generation of students at Utah and later at the University of Arizona.

At this time Eastern scholars began to move toward the promise of the Southwest. For fifty years archaeological expeditions, originating in museums and universities east of the Mississippi, were to debouch upon that field seeking answers to the riddles of man's antiquity in the New World and of his adaptation through time to varied environmental factors. In the infancy of this movement, Earl was one of the few homegrown diggers with the training and inclination to push forward regional archaeology. His opportunity came in 1915 when, with a newly earned M.A. degree from the University of Colorado and the backing of its president, Livingston Farrand, he was selected to apprentice under Nels C. Nelson of the American Museum of Natural History who at that time was doing some excavation in the Rio Grande area using methods of stratigraphy which would literally put Southwestern archaeology on its feet.

At seven sites in the treeless and eroded Galisteo Basin south of Lamy, New Mexico, and at Paako, east of the Sandias, as a result of a survey of the district of Tano-speaking Indians which he had begun in 1912, Nelson had tested a method of sequence determination (long in use by European archaeologists) wherein one worked from a known period represented in uppermost cultural levels to an unknown one, obviously older, in underlying deposits. Earl once described this phenomenon thusly, "Stratified accumulations . . . are like a book turned title page downward which one reads thence upward."[5] Before this application of stratigraphy by Nelson, it had been thought that most New World sites were of such relatively short duration that depth of deposit necessarily was too shallow (in comparison to those found in long occupied Old World sites) to be used interpretatively. Nelson, however, selected to work a cluster of ruins some of which were known to have been seats of Franciscan activity immediately following Spanish Conquest and others to have already fallen into disuse by that period. He proposed to begin with a positively recorded stage, such as would be indicated by Spanish and concurrent Indian surface material, and then, by arbitrary rather than natural layers and by the overlapping of characteristic elements to progress backward in time. For three days he worked at one site, cutting a three-by-six-foot column of trash in order to prove a chronological sequence of four pottery types which he had tentatively established during his survey.

The latest dwellings of San Cristóbal, the largest of the Galisteo ruins, situated at the base of the Trans Pecos plains and built after the advent of the Spaniards, were constructed of adobe bricks similar to those used in the Franciscan church. Bricks were considered a white man's innovation, as were the occasional corner fireplaces and paneless windows. Much earlier construction was of adobe but not fashioned into bricks. Dwellings were formed of rows of contiguous rooms, not so formalized nor defensive as earlier ground plans. In regard to artifacts recovered, broken brass candlesticks and a smashed bell gave testimony of the violence generated at the time of the Pueblo Revolt of 1680 when the Indians united in anger to drive the Europeans from their domain. More abundant in the ten-foot-deep refuse mounds than any other items were potsherds which, being virtually indestructable after firing, litter all Southwestern ruins. From the upper or most recent levels, San Cristóbal pottery was of the tan and red types, exhibiting a European-influenced decoration in two globby glaze paints of different colors known to have been manufactured by the Pueblos in late prehistoric and early historic times, probably from shortly before 1540 up to 1680. This type always was found in deposits which also contained horse bones and bones of other domesticated animals, metal tools, and bits of porcelain. Lower levels of the refuse mound produced more black-on-white potsherds than glaze-painted ones, indicating an occupation beginning at a time prior to the development of the glaze tradition. A further division of styles of black-on-white potsherds was possible, and a tentative chronology was organized.

Thus, Nelson's controlled stratigraphy clearly demonstrated the possibilities of establishing sequential dating throughout the Southwest through the use of cross-finds of pottery temporally pinpointed at one locality. The new discipline was unshackled from romantic guesswork with the publication of the Galisteo findings. Further work was needed not only to prove the soundness of the method but to more fully understand the distribution of the glaze-paint pottery of the Rio Grande. As Nelson prepared to leave New York for New Mexico in May, he was informed that, under an agreement with the University of Colorado, a young student from that state was to be under his tutelage for the summer.

Nelson's work had been in progress for a month before Earl was able to be excused from his commencement exercises at the University of Colorado to get to Santa Fe and hire a livery man and team to take him to Nelson and his wife, Ethelyn, who were tented in the slight protection of an arroyo near Domingo, some twenty miles south of Santa Fe. The men were not strangers, having met briefly in Boulder six years previously, when Nelson had paused at the university long enough to see Henderson, the museum's curator. At that time there was occasion only for the polite trivialities of introduction. Once together in the field, however, the two found a common bond in their intense interest in the work.

Nelson was a tall, robust Scandinavian with a jovial manner, a salty sense of humor, and one glass eye. His earthy approach to life and to work made a favorable impression upon Earl who, always having been conscious of his unsophisticated background, had come to the camp with reservations about his instructor. "He is by no means the type of man that one might have expected him to be. He came up from a plow hand, so he has not the arrogance and false perspective which is so characteristic of a good many easterners," was his opinion written to Henderson.[6]

Toward Earl, Nelson adopted a fatherly attitude, giving him pointers on both digging techniques and the major personalities then engaged in Southwestern archaeology. He urged Earl to go East for graduate work, offering to loan him the money, but Earl was too proud to accept.

Ten Mexican workmen and the two archaeologists dug at La Bajada, six miles northeast of Domingo, for six weeks and unearthed only one complete pottery vessel. To Earl, accustomed to rich pottery hauls in his San Juan sites, this was distressing. On Sundays for relaxation and to assure himself of the presence of pottery in the Rio Grande ruins, he explored other mounds within hiking distance. As a result, he acquired about a dozen large glaze-paint ollas which he turned over to the University of Colorado Museum. This extracurricular excavating became a pattern in which Earl indulged from time to time, always justifying it by his experience and training in archaeology. Otherwise, he felt such pots would fall into the hands of those who appreciated neither their scientific nor aesthetic value. In truth, however, this digging was both a physical and emotional escape for Earl, a carry-over from his boyhood. Unquestionably, it was pothunting. However, nearly all the pieces recovered in this way were given to some scientific institution where they could be studied by anyone who desired to do so.

The following autumn saw Earl heading into the wilderness of the Gobernador Canyon of northern New Mexico. With him were Jack Lavery and Bill Ross, both from the Farmington area. They set out to find the sources of the many Indian relics which were being brought into the San Juan valley by Mexican sheepherders. For three months in the deepening chill of approaching winter, the party clambered over the rugged timbered ridges near the Gobernador, San Rafael, and Frances canyons. What they found came as a distinct surprise to Earl.

There were round sinks marking ancient subterranean houses surrounded by surface jacal, or pole-and-mud, structures, and abundant pieces of undecorated plain gray pottery much like those he knew north of the San Juan. There were stockaded caves in Hart, Pump, and San Rafael canyons. But there also were a number of one-course, sandstone-masonry dwellings clinging to the combs of precipitous ridges or, like a rocky crown, sitting atop isolated buttes. These were extensive settlements apparently laid out to conform to all the irregularities of their unique defensible settings. Some were two storied; in Frances Canyon there was a four-story tower. Notched pole ladders were still standing in place by crevices to allow one to reach the ruined settlements on top. Although the sites had not been mounded over by fallen rubble and windblown detritus, only a few inches of fresh soil had drifted across the floors. Practically no objects of domestic or other usage were to be seen.

One surprise was that within the walled enclosures which wrapped around the larger ruins were timber frameworks of circular conical houses. Earl thought these were like the older style Navajo hogans, a feeling strengthened by the finding of portions of what appeared to be conical bottomed, fillet rimmed gray cooking vessels of a type produced by those people. Entrance to these forked-stick hogans was by means of a stone tunnel just high enough to crawl through.

A further surprise was the fact that all the plentiful timbers from intact ceilings, door lintels, and hogan frames had been cut with metal tools. Stone axes, incapable of sharp penetration, hewed beams in a characteristic rough pattern, much in the manner of beaver gnawing. The Pueblo Indians were known to have acquired metal tools only after the arrival of the Spaniards. Furthermore, there was at least one example of a hooded corner fireplace, not an Indian concept. Earl felt, too, that notched pole ladders were atypical of prehistoric Pueblos. As fragments of evidence accumulated, it became increasingly certain that the Gobernador masonry ruins were late, probably post-Spanish, in the sequence of Pueblo culture.

One noon when sliding down the splintery pole used to climb to the top of a pinnacle where a ruin defied interlopers, Earl flushed a rabbit from the underbrush. He was right after it, rapidly walking down a clay ridge some two hundred yards when he came upon a mound of fresh dirt beside an open pit. At once he knew he had come to a place where modern pothunters had told him there was ancient pottery. From where he stood, Earl could also see bones and several small, dark, metal bells. Metal objects had never before been recovered from aboriginal ruins in the Southwest. What interested him more was that the ground surface near the pit, an area approximately one-hundred-yards square, was paved with glittering fragments of crushed pottery quite unlike anything he had ever seen although it did have a resemblance to what he had recovered the previous summer in the Rio Grande Valley.

That afternoon the men gathered four bushels of potsherds from the immediate vicinity. All were of the three-color-glaze types known from the Rio Grande, with the exception of a Mexican Talavera saucer with a fleur-de-lis pattern done in blue, yellow, and red on a white ground. Other than the Navajo pottery, this deposit represented the totality of ceramics found in the late sites. Earl theorized that the departing inhabitants had crushed a number of their ollas upon the graves of loved ones left behind.

Earl and his mother worked sporadically the next winter sorting out the sherds and putting them together. In 1917 he again came to the pit's banks, this time with a screen so as to miss nothing. Ultimately forty-one complete glaze-paint vessels were restored and are now in the collections of the University of Colorado.

Largely because of this pottery and the indications of European cutting tools, Earl began to feel that he had found at its western edge the remnants of a wave of Pueblos who, as refugees in fear of Spanish reprisals, had fled the Rio Grande in the decade of 1680-90. His work with Nelson had revealed sites occupied just prior, during, and after the Pueblo Revolt. Now in the remoteness of Rio Arriba County he had discovered fortified villages, which he then thought had been constructed at the peak of the crisis, where the Indians had hoped that isolation would mean security. From the designs on his pottery he at first believed the Gobernador settlers must have come from Zuñi. Later he looked toward the towns of the Rio Grande Valley, Jemez Pueblo in particular, because Spanish documents told of these Indians having hidden out in the canyons to the west.

The pothunters' pit and nearby refuse mounds were of great interest because in their contents one could trace the course of Hispanic empire which, in 1598, had stretched northward from Chihuahua to engulf the Pueblo Indians. In addition to the human bones which lay within the pit's confines, there were small metal crosses bearing figures of the Saviour and the Virgin, metal buttons and bells (the latter subsequently found in Pueblo III sites as trade pieces from Mexico), and glass beads. From the trash heap were recovered metal tools and horse bridles. After years of cohabitation with their Iberian conquerors, it was interesting to note how few were the articles the Indians had retained from their period of association with the whites. Simple metal tools, several architectural innovations, and a few gaudy baubles were the sum total of Spanish material culture influence.

Glass beads from Venice, Italy, were one of the most common trade items in the Colonial periods in America, distributed to all parts of North America by the French, English, Dutch, Swedish, Russian, American, and Spanish traders. Certain tribes preferred particular colors. In the Southwest, where glass beads were first obtained from the Spanish and later from the English and Americans, bluegreen was popular because of its similarity to turquoise.

The glass beads from Earl's jug-shaped pit were numerous and through them Arthur Woodward, of the Los Angeles County Museum, was enabled to offer Earl an estimate of the age of his sites. One chain of beads was sixty feet in length when restored and contained six thousand two hundred irregularly shaped beads of translucent pinkish color. Another, twenty-eight feet in length, was composed of four thousand eight hundred separate beads grading from creamy opalescence to a dark blue. Woodward's verdict was that these specimens represented a period in European manufacture dating from 1750 to 1769 although some with irregular faceting might have been earlier.

If these dates proved to be correct, this meant the sites had been occupied long after the Pueblo Revolt and perhaps owed their defensive character to fear of attack from some group other than the Spaniards.

At the end of three months, Earl had excavated three sites, including a pithouse, and had mapped others. Although he began on numerous occasions to work up a report, even with the idea of using it as a Ph.D. thesis, he never completed a manuscript on the work. Five years after his trip, he learned that Kidder had surveyed through the same area several years before him, in 1912. No excavation had been done at that time, and notes taken during the reconnaissance had been lost. However, in 1920, Kidder published a brief article on the region based upon memory and photographs. For years the two men talked of collaborating on a more comprehensive paper, but it was a task left undone.

Elsewhere 1915 was a distinguished year for Southwestern archaeology because at the eastern and western peripheries of that plateau great progress was being made toward a breakthrough to the past. No one individual was more responsible than was Kidder, then associated with the Peabody Museum of Harvard University. To the incalcuable benefit of the slowly emerging science, he possessed acumen and breadth of vision.

Kidder was one of the many men bred in the East who upon his first visit to the Southwest, in 1907, found himself under its spell. He was enthralled by its elemental exuberance, the incongruity of its young and old earth, its demands placed upon anyone who chose to be there at any season. Perhaps he could not have explained the appeal of the environment, but there is no doubt but that he could have stated the excitement he found in its archaeology.

At Harvard he had learned that the great cultures of the world had had their genesis in arid-land agriculture based upon cultivation of a cereal crop. Mesopotamia and Egypt were two classical examples. However, with the time of human evolution in the Old World having been so great, the destructions and displacements of war so frequent, the cultural picture so complex—with great diversity of physical and linguistic stocks—it was impossible to retrace step by step the movements which occurred in progressing from insecure nomadism to high sedentary civilization. In the Southwest, with an assumed shorter interval of time involved and with well preserved ruins at every turn, he felt there might be opportunity to reconstruct prehistory with rare completeness of detail.

There is in the floor of a basement laboratory in the Peabody Museum a brassheaded nail which marks the spot on which Kidder and Samuel J. Guernsey stood as they shook hands and said, "Let's do the Southwest!" Out of this partnership came one of the most significant pieces of research of the early era: the Basket Makers were returned to good standing.

The Wetherills had met and recognized the Basket Makers in the deep deposits of Grand Gulch. Dr. T. Mitchell Prudden, a turn-of-the-century medical doctor from the East who enjoyed traveling and archaeologizing in the San Juan, formalized their introduction in print in 1897, and George Pepper, in describing the Wetherill and other Grand Gulch collections, did it again a few years later. But the learned men of the scientific world felt the long headed Basket Maker mummies had no proper credentials and so they were shunned, even rejected. There was no intent on the part of Kidder and Guernsey to seek them out when they took to the field in 1912.

One of the great fascinations of archaeology, like gambling, is the element of chance. Despite profound utterances and steel-edged erudition, no man can predict with accuracy what lies beneath the soil.

Quite by accident the two Harvard scientists were to learn of the Basket Makers several years after they had begun initial work.

Late in the 1914 season at a deep, narrow cave called Sayodneechee, located in the Kayenta area of northwestern Arizona, the party got its first inkling that things might be more than they seemed. There were no dwellings within the darkened recess, but a fire blackened ceiling and a fragment of a human jaw partly exposed in the soft fill soil suggested that this might be a place worthy of investigation. After digging through the odorous layer of dung from Navajo sheep which covered the surface, the excavators exposed four cists sunk into the hardpan of the cave floor. These holes had been made with long pointed sticks, their vertical gouge marks being plainly visible on the dirt walls. Each cist contained multiple burials, one having as many as nineteen bodies, all tightly flexed and packed into the hole as compactly as olives in a bottle. They were badly decayed, but each burial seemed to have had baskets placed with it or over it, the musty shreds of which disintegrated upon being handled. If these had been Cliff Dweller graves, there would have been associated pottery, but none was found. The young archaeological team wondered if, in its proximity to the Grand Gulch area north of the San Juan, the same group discovered there might not also have inhabited the Kayenta.

Back in Marsh Pass and Kinboko Gorge in 1915, with Guernsey at the helm (since Kidder was in northeastern New Mexico to open his monumental examination of Pecos Pueblo) excavations began at a cave superficially explored the year before. Straightaway the diggers hit the jackpot. Under a rubbish stratum composed of cast-off sandals, bags, basketry fragments, and the debris of long occupation were circular cists lined with slabs set on edge and cushioned with grass or shredded bark, similar to those of Sayodneechee. In all, there proved to be some sixty such cists containing twenty burials, most of which had been disturbed aboriginally. To the modern diggers, it was upsetting to have been outdone by the earlier ones because not only was it a certainty that articles had been removed from the pits, but there was the possibility that the contents of the cists might have been mixed with materials pertaining to another age.

Fortunately, before the field season ended, the men had found like remains from two more caves in Kinboko. Bodies flexed, trussed with cords, and enfolded in large woven bags shared jug-shaped graves with each other and with funerary offerings of food, weapons, and baskets. All were naturally dessicated. Hair styles, methods of facial painting, fingernails, and bodily scars could be studied if one could overcome an initial revulsion to their grotesqueness and acrid odor. Square-toed sandals, beads, cradles, coiled basketry, twined bags, human-hair cordage, rabbit-fur blankets, atlatls or spear throwers, darts, bone awls, and many other items were identical to specimens which had been obtained twenty years earlier in the Grand Gulch. Of negative significance was the complete lack of fired pottery.

The pacesetting report on this 1915 work stated, "The culture represented by the finds in Cave I, is, without much question, that of the Basket Makers. The method of burial, the undeformed type of skull, and the objects found in the graves, all being foreign to the cliff-dwelling culture, but closely similar to the Basket Maker remains from southeastern Utah described by Pepper."[7] Many of the ideas put forth at that time have stood the test of fifty years of further field work. So there it was, the Basket Makers were in contention, and in their faltering first steps would be seen the broad basis for the whole of Pueblo civilization.

Guernsey continued the Basket Maker researches for a number of further seasons, obtaining unquestioned stratigraphy to show that the Basket Makers were older than the Cliff Dwellers, and through mounting detail gaining insight into that segment of the drama of man in the Southwest.

While Guernsey continued to trace the elusive Basket Makers, Kidder took on an entire town of ancient Pueblos. Although the scene of action was far beyond the network of the San Juan, the field techniques and cultural theories formulated there were fundamental to the future research carried on not only in the San Juan but in the entire Southwest. In 1915 the names of Kidder and Pecos were synonymous in archaeology.

Pecos Pueblo, the easternmost and most populous of all the historic Pueblo towns, had had a thousand-year-old history, the last three hundred seventy-five years of which had received some documentation by the Spaniards, Mexicans, and Americans. Coronado, in 1541, had marched through the village on his way east toward the plains in an abortive attempt to find Quivira's gold. One Franciscan priest who had traveled north with that *entrada* was killed at Pecos, one of the first cases of martyrdom in the area. Fifty years later another group followed the Pecos River from its junction with the Rio Grande, reaching the pueblo in December, 1590. Ultimately, in 1598, New Mexico was taken for the King of Spain by Juan de Oñate, and Pecos, together with the other Indian villages, excepting Acoma, pledged its allegiance.

By the time of the Pueblo Revolt of 1680, Pecos had a Franciscan padre and at its southern outskirts a massive adobe-walled chapel. In the frenzy of the rebellion the church was looted, and the padre, who on a tip from a loyal convert had fled the valley, was killed enroute to join his brothers at Galisteo.

Once the kingdom was reconquered by the dedicated Spaniards in 1692, Pecos took a downward path which ended in its total abandonment a century and a half later. Not the Europeans but the Comanche, at this time on a rising tide of violence (the result of a transfiguration from docile pedestrian nomads into fierce mounted warriors), were responsible for the demise of the Pecos settlement. These savage fighters became the scourge of the southern plains, riding into northern Mexico and eastern New Mexico, taking slaves and booty, and leaving in their wake a reservoir of fear and despair. Because of them, the population and morale of Pecos was drained steadily. Finally in desperation the men of the village united to bring war to their enemy, only to be annihilated. White man's diseases further decimated the feeble ranks left at Pecos. And even the most determined knew it was only a matter of time until they must move on. In 1838 the seventeen remaining Indians flung their few possessions upon their backs and journeyed eighty miles westward to join their linguistic relatives at the pueblo of Jemez. Pecos Pueblo became an archaeological site.

Even as large and well known a pueblo as was Pecos, barely off the main road leading through the valley, it offered research appeal. More important to the archaeologist than its documented history was the record which lay in its deep refuse deposits east, southeast, and southwest of the ruin at the base of cliffs upon which the town had been erected.

Kidder proposed to slice those deposits as one cuts into a cake to see if stratigraphic layers might not be revealed, to further apply and cross-check the techniques Nelson used at Galisteo. In 1915 under auspices of the Phillips Academy of Andover, Massachusetts, and aided by Dr. and Mrs. Samuel K. Lothrop of Harvard and a crew of Pecos valley residents, he went to work and at once saw that the trash mounds were so rich and extensive that excavation in the house rubble would have to be delayed for a season or two. This in itself was a significant step forward, indicating an advance from a concern with architecture to an interpretation of a culture history as might be ascertained from the residues of living and dying.

Kidder's 1924 report[8] relates how, in his anxiety to obtain burials and their associated offerings, he promised his Mexican laborers a twenty-five cent bonus for each skeleton uncovered. In only a day or two the market for burials became glutted, and the reward was lowered to ten cents. In a week the skeletons were stacking up like cord wood, and in order to keep the expedition solvent, the bonus plan had to be discontinued. Two hundred burials came from the 1915 refuse excavations, plus an additional one hundred fifty from the environs of the church where Earl's friend of field-school days, Jess Nusbaum, was at work in stabilization efforts. The subsequent season produced four hundred seventy-five more skeletons, and each season thereafter added others. The Pecos cemetery was the most extensive one yet known in the Southwest. Its yield of bones offered a chance for significant anthropomorphic studies which were carried on by Dr. E. A. Hooton of Harvard.

Numerous trenches, some two hundred fifty feet in length, ran through the deeply drifted rubbish composed of household trash, ashes, washed and blown soil, and interments of the dead. At specified intervals, columns of earth were arbitrarily marked into horizontal sections, were carefully cut down, and their contents segregated. In the laboratory, at the conclusion of fieldwork, Kidder was enabled to begin a valid reconstruction of the unwritten history of Pecos through analysis of these findings. Pottery fragments obtained by the thousands were sorted into eight categories. They were seen to have been concentrated in specific areas and depths within the dump. Through comparative studies with sherds of Galisteo and other Rio Grande excavations, such as those at Domingo, these pottery types were assigned relative dates. For the first time, students working sites where these types also appeared would be able to fit them into a chronological framework.

Thus as 1915 ended, most of the obviously important areas in and adjacent to the San Juan basin were known and had been at least superficially tested. Scientific methodology was beginning to take shape. And Earl Morris was on the threshold of a long, fruitful career in Southwestern archaeology.

II.

Full Pueblo

T. Mitchell Prudden had written of Aztec Ruins as early as 1903: " . . . here one of the most promising of the great old pueblos lies waiting for the trained and authorized explorer".[1] It was not until 1916, however, that the American Museum of Natural History made final arrangements with the ruins' owner, H. D. Abrams, to undertake its excavation and study. Then Director Clark Wissler, acting upon the recommendation of Nels Nelson, offered Earl Morris the opportunity of heading the project.

To Earl this was a dream come true because Aztec Ruins was a place he had known for most of his life. He felt that Aztec, the largest prehistoric dwelling in the vicinity, might well have been the acropolis into which the best of all the outlying districts had been funneled. Within its rubble-caked bulk might lie incredible examples of domestic and ceremonial paraphernalia of more intrinsic quality than those of Pueblo Bonito. Perhaps its refuse dumps to the west and south, encroached upon by modern alfalfa fields, would be stratified so that, through use of the Nelson technique, the chronological position of all the hundreds of villages in the area could be established. Or at the very least, one might learn of the zenith period of man's occupation of the Animas and through that of the entire San Juan. Earl had never tried as big a job as that presented by Aztec, but he was confident that he could do it.

At the end of April from his mother's house in Farmington, Earl sent Wissler his estimates of cost and equipment needed and wrote, "To excavate the Aztec Ruin is a dream which has endured from my boyhood, and I wish to express my appreciation of the fact that you see fit to give me a part in it."[2] The name of Earl Morris would become as associated with Aztec Ruins as that of Ted Kidder would be to Pecos Pueblo.

In July when Earl arrived at Aztec, he thought the brush concealing the ruins had grown denser during the winter. It was nearly impossible to penetrate the mound area off the narrow paths beaten to the old settler entrances. Only the walls of the center portion of the North Wing projected above the rubble and plant growth. At once he set a crew of men to clearing the site in anticipation of the arrival of Nels Nelson who was coming to consult with him upon the opening phases of the project.

For several months of the spring, Nelson had been south at Zuñi aiding his museum colleague, Leslie Spier, in excavations being conducted as a related but unobtrusive part of an ethnographic study under way by A. L. Kroeber of the University of California. From there he planned to ride to Chaco to run some stratigraphic trenches through the sixteen-foot-high refuse mounds at Pueblo Bonito and then would come north to Aztec.

Earl met the Nelsons at Pueblo Bonito in July. Together he and Nels drifted the first scientifically controlled trenches into the two dumps originally explored by Earl's father. The results were disappointing because the mounds were not entirely household refuse but contained broken building materials as well. However, certain significant ceramic differences were noted between the sherds of Bonito and those of smaller Chaco houses, including the interesting absence of Mesa Verde pottery at the latter.

The work of the first season at Aztec was one of making ready for the future. A two thousand dollar gift to the museum by J. P. Morgan had to be stretched to pay for these preliminaries, which included a salary of one hundred dollars a month plus maintenance to Earl. Nelson had spent long hours before leaving New York in the effort to secure an increase in funds for Earl because, as he wrote, "I shouldn't have gotten my foot in at all probably if at one time I hadn't literally borrowed money from the bank on which to finish a piece of field work and prepare it for publication."[3] However, although it was not much, Earl was content with the arrangement, believing that a promising future lay in Aztec.

One of the main reasons why Nelson had interested the museum staff and its president, Henry Fairfield Osborne, in the proposed excavation was not only the ruin's impressive size and obvious importance but its apparent escape from wanton looting. It had been known to scientists since the middle of the nineteenth century when geologist John S. Newberry, with an exploring expedition from Santa Fe to the Colorado River, described it in detail. Twenty years later Lewis H. Morgan, distinguished scientist who popularly is credited with initiation of American anthropology, on one of his four western tours, visited the Animas villages, comparing Aztec to Hungo Pavie of Chaco Canyon in a highly readable journal narrative. Then came the homesteaders of '82 who breached a few of its walls and took away building stones and curios. By 1889 the land was patented by John R. Koontz who discouraged diggers upon his land although Earl and Scott were there in 1895. Warren K. Moorehead, of Phillips Academy, Andover, Massachusetts, and a party of eleven men in 1892, the second year of Earl's residence at Farmington, camped along the river near the ruins and spent two weeks exploring and mapping the structures. The account of this effort, published sixteen years afterwards said, "The piles of stone and earth, accumulated above them [first and second stories] to a height of many feet, converted the lower stories into what were practically underground rooms. Communication from one to the other was afforded by means of openings large enough only for a person to creep through."[4] H. D. Abrams in 1907 bought the farm lands surrounding the site, and from then until 1916 there were only reports of stray cows having been stranded in its roofless rooms and youngsters playing on the site.

Once the congestion of plant life had been hacked away, it could be seen that the ruin resembled a hollow square, three hundred fifty-nine by two hundred eighty feet in rough dimensions, standing twenty-nine feet at its highest point (along the north side) and only slightly rising above the plaza level on the south. Earl estimated that a hundred ground-floor rooms had been constructed, with the northern unit rising in set-back fashion to three stories. Here and there within the mass of rooms and in the open patio were circular depressions indicating the presence of ceremonial chambers, one being extraordinarily large and considered to be a so-called Great Kiva like those known in the Chaco Canyon ruins. Earl elected to begin his trenches at the southeast corner of the compound, working from rooms of little fill toward the deeper mounds along the north side. This was done upon Nelson's recommendation. Earl himself was still more concerned with the securing of specimens and would have preferred first to clear the refuse and what he thought would be burial mounds. He wrote, "Relatively few graves have been found in the immediate neighborhood of the pueblos, and beyond doubt in the low mounds to which I refer, there will be a great number of them together with much pottery."[5]

When work was terminated at the end of August, thirty-four rooms and three kivas had been dug. The highest walls had been repaired so that they would not collapse, and one kiva had been roofed in the manner of construction employed by Fewkes at Peabody House on the Mesa Verde.

At the outset Earl considered his ruin a hybrid, since geographically it lay between two areas of high Pueblo culture—the Mesa Verde and Chaco Canyon. It seemed to Earl that the style of masonry employed in the thick room walls was that of the Chaco, with outer facings of dressed sandstone carefully fitted and held together with adobe and with cores of rough rock and a large proportion of mortar. The roofed kiva he thought aberrant with its cobblestone walls, pilasters, and banquette suggesting Mesa Verde influence. In the matter of pottery, however, no Chaco types were found. In fact, only fifteen complete vessels were recovered, and without exception they were typical Mesa Verde.

The yield of specimens had not been as great as Earl had hoped, although after employing two men to sieve refuse dirt for two days, he was able to catalogue six hundred individual items. The fact that the rooms along the eastern flank apparently had become trash dumps in their terminal days offered hope for better returns next season, particularly in regard to perishable things which normally would not come from a ruin open to the elements. At Aztec it looked as if in the slump of upper-story rooms, lower units had been sealed and so well protected from seepage that everything had survived. Diggers found many shreds of textiles, sandals, matting, cord, rope, buckskin, and even a fragile section of fish vertebrae, in addition to fine specimens of nonperishable stone tools, arrowheads, beads, and tiny pieces of turquoise. One unique kind of artifact recovered was what Earl surmised were snowshoes. These were oval frameworks of a size suitable for footgear crossed by one taut lacing of yucca fiber and another looser one, the space between being filled with cornhusks or bundles of grass.

The 1917 season's budget was seventy-five hundred dollars, the amount Earl originally had considered necessary for the ruin's complete excavation. It was supplied by a museum patron, Archer M. Huntington, author, student of Spanish culture and the founder of the

Hispanic Society of America, and son of the president of the Southern Pacific Railroad. He had for a number of years been financing other Southwestern work, including that of Nelson. With that money at hand in June, Earl began to make the rounds of the farms to hire on a crew of local men at the two dollar daily wage of the previous summer. No one would agree to come for that figure. He was forced to go to two dollars and fifty cents. At the same time he rented a number of teams of mules and wagons. He had concluded that the trams used the summer before were inefficient because of their small capacity. Among his workmen in these early years were Oscar Tatman—owner of a poultry farm near the ruins, Oley Owens—local handiman, Sherman Howe—one of the original group who descended into lower rooms of the ruin, George Bowra—later editor of the local newspaper, Jack Lavery—"Old Jack" who taught Earl to be a first class mason, P. T. Hudson—who later served as periodic caretaker of Aztec Ruins, Manuel Chavez, Art Lawson, and others. Many of these men returned to work for Earl season after season, not only at Aztec but elsewhere, acquiring a great deal of archaeological knowledge and digging skill.

Work began with the shoveling of fill dirt up on to wooden platforms and then into the beds of wagons which would haul it off to the dump. Sometimes in the deeper rooms it was necessary to handle the dirt three times, placing it first in small wooden boxes attached to hoists which would lift it to the platforms.

No attempt has been made to keep discoveries mentioned hereafter in chronological order. However, almost with the first spray of dirt in the air in 1917, a very rich find was made in Room 41 of the East Wing. A large globular vase was uncovered resting against the breast of an adult skeleton. This was not especially unusual. But with the raising of this burial from its ancient resting place, it could be seen that thousands of olivella-shell beads literally had encased the individual from throat to thighs. Mosaic pendants of abalone shell were at the throat; an olivella-shell anklet wrapped the left leg. Dirt from around this skeleton was sacked and taken to the shack headquarters where a man was employed for a week examining the dirt with a magnifying glass and then putting it through a flour sifter and a fine-meshed milk strainer in order to recover the infinitesimally small beads. A necklace seventy-five feet long and containing over forty thousand beads was restrung as a result of this work.

Nearby an undetermined number of other burials had been laid out on the floor, covered by neither soil nor trash at the time of deposit. There were also scattered bones and bits of calcined flesh, the residue of a holocast which had started in the combustion of an estimated two hundred bushels of unshelled corn stored in the room above. This mass had burned until bits of the floor were destroyed, allowing the charred smoldering debris to fall below.

Along the west wall of the room was a continuous line of pottery vessels, enough to fill a small museum—mugs, bowls, ollas, and rarer effigies. One contained a horde of thirty-one thousand tiny disc-shaped beads. Near the room's north end was a heap of two hundred quartzite arrow-points. Everywhere through the fill there were innumerable charred fragments of bird-bone tubes, beads, and turquoise.

Earl felt almost beside himself with this greatest find of his career to date. With the same zeal his father had shown years before as he dug all night in the mound lying in the yard of the cabin where his small family was quartered, Earl was constantly on his knees in the dirt, with a paint brush and small trowel carefully pushing through the soil to make sure nothing had been overlooked. He lingered at the room long after his workmen had gone home for the day to continue the tedious task of exposing specimens for photographs and measurements. When darkness drove him indoors, he worked on the artifacts, attaching proper labels, washing, mending, and measuring. He was pleased with the discovery, but he could only regret the amount of perishables which had escaped him because of the fire. In his report upon burial 16, Room 41, he stated, "Had Room 41 been protected from fire and moisture, it would have yielded a close rival to Pepper's unprecedented finds in Pueblo Bonito."[6]

All of these tinder-dry articles were the discards or useful objects of daily living, by no means aesthetic treasures. To Earl, however, they were precious, and he handled each masticated quid or splintered arrowshaft as if it were gold. Each item, whether broken or complete, spoke of its former user. Through a study of it, Earl could obtain a picture of life at Aztec far more unbiased than that of most recorded history.

At Aztec, as would be true in other Pueblo ruins, the most eye-catching and abundant artifacts were those molded by the Indian women. Pottery, the pivot upon which much later scientific conjecture would turn, represented a paradox of fragility and indestructibility; infrequently met were the complete vessels but everywhere were their sherds. From their very quantity could be inferred pottery's great importance to each household. Vessels of clay no doubt were used for cooking, as tableware, and for storing all manner of things. And constant breakage must have meant continual replacement. The Indian woman's work most certainly was never ended, for she not only had to wash the dishes, she had to make them as well.

The process of pottery manufacture was one which involved a complex knowledge of clays and non-refactory additives and the chemical changes produced in them by fire, but it is unlikely that the women were particularly aware of this technology which had amassed through time. They were guided instead by a group tradition which called for certain materials and certain procedures. Their pots were hand-built by concentric coils of clay piled one on another, smoothed, scraped, polished, dried in the shade of a cool place, painted with designs, and then baked in a heap on the ground. Their white-to-gray base color decorated in black designs made them unique to the Southwest.

By the time Earl began his formidable tasks at Aztec, he already had had twenty-five years experience with Pueblo pottery. In print he had stated that he had personally examined over two thousand vessels from the area.[7] When he said the vessels coming from his big mound at Aztec were of the Mesa Verde culture, there was no disputing it. From the fill, on room floors, or sunk beneath them, or from grave offerings he recovered well-polished, thick-walled, pearly-white bowls decorated in close-set, neatly executed geometric designs done in a lustrous black paint; squat globular vessels with a neck flange and a handled lid; round-bodied, tall-necked pitchers with bizarre animal figures modeled on the handle; flat bottomed, elaborately decorated mugs with polka dots marching around the rim; dippers with painted bowl interiors and long vented handles; both large and small bulging jars whose corrugated exteriors still possessed sooty evidence of having seen much use in the cookfires.

To the archaeologist's great good fortune, there were regional differences in pottery which were maintained for centuries. Use of particular types of clay, temper, and paint, once accepted, persisted with relatively little experimentation. Design and form became conventionalized. In the classic period, (Full Pueblo to Earl), Chaco, Mesa Verde, and Kayenta pottery in their most characteristic forms were highly distinctive even though they were primarily all white decorated in black. Enough archaeology had been done by 1917 to allow recognition of these various wares.

There were evidences of ceramic trade with other areas—the Tularosa region of central New Mexico, the Chaco Canyon, and the Kayenta. These were unimportant in the total pottery picture for the first three years of exploration at Aztec. One trade-ware find, however, illustrates Earl's persistence. A foreign red bowl had been broken in a second-story room; some of its fragments were lying on the floor when work reached that section of the site. In the centuries following the abandonment of Aztec, sherds of this particular pot gradually had fallen through cracks which opened up in the floor and had become buried in the deposits of the first-floor room below. When excavation began in that lower room, the easily spotted red sherds started showing up on the screens through which all fill was shoveled. Earl remembered the red sherds from the overhead chamber and ordered a careful search for all such fragments. In the end, more than one hundred seventy-six cubic feet of dirt was sifted in order to reclaim fragments of the entire vessel.

Earl was hoping to find burials within the Aztec mounds because he felt that the manner in which a group treated its dead was extremely revealing. Furthermore, in the San Juan, funerary offerings already had proved to be the source of many of the finest examples of native art, and men who supplied funds frequently judged the success of an archaeological adventure on the number of specimens obtained and not on the ideas formulated. He was not to be disappointed because Aztec mounds contained the remains of many burials.

Normal burials at Aztec, mostly of aged and very young people, consisted of flexed bodies simply laid out on the floors of abandoned chambers which also might have served as trash bins or turkey pens. In time, the corpses were drifted over by trash accumulation. Less frequently pits to accommodate burials were scooped into floors or the soft trash, sometimes beneath floors of rooms in use. More burials were found in the West Wing of the compound than elsewhere, four rooms there containing as many skeletons as the entire eastern sector. Many bones had been disturbed by carnivores, rodents, or aboriginal human vandals. The one hundred eighty-six burials found could not account for all the deaths which occurred during use of the house; yet, sepulture outside the village was rare. Once in awhile farmers plowing ground near the cluster of mounds, particularly to the south, or irrigating from channels which occasionally burst and ate into surrounding terrace banks did encounter such burials.

Interment oddities appealed to the public, and the Witch of the San Juan had few rivals for attention. She was an old gray-haired crone who had been found flexed, wrapped, and propped up in the corner of a rubbish mantled room. But here similarity to normal conditions ended. A stout splinter from a broken ceiling timber had been hewn to a point and then driven completely through her pelvis and well into the dry earth below. Its frayed end showed signs of having been pounded by a heavy tool such as a stone hammer. Earl's report to the museum suggested that perhaps this unfortunate woman had been accused of practicing witchcraft. Immediately, propelled by a sensation-minded press which had been educated on Bandelier's *The Delight Makers,* tales of witchery circulated in the Animas, while the "ill fated American woman of thirty centuries ago," lying in her grisly torture chamber, had her picture emblazoned in dozens of newspapers.

Then there was the warrior. His skeleton, found in a pit beneath the floor of one of the North Wing rooms, showed him to have been approximately six feet two inches tall in life and apparently someone of importance. The body, which had an ornament on the chest and a bead bracelet on one arm, had been wrapped in turkey-feather cloth and a rush matting, topped by an enormous basketry shield, the like of which was known in only two other examples—one found by the Days in Canyon de Chelly, Arizona, and the other by the Wetherills at Mesa Verde. The Aztec specimen, some three feet in diameter, was colorful, with a selenite speckled rim outlined by a dark red band, and a central zone of blue-green. Lying across the shield were several long curved sticks which might have been fending weapons or swords. By the man's head were a small coiled basket, a bowl, and a mug. Behind the pelvis was another bowl of large size. A second bowl which had been placed between his hips and heels had had its bottom worn through at some time during usage and had been patched with a sherd of a corrugated pot ground to proper shape and size and cemented into place with gummy pitch. Between his feet and the north side of the grave pit was a third bowl. Broken over the skull was a Mesa Verde kiva jar. Other items associated with the burial were five bone awls, an antler, a sandstone rasping instrument, a chipped knife blade and several flakes. Two ax-like implements with handles attached Earl considered weapons. The description submitted to the museum called the old fellow a warrior because of the shield and sticks and commented on his height because of its unusualness among the short-statured Pueblos, saying innocently enough, "He was a veritable giant among the Pueblos." Sunday newspaper readers learned soon afterwards that a giant warrior had been "emperor of the Aztecs of the village." Obviously there was confusion over the ruin's name, as well as the physical composition of its occupants.

Another hapless male had been sealed in a room whose only connection with adjoining chambers was a ten-inch tunnel in one wall. Perhaps this was the town guardhouse. The body was found toppled forward upon a platform on which he had been seated. There were no offerings. A dessicated dog had suffered a similar fate, the plaster on his cell walls deeply scratched by his frantic claws. From this same room were removed an iron bar and a whiskey bottle left by settlers who had broken into the mound forty-five years earlier.

One ancient murder had occurred in a subterranean kiva where four children and a man had been burned to a crisp. Their cooked remains came up on the shovels like chunks of slag, pitted and honey-combed, and bluely irridescent from the burning of body fats. Earl felt that inasmuch as there was evidence that the kiva was seeing domiciliary use at the time it had burned (cooking pots at the fire-place and food bowls set around the wall bases), the conflagration had been started intentionally from above and the victims trapped below had died of burns and suffocation.

An example of primitive surgery was seen in the burial of a seven-teen-year-old girl. She must have suffered some terrible accident. Her pelvic girdle was crushed and her left forearm fractured. The Indian doctor had tried to set the bones, surrounding the forearm with six shaped splints. The girl had expired before the bones had begun to knit, perhaps from what must have been painful internal injuries.

Cremation was not the custom in the San Juan, but Earl found one instance of what appeared to be intentional burning of the bodies. He encountered a pit which had been lined with inflammable materials over and under two corpses. The entire pyre had been ignited but had only partially burned before it had been smothered out. Much later, in 1927, he came across another pyre in which five partially burned bodies and some Mesa Verde pottery were uncovered in a mound north of the East Ruin. This pile of partly burned materials was destroyed in clean-up operations around the monument before an opportunity arose for their complete study.

Aztec Ruins' architecture also made good newspaper copy, provid-ing welcome relief from the accounts of battles of World War I. Fea-ture articles were devoted to its fortress-like communal character, its stability and beauty. Apartment houses in the United States being less than a half-century old, it was of interest to note that some time long ago (and here estimates ranged from twenty to thirty centuries), in-genious Indians had perfected such an architectural style, to incor-porate five hundred rooms housing perhaps as many as eight hundred persons, terracing upper stories so that most rooms could receive fresh air and sunlight and providing ventilator shafts for lower rooms. Com-ments were made upon the lack of exterior openings on its outside walls. Descriptions were made of room walls, which were thick at their bases and thinner as one progressed to upper stories, made of carefully laid, shaped sandstone blocks from quarries at least a mile away where early day settlers had picked up many stone hammers and mauls. Two broad paths winding from the town to the quarries could be followed over mesas and across the river. Occasional partitions were of jacal, or poles and sticks plastered over with mud. Doorways in ground floor rooms were either rectangular or T-shaped and opened onto the plaza. Sometimes hatchways led to the upper stories. In one instance Earl worked by lantern light until midnight to uncover a runged ladder well polished by use from bare or sandaled feet, and apparently tipped over by large stones which had rolled through from the chamber above. Ceilings were from nine to eleven feet high and were built on a frame of two or more large stringers across the shorter span of the room. These were usually of pine, presumably from a stand twenty miles to the north but some juniper also was utilized. The beams were topped with peeled cottonwood saplings placed at right angles and evenly spaced or grouped into clusters of twos or threes and then covered with a mat formed of smaller willow sticks lashed together with yucca fibers. This was blanketed with cedar shakes and then a layer of clay which formed the floors of upper rooms.

Many ceilings remained intact when Earl and his crews gained entrance into the rooms. Some were so brittle that as soon as the pressure of the fill was removed, the men could hear splintering sounds rippling through the beams, forcing them to make a hasty retreat. Those ceilings which had collapsed prior to excavation had given way in midsection. The dangling beams had pried out chunks of the wall. Where ceilings remained, water had tended to stand on the second-floor area, gradually causing wood and mortar to rot and disintegrate.

Occasionally a room was entered which still bore its ancient coat of plaster, clay tempered with sand and spread with low-grade white gypsum from beds not far from town. Murals were painted in pale red pigment made from disintegrated red sandstone. The finest example of a painted room was in the West Wing, Room 156. Its plastered walls were dead white with a three-foot-high border and a series of triangular designs in dull red. On the ceiling beams were white hand prints. The floor, instead of being the usual tamped earth, was precisely cut flagstone. Doors had been sealed with masonry. A length of rope hung from the ceiling upon which to suspend objects, perhaps ceremonial paraphernalia since the elaborateness of the room suggested a shrine or sanctuary.

Along the exterior western wall of the pueblo ran some bands of a dark green stone, the source for which has never been discovered despite intensive search. Estes Arroyo near the mounds and Angels Peak to the southeast of the valley have been suggested. This banding mode of decoration occurred in Chaco although the color of stone most often was uniform. Earl suggested that the differences in stone used at Aztec and Chaco showed nothing more than a different source of supply of raw materials. In Chaco Canyon there were near at hand great amounts of stone which by the nature of its bedding and structure was to be had without effort in tabular, straight-faced, more or less brick-like pieces. At Aztec such stone did not occur. The material there was more massively bedded, tended to come in larger chunks, and because of its porosity was highly susceptible to destructive capillary moisture. The ranking-type of wall in the Chaco was of thin stones laid very closely one upon another, characteristically without any alteration of natural faces. Not a great deal of mud was used as mortar because not much was needed to hold the flat stones in place. In all respects Aztec masonry conformed to that of Chaco except for the variant kind of stone employed. But as yet Earl could not explain the occasional use of cobblestones in below-par efforts at construction, although he associated it with the numerous outlying ruins of the area which he considered earlier in time.

The general ground plan, degree of fortification, large size of rooms and doorways, height of ceilings, and type of masonry followed closely those observed in Chaco Canyon. The West Ruin at Aztec Ruins, which reminded Earl of Chetro Ketl in Chaco, seemed E-shaped in its principal plan when first observed; but a line of single-story rooms across the south and a low two-and-a-half-foot thick retaining wall of cobblestones faced with sandstone had completely enclosed the plaza, making it rectangular, laid out on a north-south axis. The low height of the southern side permitted the warming rays of midwinter sun to penetrate the central area of the town. Several architectural weaknesses of Chaco buildings occurred also in Aztec—joints were not broken nor were corners bonded. Doorways connecting diagonally adjacent chambers were distinctive of both Pueblo Bonito and Aztec, there being a total of five at the latter.

This fulfillment of his dreams of excavating Aztec Ruins notwithstanding, in the summer of 1917 Earl was troubled. Near the close of his school year at Columbia University where he had been studying the previous winter, the United States had entered World War I. Very little is known of that 1916-17 winter in New York except that Earl gave his first professional talk on Aztec Ruins before the New

York Academy of Science. Also, he had part-time work at the American Museum of Natural History mending Nelson's Rio Grande pots, a position which provided the opportunity of becoming well acquainted with Clark Wissler, chief of the scientific staff. Again, Earl was fortunate in his professional associations because Wissler, an Indiana scholar and author whose breadth of knowledge had made him one of the leading anthropologists of his day, was a kindly, sympathetic man sincere in his desire to further Morris's career. Throughout Earl's entire tenure with the American Museum, Wissler was the man who backed his plans and prodded him into publication.

During the next summer at Aztec there seems to have been no thought of Earl's returning East. Perhaps he had grown discouraged at the academic requirements he would have needed to meet in the face of lack of formal anthropological training at Boulder. Certainly money to continue would have been a vital consideration. And there was an often stated distaste for becoming an urbanite. Once war had been declared, the matter settled itself. Earl was in line for the military draft even though Wissler, Nelson, and Frederick Hodge wrote appeals for his deferment on the grounds that he was sole support of his mother. He simply hoped to be allowed to finish up the all-important first full season at Aztec.

At the end of August, Earl wrote his mentor that he was preparing his notes and specimens for his imminent withdrawal from the project. He divided up the materials recovered in accordance with the agreement with Abrams, who was insistent that a representative collection remain at the site, and with whom Earl was negotiating in the museum's behalf to have the ruins set aside as a permanent park. In October he wrote that he was to report for army duty and received a laudatory send-off note from Wissler which read, "I had a long letter from Nelson expressing his general approval and pleasure at the way you handled the situation."[8] Aztec work closed down. Earl took photographs from atop a tall pole securely braced with wires and wooden props. He made measurements of architectural features and packed specimens in boxes crammed with wadded newspaper and empty tin cans to prevent slightest movement. And then he waited. At month's end he sent a wire to Wissler that he had been deferred.

That fall and winter Earl devoted to the mop-up operations which follow any large-scale piece of excavation. He made a trip to New York to confer on the past work and to plan for the future and, to his amusement, had a package of bones stolen in Grand Central Station. He chuckled over what a surprised thief that must have been!

After his return West he made a ride into the Gobernador to attempt to secure more sherd fragments at the pottery-strewn graveside where he had picked up the 1915 collection. Otherwise, the long winter months were spent in Farmington with his mother.

When June 1918, rolled around he was eager to be at work. That was when the San Juan County Agriculture Agent filed a protest with the Defense Council, claiming that Earl was taking manpower needed to harvest the farm crops. Only upon Earl's statement that he would permit any worker time off at haying or harvest time was work allowed to be resumed. *El Palacio,* journal of the School of American Research, reported, "The American Museum of Natural History, in charge of excavations and reconstruction at Aztec, San Juan country, has given orders that all staff members and employees must assist in farm work in the San Juan valley whenever this assistance is needed."[9]

A fund of five thousand dollars had been set aside for the summer's digging. Earl urged a doubling-up of effort in order to get through as much of the excavation as possible in view of his tenuous draft status and the prolonged prosecution of the war. Museum president Osborne obtained a supplemental appropriation of five thousand, these two sums representing the maximum money put into Aztec in any one season. Reports of the following November stated, "By way of summary of the three year's work, it may be said that one hundred thirty seven of a probable two hundred ninety rooms have been cleared of debris, and the walls of the east wing and one half of the north wing have undergone the ultimate stages of repair. The exploration and repair of the Aztec Ruin is, then, somewhat less than half completed . . . the exploration of the Aztec Ruin will enable a more thorough and detailed reconstruction of the material culture of the prehistoric Pueblos than might be expected to result from the investigation of any other site whatsoever."[10]

The historical facts seemed to be these: that Pueblo occupation of the vicinity had been intensive for a number of centuries, the great house coming as a culmination of a long period of growth and development. The compound had been allowed to go into partial ruin perhaps twice, with subsequent repair and reoccupation. The first builders had completed its intended form, except for the low, one-story South Wing rooms, and dwelt in it for generations as testified by the fact that the silt had raised the land level along the north exterior wall some three feet above the foundations. Then the structure was abandoned and began to fall into ruin, filling many lower rooms with unconsolidated rubble. At some later period new floors were made and the building was partly renovated and remodeled, including an extension into the courtyard. Rooms were partitioned into smaller units, doorways were reduced in size, and a few smaller rooms were constructed within larger ones. Another cycle of population expansion and retraction ensued. Ultimately the few remaining families were driven off by invaders who set fire to the dwelling and ended forever its usefulness.

Two very significant aspects of the aboriginal history of the Animas village were not yet apparent. Although Earl had recognized two separate stages of occupation, he had as yet no evidence that they were enjoyed by two slightly varying groups of Indians, all Pueblos but having regional cultural differences which in part might or might not have represented successive periods over the same general area. And in his wildest dreams he never would have believed that one day he could know exact Christian calendar-year dates to demark those phases of the life of his site.

As early as 1901, Dr. A. E. Douglass, an astronomer at the University of Arizona, was engaged in studies of climatic change and their relationship to astronomical phenomena. He surmised that the annual growth rings found in tree structure might reflect precipitation fluctuations, that is a fat ring for wet years and a lean one for dry. After three years of research, he was able to measure rings on a yearly basis in some complete sections of tree trunks and then to cross-date them with a stump which had no outer rings at all but did possess inner rings which matched. Then Douglass wanted to push his rings back farther and farther into the past in order to gain a more comprehensive perspective of cycles of climatic variability. He progressed backward from living pines and firs, with a normal lifetime of two hundred years, to logs of trees, which had ceased growth at some interval during that time, gradually building up the scraps of overlapping rings into a chronology which moved counterhistorically, from this year to last. In a short time Douglass had reached the living end. He turned to Spanish churches of the Colonial period and then to pre-white Indian ruins in an attempt to get specimens which might enable him to acquire a more lengthy record.

The first archaeologist to be involved with tree rings was Earl, by profession concerned with the past beyond that place known as "white contact" (more accurately, recorded history). The first prehistoric timbers to be examined by Douglass came from Aztec Ruins in 1918. Three specimens picked up by Nelson at Pueblo Bonito were included. Earl had submitted wood from the Gobernador three years earlier, and not having heard more of it, thought Douglass had been thwarted in his attempt to count down a ladder of rings into the times of ancient men. He assumed nothing would come of the Aztec samples. Not until August 1919, when Douglass paid a visit to Aztec, did he begin to believe in the validity of tree-ring chronology.

As Earl later recalled with amusement, Dr. Douglass had arrived on an especially hot busy day after the arduous drive by touring car from Gallup to Shiprock over one of the most notoriously bad roads in New Mexico. In spite of his fatigue, Douglass wanted to set about immediately cutting wood sections which he hoped would enable him to carry his stalled modern chronology over into the past. Earl was skeptical, so much so that he paid little attention to the astronomer. He pointed to a pile of timbers from the ruin stacked beside his shack and awaiting use in reconstruction work and in effect said, "There's the wood, but what's the use?"

That evening while Earl was tediously getting notes in order and supplies ready for the next day, Dr. Douglass sat on the doorsill and began to talk about his idea of sometime being able to give archaeology a firm chronology upon which to base its findings. Earl continued with his work. He was reluctant to become engaged in conversation, not because of any objection to listening to Douglass's theorizing, but because he had a thousand details of administration before him and he had been at work in the ruins since sunup. Douglass did not seem to notice his preoccupation and talked on, as much to himself as to Earl.

As Douglass continued to talk, Earl's interest increased. He laid aside his notebooks and pencil and went with Douglass to examine his specimens, listening intently as the older scholar explained his methods. In their enthusiasm the weariness of travel and of work melted away as they sat up most of that summer night discussing the exciting theory.

The next few days Earl took Douglass to Basin Mountain and to Sullivan's lumberyard where he could take samples of modern pine and spruce growing in the vicinity. It was not yet known how to read juniper or piñon, and since juniper was the most long lasting and frequently used wood, Earl wondered how far the dating process actually could go. The two men discussed methods of obtaining specimens from aboriginal beams still in place without weakening them. Together they planned a specimen borer which would consist of a piece of steel tubing one inch in diameter with fine saw teeth at one end and a brace at the other.

After Douglass had departed, he wrote back from the Harvey House in Gallup asking for a set of four or five pieces of wood from one specific room and examples from the most probable aboriginal source. Earl, using the implement which Douglass shipped, took cores from twenty-six beams in sixteen different rooms.

Several months passed before the anxiously awaited report came from Douglass. Earl was surprised by what he read. First of all, every sample submitted had been cut or girdled in winter. This was surprising, for Earl had felt that the bark would have been too tightly set to allow such unmarred removal as had been accomplished. He reasoned that a great amount of timber must have been felled at one time, a two- or three-year supply, and then it had been stacked to season, since green wood was too difficult to work with stone tools. Furthermore all the timbers covered only an eight-year span. It had seemed that a sizeable structure built by such primitive means as were at the disposal of the Old People—the laborious hand-shaping of stones hauled from a source miles distant, the felling of large timbers in the mountains and floating them downstream, the actual work of erection—would have required many more years of communal effort.

The biggest surprise of the report came through comparison of Aztec timbers with those of Pueblo Bonito forwarded from Pepper's collections of twenty-five years previously. Douglass announced that the Bonito wood had been cut forty to forty-five years before that at Aztec! He selected a particularly fat, easily discernible ring and called it 500. From there he assigned Aztec beams a *relative* date of 523 to 528 and Bonito, 476 to 486. It would not be known for ten more years just where these *relative* dates tied into the modern calendar with its *absolute* dates.

From that moment in 1919 until his death in 1956, Earl was the most avid collector of tree-ring specimens Southwestern archaeology has ever known.

The year of 1918 saw Earl make another contribution to knowledge of the region's past: that at least once, local prehistoric residents had experimented with the manufacture of bricks made of adobe mud, a method of manufacture universally used by the Spanish in the Southwest. In two small kivas at a site three-eighths of a mile from the main ruins were observed wall veneers of adobe bricks.[11] Another find of these forms was made in later years upon the Abrams farm. Apparently the experiment had been considered a failure by the eleventh-century architects because stonemasonry continued in style. Adobes also had been employed in some of the Kayenta structures as well as in White House at Canyon de Chelly, as Earl would learn later.

B. T. B. Hyde, one of the brothers who had sponsored the Wetherill work in Grand Gulch and Pueblo Bonito and a former student of Frederick Ward Putnam of Harvard and the American Museum of Natural History, had been associated with that museum in various capacities since the 1890's. In 1918 he was sent to Aztec to relieve Earl of the many routine chores consuming his time. This was not a completely happy arrangement. Earl thought Hyde an impractical rich man with a propensity for grandiose schemes, and with little understanding of the particular problems of Aztec. Also, he found it impossible to delegate the director's many duties and accordingly wrote Wissler: "In so far as I am able, I shall follow your instructions as to having a more comprehensive publication well under way by the end of the season. However, I cannot bring myself to be away from the excavations while they are going on for many minutes at a time. My conclusions as to conditions and relations are based chiefly upon a careful scrutiny of the digging as it progresses, and I do not want to lose a single detail which would help to answer one of the numerous questions with which my mind is filled."[12]

There were several specific areas of disagreement between the two men. Hyde wanted burials and artifacts left in place so that visitors might see them just as they were found, and he proposed to organize a local volunteer committee to guard the ruins from despoilers and collectors. Earl objected to these plans, pointing out that his future and that of the site were filled with wartime uncertainty. Furthermore, since this was not museum property, they could not patrol Mr. Abram's farm. They could, however, continue negotiations for the property.

The structure then being exposed was but one of six complexes in the immediate area. The museum, through financial gifts of Archer Huntington, proposed to buy a twenty-five-acre tract encompassing some of the mounds for sixty-five hundred dollars, or what it would cost Abrams to replace the ruin area with additional cultivable land. Institutional regulations debarred the museum from permanently maintaining a park at the site, hence it was planned, once the excavations were completed, to deed the property to some public body such as the United States government, the state of New Mexico, or the town of Aztec. Abrams remained adamant in his insistence that provision for a museum be made a part of the transaction. The law of the land prohibited the government, should it accept the gift, from entering into such an agreement involving mandatory expenditures; war conditions delayed an early settlement. It was not until April 1920, after Wissler had come to Aztec to confer personally with Abrams, that a transfer of title was made, the American Museum of Natural History becoming temporary owner of the site.

In the fall of 1918, with the war at an end and Earl free of uncertainty of military induction, Wissler made him an offer. He asked Earl to take up permanent residence at the ruins and for twelve hundred dollars a year to act as museum agent there. He could continue work at Aztec on a smaller scale inasmuch as there would be no rush to meet a lease expiration, and he would be allowed time to do collateral field work as he desired. Earl accepted. For the next fifteen years, Aztec Ruins would be his home. He wrote, "My attitude toward this piece of work is not that of one who labors because of the financial consideration involved. My interest in it is the same as if I were doing it upon my own initiative, and with my own funds. Therefore as far as the future is concerned, you may depend upon me to the limit of my powers."[13]

The budget for 1919 allowed a thousand dollars for Earl to build a home at the site. As many other home builders have learned, it cost twice the estimate. At a location just south of the village entrance and with stones and timbers salvaged from fallen portions of the ruins, work was commenced in the slack days of the fall, Earl and several helpers doing the construction. The small house, unobtrusive in its similarity to the pueblo behind it, was ready for occupancy in November, 1920. The headquarters shack in the plaza became a temporary exhibit hall until such time as a more suitable one, to be attached to Earl's new home, could be completed. Two rooms in the southwestern corner of the ruin were converted into a combination blacksmith shop and tool shed, as well as a garage for the institution's model-T Ford. In this housing arrangement Earl achieved a unique status among Southwestern colleagues, previously enjoyed only by Richard Wetherill at Pueblo Bonito: he was a practicing archaeologist living amidst the object of his attentions.

The first hints of the distinctive occupations of Aztec were revealed in a letter of January 12, 1920, to Wissler in which Earl reported, "Saturday we finished clearing out a room whose contents I feared might be damaged by melting snow. Most interesting evidence of superposition was obtained. Pottery was obtained both above and below a secondary floor. There is a marked difference in composition, form and ornamentation between the wares from the two levels."

The apparent stratigraphy found in 1920 was not sufficient to enable excavators to make positive conclusions concerning the two sequences of occupation, although Earl did wonder about the few hollow figurines which had come from the diggings from the very initiation of work. He had considered them alien trade pieces, the sort of whimsical bric-a-brac women might have bartered some valuable possession to obtain, but perhaps they were more important. Not until work of the following year would he be sure.

At that time workmen sank a pit in the southwest corner of the barren windswept plaza and there found graves with associated pottery in a room of a building which had been dismantled in prehistoric times. This led to further exploration and one of those lucky archaeological accidents. Two kivas, one built beneath the other, were encountered eight feet below the level of the plaza where Earl had previously decided there was no further need for excavation. They were filled with occupational refuse incorporating many fragments of broken pottery. In the lower kiva, sealed over by the floor of the one above it, pottery was of unmixed Chaco types, two hundred pounds of sherds and thirty restorable vessels. Further proof of Chaco occupation came from a compacted layer of earth where there were two prizes—effigies of a seated hunchback figure similar to one recovered by George Pepper at Pueblo Bonito and a sad-eyed spotted deer.

Anxious to base this excavation accident on proof, Earl put diggers to work in the northeast sector of the plaza, cleared in 1917 down to a packed, old surface level. Beneath four feet of fill another kiva was encountered, this one a mere pit in the ground, plastered but without bench or pilasters. This, too, was loaded with Chaco deposits which Earl considered the richest ceramic complex he had yet found.[14] Included in this find was an effigy of a human male with conspicuously represented genitals and a line representing a sandal tie on one foot.

With tenacity, Earl pursued the Chacoans. The plaza was plugged here and there but no more hidden chambers were found even though Earl was positive that a full excavation of the southeast and southwest corners of the court would reveal a complicated maze of buildings piled on top of, or crosscutting, each other. Then he turned to the house itself. Beneath the floors of some of the ground-level rooms he found circumstantial evidence. Chaco refuse, in places five feet thick, had been floored over, sealed off as neatly as jelly under paraffin. Above it drifted the Mesa Verde refuse. After five years of intensive study, quite by accident Earl was approaching the truth, and the pieces of the complex puzzle were falling into place. Had he realized that the old courtyard was the true heart of the town in all its stages, he might have commenced his explorations there in 1916. Dr. Wissler, amazed at the turn of events commented, "It seems rather curious that we should have begun at just the wrong end of this ruin, but perhaps it is best as it is because we shall have worked over the whole in anticipation of the solution."[15]

The range of Chaco culture had not been defined nor had its temporal relationships been determined. But to Earl in 1921 it seemed unquestionable that people bearing that tradition had settled on the fertile terraces of the Animas. They constructed a town as fine as those in their relatives' area to the south, they worshipped in similar chambers, and they shared the same craft traditions and channels of trade, even like Pueblo Bonito acquiring goods from central Mexico. How they disposed of their dead remained as much of a mystery at Aztec as it had at Chaco Canyon. "A point of interest has just turned up here. I found a skeleton sticking out of the bank of Nelson's test pit in the southeast refuse mound, and with it two fine pieces of Chaco ware. The design on the pitcher is the same as the major element of the decoration of the painted board shown in Pepper's plate S. Today I found another grave on the opposite side of the pit, also accompanied by the older pottery. It has always been very much of a puzzle where the Chaco people of this place put their dead, as only one skeleton identifiable as of this age had been found previous to these two. It now looks as if there may be quite a few in the southeast refuse mound. Of course, it has been pretty well prospected, but in the untouched parts there is room for scores of graves. I hope they prove to be there."[16]

They did not. Only a total of five positive Chaco burials were uncovered at Aztec, one in a pit beneath the floor of a dwelling, one in refuse within the building, and three in the southeast refuse mound Earl's letter mentioned. Several other burials might have pertained to the Chaco occupation, but Earl did not feel certain of the cultural association.

Presumably Aztec and the Chaco towns like Pueblo Bonito were roughly contemporaneous if Douglass's dendrochronological determinations proved correct. Aztec even might represent a colony of Golden Age Bonitoans, an actual migration from the canyon rather than a generalized sharing of culture traits. At any rate, the people lingered in the northlands for considerable time if one could judge the length of occupancy by the average one yard depth of accumulated refuse and the sherd-littered, eight-foot-high trash dump beside the city's walls. Then, for reasons as yet unknown but no doubt similar to those which have banked the horizon of other cultures at other times, Chaco culture faded from the valley. There was no evidence of strife. It was simply a matter of walking away and never coming back.

From that point on the story of Aztec was much as Earl had always thought. Deserted, the great city began to decay. Just how long this might have been he had no way of knowing. Then, perhaps in a final push outward from overpopulation farther north or as a result of an increasing occupation already present in the Animas Valley, Mesa Verde folk arrived and reclaimed the structure. They moved into portions still in good condition, razed others where necessary (particularly the West Wing), and added on as they desired, often reusing materials of the older house. Their remodeling changes are to be seen in introduction of T-shaped doorways and kiva styles as well as minor architectural variations. And they built other structures adjacent to the West Ruin, some of circular form. At the same time, other individuals of the same stock were building along the valley terraces, often using the most plentiful materials—cobblestones. The Old Fort, scene of Earl's childhood digging, was one of the larger settlements along the San Juan born of this impetus.

Mesa Verdians had arrived at Aztec Ruins, though not in the Animas valley in general, with their ceramic, architectural, and other features fully developed. They thrived for a time as had their predecessors, perhaps had occupied the town in larger numbers, but like those earlier people, their culture became beset with problems of drought, disease, and general decline, all of which is eloquently described in the final paragraphs of Earl's last report on Aztec Ruins.

> But there came a time when they had become a dwindling remnant, huddled into filthy quarters, their women and children dying off rapidly, and being laid away in rooms beneath and beside those in which they dwelt, with few or no accompaniments. Architecture had become a dead art. Their last buildings were tawdry makeshifts, weak and flimsy to the limit of belief. The same condition held in the field of ceramics. There is recognizable at the close a distinct variant of the Mesa Verde pottery complex in which the paste is very frail and friable, the pigment impermanent and poorly handled, the decoration not crude but decadent, and grace of form almost entirely lost. Upon this condition of cultural senility or disease came the fire of intentional origin which for an interval transformed all but the western side of the pueblo into a veritable furnace. Whether the remainder of the Mesa Verde people evacuated the place and then fired it, or whether an enemy was the incendiary, may

never be known, but the burning thereof marked the close of human occupation of the Aztec Ruin. During the centuries which followed, there labored within the great house only the effacing hand of time.[17]

Archaeology was not at a standstill elsewhere in the Southwest while Earl was absorbed in Aztec. Nelson had continued for several years with his Rio Grande pottery surveys. The pressure of his museum duties kept him from writing the results of this fieldwork and in time removed him from the Southwest entirely.

At Pecos, Kidder continued his mammoth undertaking, in 1916 doing further stratigraphic work and discovering that he had a New Mexico counterpart of Troy with city built upon city. The following season he was off to war, but testing was continued in the vicinity by Carl Guthe. The work in the field was suspended until the summer of 1920 when digging in the houses was resumed by Kidder and the harvest of artifacts kept pace with all standards previously set.

Work had gone on also in the Kayenta, early periods being further studied by Guernsey and a late site, Betatakin, being restored by Neil Judd.

In 1920 Judd, working for the United States National Museum, was assigned the task of appraising the ruins of Chaco Canyon with prospect of excavation in behalf of the National Geographic Society. He invited three old friends—Morris, Sylvanus Morley, and Kidder—to accompany him on a reconnaissance of the canyon to select a site for study. They were to rendezvous at Aztec. After a brief stay there, they departed for Chaco Canyon.

At Chaco, the four archaeologists explored many of the ruins, weighing the research possibilities of each. The canyon is one hundred feet deep, nearly a mile wide in places, and fifteen miles long and cuts through a desolate section of northern New Mexico. In times past this dry realm was occupied by one of the largest concentrations of aborigines anywhere in the San Juan. More than a dozen multiroomed several-storied structures stand along the canyon bottom or on the mesa tops to the north or south, and over two hundred smaller archaeological sites have been mapped within the limits of the monument. It was believed that these rubbled wrecks in the desert once had experienced an efflorescence of Pueblo culture such as had occurred in few other regions. Their inhabitants seemed to have found stimuli to create a high level of artistic achievement but then had known hardships which drove them from their homes. What might have transpired thereafter was hinted at in Nelson's observation of Mesa Verde sherds in the dumps.

Huge Pueblo Bonito, or Beautiful Town, was a natural center of attention because of work already done there by the Hyde Exploring Expedition. Its size—estimated at eight hundred rooms and thirty-two kivas sprawled over nearly three acres of land along the north side of the canyon—and its apparent wealth of material objects indicated that once it had been the metropolis of the Chaco. Pepper's work had touched less than half of the town. Furthermore, he had failed to note temporal phases of development. Kidder, fresh from the superpositions of dwellings at Pecos, thought it probable that older habitations might occur beneath the large structure. Hence one might gain insight into early times of Southwestern occupation, periods little understood at that time because of the fact that most excavations had been of either what Earl called Full Pueblo levels or the very early Basket Maker.

Pueblo Bonito sat impressively against the face of a sheer cliff one hundred feet high. One mammoth block of stone one hundred fifty feet long and some thirty thousand tons in weight had broken loose from its stratum to lean toward the town and had been treacherously undercut by scouring action of wind and water. The reconnaissance party knew this rock as "The Cliff Braced Up from Beneath", the Navajo description; the National Park Service called it Threatening Rock. They realized that it had been in that seemingly hazardous position at the time of the Indian occupation of the canyon. In 1916, Nelson and Earl had made a brief examination of the practical attempts Indian masons had made to hold it steady by the erection of retaining walls of masonry, pine props, and banked platforms of adobe.*

After much discussion with Hewett, who had launched a campaign at neighboring Chetro Ketl, Judd determined to recommend excavation of the site of Pueblo Bonito and a smaller ruin on the banks of the Chaco arroyo, called Pueblo del Arroyo. Morley, on the National Geographic Society Board, would carry such a decision to a meeting in Washington and would request the American Museum of National History to relinquish its excavation permits for Pueblo Bonito.

The National Geographic group continued on southward to an ancient Zuñi town called Hawikuh. This site, one of the fabled Seven Cities of Cibola for which early Spaniards had searched, was being

* In January 1941, almost a quarter of a century after Judd's reconnaissance, the rock came thundering down upon the ancient town, smashing beneath its tremendous weight the highest standing walls of the northern portion of the site, even though the National Park Service and Civilian Conservation Corps crews had attempted to cause the stone block to settle back against the cliff.

studied by Frederick Hodge, former head of the Bureau of American Ethnology and then associated with the Museum of the American Indian. Two of his field helpers were names often repeated in the story of Southwestern archaeology—George Pepper and Jesse Nusbaum. Earl had met Dr. Hodge first in 1912, when he, Hodge, and Morley had made a visit to the Rio Grande pueblo of Santa Clara. Later Hodge had assumed a role of adviser for Earl's first scientific publication. This early acquaintance had been renewed when Earl and Talbot Hyde, on word from Wissler, had gone to Hawikuh to observe field techniques.

From Hawikuh the men went on to Inscription Rock, a sheer-faced promontory where the conquistadores had placed their signatures under an inscription beginning with the words of "Paso por aqui." By auto they rode to Chinle and Canyon de Chelly in northern Arizona, Earl being completely unaware that in three years he would be caught up in the fascination of that colorful region. At the Hopi villages farther on Earl witnessed his first Snake Dance and took the occasion to acquire some old historic pots as gifts for friends and to add to his own growing collection. On return to Aztec he noted, "My trip with Judd was very pleasant and instructive. Things seen at Zuni and the Hopi towns have clarified much that was obscure in my mind in regard to conditions observed in the ancient ruins. The various intervals spent with Kidder, Hodge, Judd, and Hewett, and the discussions which arose gave me a broader perspective of the problem as a whole which will bear fruit in due time."[18]

The first fruit was an article which appeared in the *Proceedings of the National Academy of Science* outlining Earl's views on the chronology of the San Juan, a paper that resulted from Wissler's prodding him to attach his name to the archaeology of that area and thus establish a priority. By this time Earl already had almost a dozen publications on various aspects of this research dealing primarily with Aztec. He had been urged to report as work proceeded rather than to wait until the ruin was completely cleared. Nelson and Wissler wanted to avoid another Pepper affair when a twenty-year lag between excavation and publication had occurred.[19] Like many other scientists, before and since, Earl found much of the effort necessary to compile a detailed report sheer drudgery. There was little doubt in his mind but what excavation was easier and a great deal more fun. Wissler sensed this attitude and constantly reminded Earl of the need of publishing lest accumulation of material objects rather than growth of scientific data become the goal. He reminded Earl that archaeological remains are unique and irreplacable records of human history and once dug up, their value is lost unless presented fully.

Earl's chronology paper was particularly significant for it revealed a maturing of his thoughts and showed the great breadth of his background as well. Also, in its lack of complexity it indicated the work yet to be done. Earl claimed to have examined one hundred forty-eight sites in the San Juan, after having visited two hundred fifty, in a ten year period, an astounding feat inasmuch as he had been a true professional for only five of those years. He recognized four stages of culture beginning with long-headed Basket Makers in a twenty-five mile radius of Bluff City, Utah, who produced the array of baskets, sandals, and bags found by Kidder, Guernsey, and the Wetherills; a nebulous, widespread Pre Pueblo characterized by flimsy, irregularly shaped dwellings of poles and mud, and plain pottery; an as yet unstudied early black-on-white pottery stage whose people were round-headed, had stone houses and kivas, and fashioned corrugated pottery; and a late black-on-white pottery stage which was found in two types of settings—those in cliff shelters as at Mesa Verde and those in great houses in the open, Aztec Ruins being a typical example.

Another direct result of the Judd trip was a strengthening of Earl's determination to undertake excavation of the Great Kiva which lay in the southern section of the Aztec plaza. It is curious that Moorehead's engineer in 1892 had failed to observe that this kiva pit was of far greater size than any others visible in the Aztec rubble, a fact which had not escaped Earl upon his first visit there as a child three years later. However, because of the very size of the kiva and the laborious excavation involved, this was a phase of the work which had been delayed. In the early summer of 1920, while doing some clearing at the rim of the kiva depression, workmen had revealed a concentric ring of chambers around the kiva, a situation which Earl thought might prove to be unusual. Also he felt a sense of urgency to have his Great Kiva cleared before those of the Chaco sites were done, giving him a type example to which other archaeologists would have to refer. In October he recommended to Wissler, "The Great Kiva in the court, and the surrounding row of chambers should next be attacked. Groups of this type occur in the courts of Pueblo Chettrokettle and other ruins in the Chaco group. It would be desirable for us to publish on our example of this new type of structure before someone else gets ahead of us,"[20] and later, "I am most desirous of opening and describing this at present unknown type of structure before the Chaco Canyon people dig out a similar one."[21]

But there was no money. Nevertheless Earl asked and received permission to proceed with the Great Kiva excavation, hoping to make up the expenditures from his own pocket with the next museum appropriation and a contribution from Huntington. By February 1921, he was able to report, "It is proving to be a most remarkable structure. The outstanding point revealed thus far is that on the north side, connected with the kiva by a stairway, there is a raised alcove room containing an altar and other unusual features as yet not wholly uncovered."[22] Work was completed by the end of March. Earl at once sat down to write a report for the anthropological series of the museum. It took the place of a planned ceramics paper which was delayed by the finding of the Chaco cultural layers; no publication dealing specifically with the pottery was ever written although many of the ideas as to the comparative qualities and time of manufacture of Chaco and Mesa Verde pottery were incorporated in a voluminous report on the La Plata to be completed years later. Earl accomplished his aim of beating Judd in the Great Kiva study for in June, three months after Aztec work was done and an article was in press, he wrote Wissler: "Judd has just finished digging out the great kiva in Bonito. It presents some variations in detail, but in all essentials is the same as the one here. Strangely enough on the topmost of its several floors were numerous Mesa Verde sherds, apparently with no admixture of Chaco ware."[23]

The Aztec Great Kiva, which Earl likened to a wheel, with the kiva being the hub and the arc-shaped surface rooms being located between the radiating spokes[24] was approximately forty-one feet in diameter at floor level, sunk seven-and-one-half feet below the plaza. It was a super-sanctuary for the village, a kind of primitive cathedral in which the most important religious ceremonies could have been held. It was encircled by two masonry benches, one perhaps being the remains of an earlier razed kiva and the other representing a convention of San Juan kivas. On its north and south sides were stairs, the southern one leading to a passageway to the outside and the north one to a surface-level, three-sided alcove with unique features which Earl interpreted as being of special ceremonial significance. A built-in altar, a backdrop indicated by the charred stubs of three posts, and a symbolic hole to the underworld called a *sipapu* gave this the appearance of a shrine. From there a priest might have had a dramatic position overlooking rites carried on below in the kiva. A series of vertical slots up the walls once might have held cross poles to create vertical ladders to each of the dozen encircling one-story surface rooms. On the kiva floor were the remains of four pillars composed of alternating layers of masonry and mud-embedded, peeled cedar poles, a technique which would have produced the strength and stability necessary to support a heavy roof. The highest pillar was only three feet six inches when found, but from the amount of fallen materials, Earl estimated that the pillars once had stood sixteen feet high. Two vaults in the floor, eight feet long and three feet wide and three feet deep, might have been large drums upon which participants in ceremonies danced, or they might have been stage pits from which figures could have emerged as if by magic at specified points in the proceedings. A square masonry box between the southern pillars was filled with fine white ash, showing its usage for a long period as a fire pit. Earl suggested it might have housed the sacred fires of the community. Other numerous potholes, presumably for caches of offerings or valuables, were scattered haphazardly over the entire floor surface.

The walls of the kiva were masonry composed of a thin veneer of sandstone and a massive hearting of river cobbles; walls of the surrounding chambers were unusually thin and were of coursed sandstone on a foundation of cobblestones. In time of use all surfaces had been plastered, with evidence that a two- to three-foot basal border had been red and the upper portions had been white. Earl felt there had been several refurbishings of walls with at least nine renewals of the smoothed adobe floor.

The roof of the Great Kiva exemplified the immense skill of the aboriginal engineers. An area of almost nineteen hundred square feet had to be roofed over without use of mortice or tenon, wooden peg or metal nail. A wooden framework would have had to support not only its own weight but a covering of at least a foot of earth, or a direct load of an estimated ninety tons. Earl thought there was no evidence of a vaulted roof such as was seen in most of the smaller kivas at Aztec because of the absence of pilasters spaced around the kiva walls. Therefore, he concluded that the roof had been flat with a central ventilating opening and that a rectangular core of four heavy girders had rested on top of the large pillars. Radial timbers, found in quantity but in a carbonized condition throughout the fill, had rayed out from this core to the tops of the outer walls of the encircling rooms. Over these were lashed smaller poles and splints which were topped with earth. Thus, the depression of the kiva and the rooms which were placed around it at ground level were under a single roof and stood like a giant hatbox in the south courtyard.

In 1921 it seemed to Earl that the Great Kiva was a late elaboration of the ordinary smaller ceremonial house and that its presence at Aztec represented not only the flowering of a more complex ritualism but was another tie to the Chaco where there were at least ten similar structures. For the first time in print, because of work earlier that season which led to the accidental finding of Chaco deposition, he made the definite statement of two occupations at Aztec, a reversal of his earlier theory of a hybrid culture. He postulated that the Great Kiva had been remodeled by the Mesa Verdians who moved into the town after the Chacoans had departed and that it had burned in the fire which brought about the final ruination of Aztec.

There was a notable postscript to Earl's work in the Great Kiva which came thirteen years after original excavation when Earl was no longer in residence at the ruin nor employed by the American Museum of Natural History. But the results were destined to stand as a living memorial to Earl's skill, one which would be of utmost interest to visitors to the site. He was asked by Arno B. Cammerer, Director of the Office of National Parks, Buildings, and Reservations to undertake reconstruction and stabilization of structures at Aztec, as well as at Mesa Verde.

At Aztec the job was to be restoration of the Great Kiva, to restore it to the appearance it might have had when in use. In early spring, with recruitment of the best stonemasons and carpenters to be had in the area, work commenced. One of the principal helpers was Gustav Stromsvik, a Norwegian who had worked for Earl in Yucatan and in the Southwest. Men were needed to gather and sort building stone. When local supplies were exhausted, rock was brought by truck from La Plata sites excavated earlier by Earl. Poles for the ceiling and pillars had to be peeled; cedars had to be made into shakes. The amount of deterioration since excavation was great, the kiva by 1934 resembling a yawning circular bowl strewn with scattered stones, with little definite indication of the features which had been found in 1921. In a short time, however, with diligent efforts on the part of the crew, the surface was cleared sufficiently to allow actual reconstruction to begin. Stone walls started to rise around the circumference of the kiva. The vaults and fire pit took shape after they first had been completely dismantled and a new foundation had been prepared.

Then Earl made a hurried trip to Chaco to get ideas on constructional details. By this time the larger Great Sanctuary of Chetro Ketl, which was originally dug in 1921 by the School of American Research, had undergone further study in 1929 and several subsequent seasons, with the discovery of an older building period at more depth and wall niches containing remarkable caches of native jewelry. The mammoth sandstone disks bedded on coal shale found under Chetro Ketl pillars inspired Earl, upon his return to Aztec, to sink pits below the Aztec pillars. What he found enabled him to fill in more of the mosaic of the past and further pointed up the fact that no excavation in the Southwest could be considered complete until work had been carried down to virgin soil. His experience duplicated that of Hewett's at Chetro Ketl: an older kiva had been erected on the same site.

Before the Great Kiva had a roof in place, all the appropriation money had been spent. Many of the planned repair projects on the rest of the ruin still had to be done. Appeals had to be dispatched to Secretary of the Interior Ickes for additional funds. Once these were secured, the Great Kiva assumed a finished appearance. A formula for a suitable plaster color was secured from John Meem, the Santa Fe architect who designed the Laboratory of Anthropology located in that city. It was a mixture of reddish sand, hydrated lime, mineral-red mortar color, burnt umber, brown, and raw sienna.

Not everyone liked what he now saw in the Aztec plaza. Archaeologists argued over details of restoration. The flat roof, in particular, bothered some students, but no one had a better solution to offer. The shiny newness of the building was distracting. Many felt disturbed at reconstruction, believing a ruin should be preserved but not rebuilt. Earl, however, was satisfied. He had not added a single feature for which he did not have concrete evidence with the exception of high niches in the pillars to accommodate modern-day lighting. Time would mellow the walls.

Tourists to the monument expressed a totally favorable reaction. In the coolness of the kiva's deep interior, in its quiet massive grandeur, they sensed the moving religious vitality of a foreign people who centuries past gathered there for worship. Enclosure itself created a feeling which never could have been gained from an unroofed structure. This particular building was the memory that most visitors retained of old Aztec; in this Earl rejoiced.

The Great Kiva was the last major piece of excavation done by Earl at Aztec. There was a chronic shortage of funds at the museum, and Nelson wrote that Huntington seemed to have lost interest. In 1920 Earl was disheartened by the rumors of the museum's withdrawal from an active campaign there. He wrote, "My feeling is that our knowledge of the ruin will not be complete until we have found out the condition and contents of every chamber in it."[25] And to his old friend Nelson he confided, "If there is nothing more done at Aztec, the future is practically a sealed book to me. I have turned down other positions to stick to this job, and I shall continue to stick as long as there is a hope or prospect. I shall go on with research in this region as long as I can keep the pot boiling."[26]

There remained one hundred seventy-five rooms to be cleared and repaired at an estimated cost of thirty thousand dollars. Although there was little prospect of continuing in as grand a scale as in the past, there was much for Earl and his reduced crew to do. Walls were capped with cement to prevent collapse from rains, freezes, and thaws. Unsightly piles of spoil dirt were removed from the plaza and dumped into holes in the roadways. Weeds were cut and burned. The surrounding land was cleared away from exterior walls and then leveled. In doing this work a great amount of charcoal was noted along the north side of the house causing Earl to suspect the former presence of a balcony at the second-or third-story level. Notes were reworked, and manuscripts on the burials, the splinted skeleton, and the rooms of the dwellings were prepared. The tool shed was moved from the plaza, and a cobblestone annex to the west, which apparently had been erected over an early destroyed structure of Chaco affiliation, was excavated in order to prepare a suitable position for it. Earl continued to show an increasing number of tourists around the ruins. He pushed new negotiations with Abrams to acquire land containing more of the cluster of ruins although he anticipated that discovery of gas in the vicinity of the valley would raise the price of land. A deed for this second purchase from Abrams was signed in the fall of 1922. He initiated propaganda to bring about a change of route of a proposed paved highway from Durango to Farmington so that it would run down the Animas to Aztec rather than come down the La Plata as did the old road. He planned a reconstruction of the painted room in the West Wing which was to be built in a hall of the museum in New York. In the early mornings or after work had ceased for the day, he took his worn shovel and trowel and went off to the cobblestone ruins up and down the valley where he dug for pots—his form of recreation.

Earl's services were sought by colleagues who had been impressed by the painstaking work done at Aztec. Fewkes offered him employment at Aztec Springs where he thought he had another Great Kiva. "Dr. Fewkes went so far as to say that you had set the standard for excavation and in restoration and that it would be his endeavor to live up to it. If you know Dr. Fewkes very well, you will know that this is saying a good deal," was what Wissler wrote.[27] Earl declined the

Aztec Springs work. Instead he joined Judd's Pueblo Bonito camp at the end of the Chaco arroyo, but other commitments called him away after three weeks.

By no means was Earl idle just because there was no appropriation forthcoming for Aztec. He was digging periodically in several other localities which did not require great expenditures and, in enthusiasm for the new fields, lost some of his ardent desire to clean out every single unit in the old house. However, he felt a deep attachment for the ruin and was quick to accept a lease proffered by Wissler. On January 24, 1923, Aztec Ruins was proclaimed a national monument by President Warren G. Harding. The American Museum of Natural History was granted a three-year excavation permit. Earl was made the first custodian with an annual stipend of twelve dollars, about enough, as he remarked, to pay the notary public to place his stamp upon the required oath. He also was given a lifetime lease for one dollar a year on the portions of the Abrams land which the museum retained, including the house he and his mother occupied. He wrote as if in prophecy of the future, "There are still many years of fruitful archaeological research to be done in the Southwest, and as long as I have sufficient financial backing to continue therein, I would be glad to have our establishment at Aztec as home and headquarters. But the time may come when circumstances will force me into other lines and other localities. Then I should have no alternative but to cut loose entirely from this ruin."[28]

For the next decade, Earl was at his home at the ruins only for brief periods between field trips. He put together a report on details of secular rooms and had planned another on the kivas. This latter was not done because of the loss of his notes. He sorted out a representative collection of artifacts for Abrams' widow. He remained in nominal custodianship until 1928 when, in the face of over five thousand annual visitors, the government provided for a full time employee, George L. Boundey, an assistant to the Superintendent of Southwestern Monuments. Earl obligingly continued to act as consultant for all repair work done at the monument but gradually came to the view that further excavation should not be undertaken so as to give viewers a clearer conception of just what had taken place and to retain for future archaeologists a fragment suitable for cross checking by more advanced means.

In 1933, having purchased a home in Boulder, Earl vacated the house at Aztec Ruins and deeded it over to the monument. His active association with Aztec came to a close a year later after the restoration of the Great Kiva. By 1940 he felt dejected and so out of touch with his former home he wrote, "Once I regarded the Aztec Ruins as a hen might an only chick. But that was long ago. The bitter disappointment of having to give up excavation when the venture was, as I planned it, only well begun, and the time that since has passed, have brought me to the point where I view the place just as impersonally as I would if I had not devoted to it in a misguided way some of what should have been the most productive years of my life."[29]

III.
Pre Pueblo

THE SUMMER OF 1913 WAS ONE OF severe drought in the Four Corners. Ephemeral streams disappeared. Bunch grass withered and turned brown from lack of moisture. Adobe flats cracked open. Because of the dry hot weather that June and July, Earl was forced to change his plans.

He had come back to Farmington at the close of his first year in graduate school at the university, named by Hewett as a field assistant for the School of American Research, with five hundred dollars from the University of Colorado Museum to do archaeological collecting in an area new to him but which, according to rumor, had been thickly populated in ancient days. His application to the university had read: "Because of my extended experience in outfitting and maintaining a camp, my acquaintance with the people with whom it would be necessary to deal, and my intimate understanding of the varieties of relics to be found in the region, I do not hesitate to say that for amount of money involved, I can secure more material than anyone else you might send to this particular field." He proposed to explore the La Plata country which lay some miles north and west of Farmington, embraced by the lofty escarpments of the Mesa Verde to the west and to the north by the jagged crest of the La Plata Mountains usually snow crowned in early summer but gaunt and greyed in this cycle of dryness. A rolling mesa land probed by deep perpendicular canyons along its western skirts, it spread green and inviting from the La Plata River on the east to the Mancos River on the west. Piñon and cedar crowded over higher elevations, interspersed with clumps of wild gooseberries and chokecherries or open glades of sage and thorny chaparral. It was, and has remained, a region seldom visited by white men because it was largely the Southern Ute Indian Reservation. One wagon road passed through the La Plata Valley itself and cut westward from a junction south of Dale's, a farm of an early settler which became a favorite stopping place, through a basin called the Meadows to reach the Mancos River below the gorges of Mesa Verde. Earl had planned a thorough survey through the island of mesas demarked by these routes and had a government permit to include Montezuma and La Plata counties in Colorado and San Juan County in New Mexico, exclusive of Mesa Verde National Park in the former and Chaco Canyon National Monument in the latter. "I wish to traverse every mesatop in the area, and to locate every ruin."[1]

He had in part been preceded by at least three competent observers. W. H. Holmes in the employ of the Hayden Survey of the 1870's had visited and described a sprawling aboriginal residence on the east bank of the La Plata opposite a later village of that name. Moorehead, in the spring of 1892, had traveled over a portion of the region. Prudden, an Eastern doctor by profession but a summertime archaeologist by avocation, also had passed that way, guided by Clayton Wetherill.

With the strenuous goal of searching out all the ruins, Earl had saddled up a pony, tied on a blanket and small pack of food, and had ridden north from Farmington along a rutty wagon trace which was the main highway to Durango. He recalled the note he had posted to Hewett on his way out of town in which he said, "I wish to thank you for obtaining me this position, for it suits my interest and desires in every respect. I have long tried to interest the university in some relics from the Farmington region, and your recommendation has accomplished what I had been unable to do."[2]

When he arrived at a small cluster of farm houses in southern Colorado named Red Mesa, the vicinity of which was described by Prudden as vacant of ruins,[3] he hired as guide a Mormon cattleman familiar with the region lying westward to headlands. He was told of remains near Red Mesa of an ancient settlement of which he had never heard. It proved to be of special interest. Covering some forty acres on the east bank of the river, this extensive ruin gave Earl his first shred of evidence for a culture different from and presumably older than that of the ruins closer to the San Juan with which he was familiar. This was an unexpected development, the sort of turn which gives the study of archaeology an eternal appeal.

Once at the ridge to the west, Earl's sharp eyes sought the horizon ahead where the land fell away toward the embattled cuesta of the great Mesa Verde and Sleeping Ute Mountain beyond. Nowhere since leaving the La Plata had he seen running water, only murky, scum-covered pools hidden in unobtrusive places along a secluded rocky bed and aswarm with irridescent dragonflies. The La Plata itself, in its upper reaches, was so lowered one could leap across it with no difficulty. Mancos Springs, a moss-lined seep near the head of a box canyon feeding into the Mancos, was the only source of drinking water for miles in any direction. He knew he would not be able to stray far. When he returned to town, he explained, "To my great disappointment I found that the dryness of the season prevents the exploration of the central portion of the area. To work there at all would necessitate carrying water for all purposes by pack train, and the money at my disposal would not allow of such an expenditure as that would make necessary."[4]

Even though work could not be done over as wide a terrain as originally planned, Earl felt that by using Mancos Springs as a base camp, a survey of a sizeable area could be accomplished on foot. He secured the services of three local men whom he knew to be interested in the antiquities—Bill Ross, who had spent thirty years digging for pots in the ruins around Farmington and had developed a sensitivity which led him almost magnetically to specimens; Jack Lavery, who would become the principal mason at Aztec Ruins and Pueblo Bonito; and E. K. Hill. Upon a request from Fewkes, Earl also included in the group for part of the season a young undergraduate of Swarthmore College, Ralph Linton, who in years ahead became an outstanding anthropologist on the staffs of Wisconsin and Columbia universities. They piled their camp gear and digging tools into a wagon, together with thirty-seven dollars worth of beans, potatoes, bacon, coffee, flour, and other groceries, and turned back toward the north. In the course of the next nineteen years, Earl would retrace most of those steps for ten separate seasons.

The report to Hewett made at the conclusion of this first summer's work in the La Plata country is quoted fully because it reveals significant ideas of differences from classic Pueblo which would be verified in seasons to come.

> I have carried the exploration of the country between the Mancos and La Plata rivers as far as the funds at my disposal will allow. This exploration has brought to my notice the cliff ruins of Johnson Canyon,

which winds to the northwest into Mancos Canyon; numerous house sites upon the surrounding mesas; the remains of a very large settlement on both sides of the La Plata river at Red Mesa, Colorado; and scattering ruins thence down the La Plata river.

The culture represented by the cliff ruins of Johnson Canyon differs in no great particular from that of which the large ruins of the Mesa Verde are a type. However, the house sites upon the mesas present puzzling problems to the investigator. Practically without exception the walls of the buildings were constructed of sticks or small poles anchored in the ground by being set between two rows of large stones. The poles were then plastered over with mud which often formed a coat two to three inches thick. Apparently the roofs were of the ordinary type. Most of the house sites are small, and bear no evidence of more than one-storied structures.

One exception to the above was observed. Upon a high hill about one half mile northwest of the waterhole known as Mancos Springs, are the remains of a structure roughly 195 to 100 feet. The mound is rectangular, and about five feet high at the highest point. Investigators revealed but one stone wall, that being only one foot high. Much burned clay bearing the imprint of twigs and sticks supports the theory that this too was a mud and stick house.

A short distance south of the house-mound is a roughly circular mound seventy feet in diameter, and four-and-one-half-feet deep in the deepest part. A vast quantity of broken pottery strewed the surface of this mound, and the black soil composing it made it appear to be a burial mound. Excavation was commenced at the southern edge, and the mound was removed to a point a few feet north of the center. Only seven burials were found, although detached fragments of human bones were scattered throughout the soil. It seemed evident that the mound is chiefly a refuse heap. Astonishing quantities of pot shards were unearthed, and broken metates, axes, etc. were common. The earth of the mound was made up almost entirely of housesweepings, ashes, and similar debris. Badgers had burrowed through the mound most extensively and without doubt many burials had been wrecked, and the pottery broken and scattered by this agency.

The object of the expedition being primarily to obtain museum material, when it was seen how poorly the mound yielded, it was abandoned.

The pottery type represented by the major portion of the shards from this locality was an entirely new one to me. Fragments of coil-ware were rare. The cook pots which served in their stead were mostly globular in form, with straight necks two to four inches high, laid off in raised bands three-eights to three-fourths of an inch wide. One complete specimen of this type was recovered.

The black and white ware presented a great diversity both of form and symbolism. In general the ware was crude, although occasionally a fragment showing most perfect execution came to light. However, hardly a familiar design appeared. One water jug was found whose decoration was the familiar square with arms extending from the corners, but aside from this, all the decorations were utterly unlike those upon the pottery from the near-by cliffs, or those of the dominant culture of the La Plata valley.

Various blends of red and brown ware were common among the fragments, and one complete specimen of very fine red ware was recovered.

It seems permissible to conclude from the type of house construction, and from the different texture, form, and symbolism shown by the ceramic remains, that this ruin, and the ruins of which it is a type, represent a culture different in most particulars from that already known in the surrounding country.

This culture modification extends eastward to the La Plata valley. On the east side of the river at Redmesa are the remains of a settlement which covered more than forty acres, and beyond it both up and down the river are scattered remains. From the pottery fragments and other surface indications the culture here seems identical with that previously described.

On the west bank of the La Plata just across from this village is the ruin of a most unique structure. It is a rectangular pile 35 by 70 feet, and 9 feet high. It is the nearest approach to a temple ruin yet recorded from the cliff-dweller area. The main axis of the building runs east and west. Three kivas form the south side. They are flanked on the north by a single row of rooms, apparently four in number. Both kivas and rooms are entirely above the level of the surrounding country. This is the one stone ruin which I saw in all the region. The masonry is exceptionally good. The kiva at the southeast corner was partially excavated, the room north of it cleaned out. The kiva is 15½ feet in diameter and the walls are three feet thick. The kiva is a variant from the type common to the Mesa Verde. The banquettes are only four to six inches deep, and the pilasters extend to the top of the wall. I regretted that my funds gave out before the excavation of this ruin could be completed, for it is most unusual and interesting.

The culture previously indicated extends a few miles down the La Plata river from Red Mesa. Eight miles below that point, while stopping at noon on the return trip, a skeleton was found beside the wagon road. Subsequent investigation brought to light ten graves, and several specimens of pottery. These graves were of exceptional interest both because of the skeletal material and the pottery they contained. The skulls were exceptionally dolichocephalic, the foreheads being very narrow. Not one of the skulls bore evidence of posterior flattening due to being bound on a papoose board. I have never before seen a skull from the San Juan drainage which was either dolichocephalic, or failed to show artificial flattening.

No coil-ware appeared among the pottery. The cooking pots were all smooth. The bowls were gray with red and brown markings. The designs are entirely new. They extend down across the bowls much after the fashion of those upon the ancient Hopi ware. The exterior of each bowl had been painted a bright red which in many cases had mostly weathered off from contact with the soil.

Two or three miles farther down the La Plata river the large ruins of the culture common to the San Juan, Animas, and in the La Plata valley, begin. From all this I would conclude that in the upper La Plata valley, and thence westward into the drainage of the Mancos river there existed a culture which if not a different culture, was at least a distinct modification of the surrounding culture; that heretofore this culture has not been known or mentioned; and that further investigation of its remains would be highly instructive.[5]

The summer of 1914 saw Earl again in the La Plata Drainage, this time working solely for the University of Colorado. With his group, he traveled by wagon north along the La Plata River, past Long Hollow where he had discovered the long-headed skulls during a noon rest stop the previous summer, to Red Mesa. There he again turned westward toward Mancos Springs after having hired a pack outfit to carry in supplies. The weather being more favorable than that of 1913, the group was able to range far from the permanent springs at the old headquarters and to rely on pockets of clear water imprisoned in cups of the hard sandstone strata or on revived springs situated along the bases of cliffs. They rode south across Red Horse Gulch, named for a Ute painting on an escarpment, along a crest which marked the boundary between La Plata and Montezuma counties and onto a dividing spur of land between Salt Canyon in New Mexico and Grass Canyon in Colorado. What was seen that summer of 1914 was the same as what had been seen in 1913.

Some group of people perhaps fifteen hundred years before, according to Earl's estimate, had occupied these mesa tops. They had not possessed Full Pueblo culture but might possibly have been the beginning. The fifteen sites examined in the two seasons formed the basis of a report later published by the Bureau of American Ethnology. Earl became the first to excavate and publish upon a pit-house type of architecture in the northern San Juan, the first to describe the regional variation of the plain and poorly decorated pottery, the first to put forth the idea of the germ of Pueblo culture being localized in the San Juan Basin and later distributed from there. "The discovery in the northern part of their domain of a more ancient culture than that of the cliff-dwellers should be of special interest, since it appears that the region north of the San Juan River is the center from which migration carried the true Pueblo culture to the south, southeast, and perhaps to the west."[6] He called his newly found culture the Pre Pueblos but he failed to recognize a most significant fact: that the undeformed dolichocephalic crania obtained at Long Hollow were associated with a unique pottery assemblage different from that of the plateaus surrounding Mancos Springs and that in effect he had discovered not one new culture but two.

The very same season of 1914 the Harvard team of Kidder and Guernsey operating through the Kayenta area of northeastern Arizona found evidence for a similar cultural stage. They were unaware of Earl's work, just as he was of theirs.

In the dry, sandy Hagoe Canyon which opened into Monument Valley was a small cave whose entrance was clogged with Jimson weed and box elder trees. Within its confines were seen tumbled remains of a small, four-room, masonry structure practically identical to others in neighboring rock shelters and which the Kidder and Guernsey party called Fluteplayer House because of a series of figures playing musical instruments which had been pecked into a nearby cliff wall. Kayenta masonry was of consistently poorer workmanship than that of either Mesa Verde or Chaco, being composed of carelessly shaped sandstone slabs laid up with copious amounts of mud mortar into which were inserted numerous spalls of rock. But there were other structures within the cave which seemed unusual. These were semisubterranean and could be described as rectangular with rounded corners. Instead of being erected of masonry, they had foundations of sandstone slabs set on edge and topped by irregularly rounded lumps of clay laid up in brick fashion. After these so-called "turtlebacks" of clay had dried, cracks had been pointed up with more clay.

There was no superposition of architectural features at Fluteplayer House but refuse deposits were more rewarding with two distinct cultural layers being separated by a drift of sand and ashes, allowing for cultural interpretations based upon stratigraphic evidence, one of the first scientific applications of that principle outside the Rio Grande valley. From the upper stratum came black-on-white, polychrome, and corrugated sherds of the usual Kayenta array; these were considered associable with the masonry house. But from the lower layers were removed pottery fragments unlike anything yet observed in the area. The Harvard men named the lower level of occupation the Slab House culture.

Actually, credit for the first observation of this early stage of development, which was neither Basket Maker nor Full Pueblo must go to Dean Cummings who, in his only publication on fieldwork in the Kayenta, which appeared in 1910, mentioned such remains in Sagiotsosi Canyon, a gorge which cut into Monument Valley from the west. In a paper dealing with the kivas of the San Juan drainage he wrote: "In other sections as in Sagie-ot-Sosie canon, a branch of the Moonlight, and in Water Lily canon, a branch of the main Sagie, we have found numerous instances of circular rooms constructed of flat stone set up on edge, braced by posts and poles and holes filled with grass, cedar bark, or clay.[7]

The Slab House people of the Kayenta and the Pre Pueblos of the La Plata would prove to be one and the same excepting such variations as might be expected in their areal separation from each other. They were eclipsed for a few years because of the excitement generated for the newly reinstated, artifact-rich Basket Makers. No further study of this horizon was undertaken by Guernsey until after World War I.

In the La Plata area their counterparts, the Pre Pueblos, were neglected for a summer since Earl and Nels Nelson chose to dig in a more recent cobblestone ruin on their way from Mesa Verde to Farmington. Methods employed on that occasion later led to adverse criticism, although they were not unusual during the formulative period of archaeological techniques.

Site 36, as it was termed in a report, was a heap of stones which rose as a sagebrush hillock from the middle of a cultivated field on the Emery brothers' farm in the rich bottomlands near the junction of Barker Arroyo and the La Plata. The site had been dug into sporadically by local collectors for twenty-five years, at one time producing a collection of several hundred pottery vessels, most of which were highly typical of the Mesa Verde pots obtained in the region. In 1915 the owners wanted the nuisance of the ancient house removed from their property. They agreed to allow excavation if the mound would be entirely leveled in the process. The work was done with a plow and scraper, banks being caved down in slices and worked over with a pick and shovel until both the aboriginal trash mound and the twenty-room dwelling were obliterated. Sketch maps were drawn of both as demolition continued. The most interesting finds were thirty-four, large, corrugated pots which had been sunk beneath the floors near walls, or were arranged in a row parallel to the walls to serve as storage chambers or cists. This was a common custom in the San Juan area but the number of such cache vessels at Site 36 was unusual.

It was at this ruin where Earl had an amusing encounter with a local bewhiskered elder of the Mormon sect which became a favorite story. One day while on his knees in a trench, he looked up to see an overall-clad stranger standing on the mound intently watching the work. After the usual introductory remarks about the hot summer, the aged visitor said, "What Ye doin'?"

"We are arch. . .," Earl started to explain.

"Looking for the ark, be ye!" the old man gasped in astonishment. "I thought that was on a mountain on the other side of the world!"

During the spring of 1916 Earl continued his archaeological explorations along the La Plata drainage. The site selected for study was a community of mounds, domiciles and trash scattered over the surface of an isolated triangular mesa thrust high above the arroyo. There were innumerable gaping holes and piles of dug-over earth in nearly all the mounds because this ruin area had been known and potted for at least a quarter of a century. Previous to this spring of '16 Earl had observed that the largest mound at the end of the promontory had remained untouched, presumably because of the considerable efforts involved in reaching its occupational levels. He set his crew to work at an edge of the mesa, running a series of trenches in toward the highest part of the untrenched mound.

Earl employed a method which had proved successful in the past and one which would be resorted to repeatedly during the course of his career. One man was given the assignment of breaking the hard rind of the surface with a plowshare. Other members of the crew followed behind searching the furrows for any sudden change in soil color, a concentration of charcoal, a lens of refuse, or other signs of man-made disturbance which might indicate a burial pit. It was a reading of the soil, a skill demanded of all archaeologists. Through misunderstanding, it was interpreted by critics as plowing up a graveyard. In 1916 it did not pay off since no signs of graves were visible in the plow-turned earth.

There were, nonetheless, startling finds. At eight feet below the masonry house-foundations pithouses piled on top of each other or dug side by side had honeycombed the point. These had been filled and erased from the surface before the later sandstone masonry house which was responsible for the modern high mound had been constructed. Here Earl was to gain the stratigraphic information which would prove the position of his Pre Pueblos.

There were three distinct periods of occupancy represented at the site. In the earliest times there had been a sizeable settlement of houses sunk into the subsoil. These were roundish in form and had their sides plastered with mud. Earl did not search for a ventilator doorway, a feature which subsequent experience would reveal to be located at the southern wall of such pit dwellings. Associated pottery was of crude form and workmanship with painted decorations being used sparingly upon an unslipped gray base. Occasional exteriors of such vessels had been coated with a red paint which Earl judged had been applied after the vessel had undergone firing because it was easily removed with water. This red would be later termed "fugitive red" because of its impermanence. Corrugated pots were absent.

The second tenancy was represented by dwellings of cobblestones and adobe. They were of irregular shape. Kivas were present. Pottery was of more variety in both form and decoration than that of early levels. Sam Guernsey, who made a brief visit to the camp while on his way south for another session in the Kayenta, was startled at the similarity of these pots to those he and Ted Kidder had found at Fluteplayer House.

The house of dressed sandstone represented the final occupation of the mound. At the time of excavation all pottery from the structure was classed as Mesa Verde type, but in the experience gained through a number of further digs on the La Plata and at Aztec twenty-three years later, Earl made a distinction between a Chaco complex which underlay a Mesa Verde complex.

For the entire first month at Site 39, as this particular group was numbered, not a single complete vessel was recovered. Since Earl had been commissioned to add to the museum collections, this was considered a deplorable state of affairs. Daily he fretted as he diligently dug around the mound in all the likely looking spots to which his intuition and experience led him. But pots, like the trout Earl coveted, have an annoying ability of staying concealed when wanted most. He began to dispatch notes of despair back to Boulder. Data there were, exciting stuff to the retracers of history. However, data could not be placed in a museum display nor do they carry much weight with most tenders of legislative pursestrings. To Earl's relief, President Farrand, himself a trained anthropologist, shrugged off the obtainment of specimens as of secondary importance.

With dogged persistence Earl kept on looking for the elusive pottery, which he knew was somewhere on that mesa top even though others had dug before him. One morning, after getting the workmen started at their assigned jobs, he tramped out into the flat country which lay away from the main ruins to look for graves, the best known source of pottery. Before noon he had unearthed a grave in which lay a tightly flexed skeleton and four pots.

By May 28 he was able to tell Farrand, "The problem of securing specimens need give no further concern, since during the past week a burial ground was discovered from which some fifty specimens of pottery have been taken, and the richest portion is still to be excavated."[8] When he finished the work at Site 39 for the season, he had amassed an imposing collection of one hundred sixteen pots representing each of his three stages of development, some of them complete when exhumed, others mended by the light of a kerosene lamp at the adobe house which served as camp headquarters. This was the most extensive and diversified haul of early pottery reclaimed to that time. Earl's phenomenal luck, aided by tenacity of purpose and skill of excavation, had not deserted him. Through a study of the contents of this sample, he was able to take one more step toward total understanding of the course of development of pottery in the San Juan.

With the mounting excitement of the exploration of Aztec Ruins beginning to absorb him, Earl felt the research in the La Plata was finished. However, he was to learn, as others also have learned, that the answers to many of the puzzles of human history are not to be found in the largest towns nor in the richest burials. He would return again and again to the stone heaps of the La Plata conutry in order to piece together the jigsaw of lifeways of the Old People.

The next encounter with the Pre Pueblos came four years later when Earl undertook to drive Wissler in his 1917 Model-T Ford from Aztec west to Shiprock and then due south along the eastern flank of the Lukachukais to Gallup.

When Earl got his first car, he found that driving it through the trackless wastes of the Four Corners country was a challenge which almost rivaled the lure of trout and pots. It was a point of honor with him to go anywhere regardless of the odds. With his open touring car equipped with extra gas and water, spare parts, ropes, and shovels, he recaptured some of the spirit of his freighter father as he shoved aside obstacles such a quicksand, flash floods, tires pierced by cactus thorns, oilpans cracked open by jagged boulders, beating storms of sand, rain, or snow. He acquired an unrivaled reputation for ingenuity and dexterity. Many persons came to believe that if Morris could not get through, the way was closed to all others.

One of the episodes about which Earl liked to tell concerned a leaden-colored day when Captain Tom's Wash ran bank to bank across the road to Gallup. When Earl reached the brink of the arroyo on a drive back to Aztec from the south, he made a sudden decision to plunge into the churning waters and make a try for the opposite bank. Once into the swiftly moving torrent when there was no turning back, he felt his power lapse and the wheels begin to fight for footing. He knew he was doomed. But suddenly, with the throttle wide open, the car found a firm base and shot forward to the dry bank. Earl stopped and walked back to the crossing where several men were standing. When he informed the spectators that he seemed to have encountered a solid base at midstream, one man turned to him with a wry smile and said, "Of course you hit a solid base. You ran right over the top of my truck!"[9]

In June 1920, with Wissler as a passenger, there were no such accidents. Instead there was an exciting archaeological find. Earl recounted it in this way: "The discovery of hundreds of pottery vessels, scores of ancient tombs, and numerous unexplored Pueblo ruins and cemeteries rewarded our recent expedition into the Navajo country. Mere chance led us to the richest find of the season. Thirty miles south of the Shiprock Agency we noticed a number of low mounds scattered here and there over the breast of the desert. They glistened in the sunlight as if strewn with bits of mirror. Upon investigation the elevations proved to be the ruined buildings and cemeteries of a prehistoric village nearly a mile in length. The mounds were literally covered with fragments of broken pottery, the polished surfaces of which had reflected the sun's rays, and so drawn our attention."[10]

Earl was filled with his usual desire to commence digging at once and, although cautioned by Wissler not to use up his funds, he began the next month. A permit from the government did not arrive until mid-October to legalize digging which had been carried on in July and early August.

Another find of interest and material rewards was chalked up to Earl's credit. The press release said, "There had been more than twenty buildings in the village, varying in size from four to as many as fifty rooms. Aside from determining that the rooms were small, and that the walls of the structures were composed of thin unworked slabs of sandstone laid with adobe clay for mortar, we did no excavating in the buildings. The cemeteries, however, one or more of which were found southeast of each residential structure, were extensively explored.

> The winds of centuries had blown away the dust and ashes from the refuse heaps in which the dead were interred until bones and mortuary vases were left protruding from the soil. Each body lay in what had been a pit dug into the refuse. In preparation for the burial, the knees were drawn up against the chest, and the feet thrown backward toward the hips, evidently to make the body take up as little space as possible. Invariably clay vessels were placed beside the head, or in front of the breast or abdomen. Usually the grave pit was covered with a great stone slab, sometimes held up by cedar poles. The wealth of objects accompanying the skeletons of children was pathetic evidence that the hearts of this primitive people were deeply riven by the loss of their little ones. Covering the bones of one mere infant were an elegant red bowl, a slender drinking vessel, and a small vase filled with jet ornaments and shell beads and pendants from the far Pacific, the latter a treasure which may well have meant the entire wealth of a family.
>
> The two hundred pottery vessels taken from its tombs prove that this desert settlement belongs to a culture period more ancient than that represented by the enormous community dwelling at Aztec, New Mexico, in the exploration of which our efforts have been centered for the last five years. In that period the Pueblo lived in scattered settlements, unoppressed by the dread of enemies which later impelled them to build such impressive strongholds as the apartment house-fortress at Aztec.[11]

The initial work on the reservation was essentially a salvage operation. Earl meant to return at a later time to make a detailed, controlled examination of the associated house structures which he classed as early Pueblo and for which no type site had yet been dug. This was never accomplished. Instead, in the fall of 1921 with an allotment of one thousand dollars from the American Museum and accompanied by Oley Owens and Oscar Tatman from his Aztec crew, Earl began operations fifteen miles farther south. His party pitched their tents near the A. J. Newcomb Trading Post on the crossing at Captain Tom's Wash where they could secure drinking water from a well.

That basin, just beginning to cool from the heat of summer, developed into an archaeologist's dreamworld with ruins and relics at every turn, and was called "Cemetery Ridge" by Earl. There were four extensive ruin areas within a mile radius and Navajos met at the store told of others. Small house sites in the bottom of the wash were being exposed and removed by erosion. Cemeteries upward on the slopes were caving off and being devoured by floods. Age-old treasures lay eroding in the dust just waiting to be gathered. Other artifacts were covered by shallow deposition easily probed by knowing jabs of pick and shovel. Earl basked in a constant wave of excitement over new finds, not only of specimens but of data which would confirm the occupational sequence he had worked out farther north. From daylight to dark he trod the mesas and shoveled along side his helpers. After the evening meal he dismissed inclinations to sleep in order to wash and repair pottery, until he had a collection of four hundred seventy five specimens. The report of November 1921, filed with Wissler, read:

> Excavations were principally confined to the mounds on the mesas immediately overlooking Newcomb's post, and to certain isolated sites in the lower country southeastward of the mesa. Most of the digging done was in refuse mounds which with few exceptions were rich in burials. Skeletal material and pottery to the extent of approximately four hundred seventy five catalogue entries were recovered.
>
> It now appears that from the time of the first pottery makers to the abandonment of the San Juan drainage by Pueblo peoples, occupation of the territory within a mile of the Newcomb post was nearly if not completely continuous. Consequently here in a limited area the ceramic chronology of the San Juan area is more thoroughly epitomized than in any other known locality. Not only will thorough examination of the ruins within this scope confirm the stratigraphic order of the principal ceramic periods previously excavated, but it will make possible the localization of certain transitional types whose chronological position the writer has not as yet been able to establish.
>
> About eight miles eastward from the site where this year's digging

> was done there are unusually extensive slab houses dating from early Pre Pueblo times. They are situated on low hill tops or in little valleys on the outskirts of a cluster of ragged sandstone mesas in the cliffs of which there are shelters favorable for human occupation.[12]

A follow-up personal letter sent to his superior further discussed the reservation work: "As to the importance of the site, I may say with justifiable enthusiasm that it will provide more data on chronology than any other I have ever examined, or ever expected to see in the black-on-white area. Given another season there I have no doubt whatever that I should be able to give you an account of the ceramic chronology of this region which would stand for all time.

> Moreover the possibilities presented for a study of the architecture of the various periods, especially the earlier ones, are quite alluring. The slab houses mentioned in my report situated eastward of the focus of our activities, are unusually extensive and clearly defined, and would well repay the small amount of digging their exploration would entail. And on the mesa where we dug, buildings stand on top of buildings of an unknown depth, while under some of the refuse mounds there are fairly well preserved archaic structures of which not a trace would have remained had they not been covered over with a secondary deposit. In all probability the life history of the kiva is to be read among the remains on this mesa. That there are a great many subterranean chambers is proved by the fact that in every refuse mound examined were found quantities of clean gravel such as lies beneath the thin layer of soil constituting the natural surface of the mesa. We intentionally avoided opening kivas, as much as possible this season, but it would be altogether advisable at some future time to ascertain the various types which exist at this site.[13]

A letter on the new site written to his friend, Ted Kidder, brought the following cheery reply: "I was most interested to hear of the La Plata and reservation finds, the latter particularly must have been a stem-winder. That site with Pecos carries the whole story from Lord knows when down to 1838 in two jumps—for at Pecos I have gotten from the lowest levels several unmistakable Mesa Verde sherds and one 'beer-mug'. We are getting at things, aren't we?" (Kidder letter of December 16, 1921). Earl's confident response was, "Yes, I believe we are getting at things most satisfactorily. Before long we will have the chronology of the San Juan lined up about as nicely as anyone could wish for." (Letter of December 28, 1921). Forty-five years later workers still would be trying to fill in lacunae in the itinerary of man's trip from savage nomadism to sedentary civilization, but it is true that by 1921 the fundamental steps of at least Basket Maker-Pueblo culture had been determined.

In spite of the often stated desirability of studying domiciliary remains such as dotted the uninhabited piedmonts by the mountain skirts, the quest for specimens remained supreme. Again in a frigid December of 1922, when a fall storm had frozen the soil and left a foot of snow on the mesas, Earl returned to that region on a reconnaissance paid for by a new patron of the American Museum, Charles L. Bernheimer.

Earl struck out from the Barnard store to make a survey of the valley of the San Juan from Shiprock westward and then east, north, and west over the flanks of the Carriso Mountains and into a portion of the Chuska Valley. He drove the reliable old Ford as far as possible and then sought ponies at the widely separated Navajo hogans to carry him over rougher ground. In the circular valley at the northern head of the mountain mass separating New Mexico from Arizona he observed remains of many small cobblestone foundations of rectangular rooms composing irregular structures of Full Pueblo age. A slab house of Pre Pueblo type was met infrequently. Pottery revealed a meeting ground of Chaco culture from the east and Kayenta culture from the west with a general absence of Mesa Verde types. He found the rolling tableland west of Carriso Mountain devoid of ruins, noted slab houses along the south side of Keetseel Wash, and heard about but could not verify the presence of cliff houses in the land of the Tseachong and its tributaries. Then he turned his attention back to the expanse which lay between Bennett's Peak and Newcomb's post, scene of his diggings for the two previous seasons. Of this work a single sentence written almost as an afterthought remarked: "Incidentally I ran across some groups of ruins I had not heard of, and secured from them an excellent collection of some 325 specimens, together with data that is well worth while."[14] The plethora of pottery was dulling the pleasure of its discovery.

The next year, digging on the reservation was directed at the specific objective of securing skeletal material. This, of course, was to be found in burial grounds and not in houses, and so again the architecture was neglected, still with the feeling that it would be got to in due course. The plans for the season hinged upon the health and desires of the physical anthropologist for the museum, Luis R. Sullivan, who had suffered a physical collapse requiring his resettlement in the arid desert of southern Arizona. Sullivan felt he could profitably spend time while recuperating in a study of the bones which his archaelogical colleagues were obtaining in the areas south of the San Juan and near Galisteo, New Mexico. So in July he joined Earl in camp near Mitten Rock, a local landmark twenty miles southwest of Shiprock.

Bone were plentiful and ranged in age from Pre Pueblo to Full Pueblo. Unfortunately, the prevailing shallowness of burial had allowed for advanced decay. One very intriguing find, and one which brought Earl further newspaper publicity, saved the expedition from the now routine acquisition of more and more pots and shattered bones. A letter to Wissler at the museum, August 1923, graphically described the discovery.

"A most remarkable specimen was unearthed today in our excavations at Mitten Rock in the Navajo Reservation, New Mexico. From a shallow grave there was taken a skull which presented an unusual appearance. When freed of earth it was found that the entire upper portion was knobbed and pitted as the result of disease of long standing. In addition the right side had been extensively trephined. An oval section approximately two inches in length and one in width had been removed from the frontal bone immediately above the right eye. Presumably this operation was performed as among other primitive peoples, in an attempt to relieve pain. The skillful manner in which the ancient surgeon used his flint knives is revealed by the smooth even edges of the bone. However, the fact that these show no evidence of healing proves that the individual did not long survive the ordeal.

"The person to whom the skull belonged was of brachycephalic or short-headed type, and of small stature. A people possessing these physical characteristics inhabited the San Juan valley before the development of the Pueblo-Cliff Dweller culture which was in existence for many centuries if not for thousands of years previous to the discovery of America by Europeans. Thus the trephined specimen is of relatively great antiquity and of commensurate scientific importance. No other instance of trephining has been observed among aboriginal skulls from the Southwest, and only two others have been recorded from North America north of Mexico."

Whether the holes in the skull had been caused by purposeful aboriginal surgery was a point of debate. But the skull remained an interesting specimen nonetheless. Sullivan later found another such skull at San Cristóbal in the Galisteo area. Neither were as old as originally believed.[15]

As the years passed, pressures of work elsewhere kept Earl from returning to complete the reservation research in detail. And then it was too late. The antiquities, straddling as they did a main north-south road, and the publicity they received largely because of Earl's stupendous hauls were too tantalizing to be ignored. Pothunting by whites and Indians swept through this territory to thriving tourist markets at Gallup. In the space of a few short years all sites were gutted and forever ruined for scientific work. Bones lay in bleaching heaps where they were tossed aside by eager diggers. Sandstone slabs which once had covered burial pits strewed the surface of mounds. Pits and trenches destroyed stratigraphy and knocked walls apart. Although a thorough analysis of a total culture became an impossibility, Earl had gained strong ideas and impressions from his work there which would be incorporated in publications on pottery development and chronological sequences.

With hope of continued excavation gone, Earl turned to acquiring pots for his private collection. Whenever he drove that way, he always paused for an hour or two of digging. Many of the finest specimens of his collection came from that source.

The question of when was a man a Basket Maker and when was he a Pueblo was a basic one which Kidder and Guernsey had answered in an unchallengeable fashion during the course of their prolonged exposure to the noxious dusts of Kayenta caves. However, it was believed that there must have been developmental phases of both cultures when all attributes assignable to the peak periods of each had not been present. It was very much an open question as to whether Basket Makers were ancestral to Pueblos or whether they had been a group submerged by an incoming wave of foreigners. In 1920 an unbridged gap lay between the two peoples.

In that year, in Tsegi Canyon of the Kayenta country, Sam Guernsey excavated what appeared to be Basket Maker remains directly associated with poorly developed pottery and architecture reminiscent of some Pre Pueblo types which were found in overlying strata but with the typical Basket Maker skull type still being present. It appeared to Guernsey that he had uncovered a cultural link between the two populations which was most closely allied to the earlier horizon. Then a hasty reexamination of sherds excavated in Hagoe Canyon in 1914, and at that time considered to be Slab House or Pre Pueblo in age, showed them to be identical to those Guernsey now regarded as earlier. Thus the following year he and Kidder coauthored a report suggesting a cultural level they called Post Basket Maker because the cranial type and most material items remained Basket Maker in character but which exhibited some important advancements, such as pottery and architecture, which were to become an important part of the later Pueblo tradition.[16]

Similar discoveries began to be made elsewhere in the San Juan as the tempo of research increased. In Chaco Canyon Judd accidently found evidence for the so-called Post Basket Makers when a crumbling bank of the Chaco arroyo revealed a pithouse six feet below the modern surface. In the fill were fragments of the same early pottery.

Earl's work on the problem of the Post Basket Maker was initiated by Kidder who suggested that in addition to the Pre Pueblo materials found on the La Plata the Post Basket Maker phase was represented there in the Long Hollow long-headed skulls and the associated groupings of pots. Earl was stunned by this idea. Quickly grubbing through notes and photographs still in his possession, he had a sneaking feeling that his Eastern colleague was quite right. He had made exactly the same mistake on material excavated at the same time as had Kidder and Guernsey in the Kayenta, but he did not have the satisfaction of knowing it until some time later. For now, he only felt dismay that such a distinction had not become apparent to him sooner. He laid plans for testing Kidder's hypothesis. "Your review of my paper on the La Plata-Mancos region pleased me very much. It seems indubitable that the pottery from the mesas is of two distinct types. Certainly the group of vessels from Long Hollow bear no more resemblance to those from sites to the westward than do the latter resemble the typical pottery from the cliffs. Why the difference did not impress me long ago is more than I can understand. For the early spring I have mapped out a campaign to determine the exact status of the Long Hollow sites. There may be some difficulty about securing funds, but I believe it can be managed."[17]

Just as soon as work underway at Aztec would allow him to do so, Earl drove back to Site 22 at Long Hollow in late summer. Finding only a few graves near those stumbled upon in 1913, he shifted work to a clay-blanketed mesa on the opposite bank of the river where surface indications seemed similar. The brick-like hardness of the soil hampered the intact removal of bones but the evidence Earl sought was there—twenty-eight skulls all long and undeformed and forty-two pieces of pottery true to types found in 1913. What Kidder had guessed at from photographs was verified in the dirt, and Earl had to deal with yet another chapter of the increasingly complex aboriginal story. Beyond doubt the post Basket Makers of Tsegi were the same as those of Long Hollow with only minor differences, at least insofar as pottery and skull type were concerned. Furthermore the same association would be observed later that year on the reservation but not in a culturally unmixed situation. Earl was reluctant, however, to consider them Basket Makers because the mounds had been exposed to the destruction of weather, and he had recovered no perishable materials nor had he yet dug houses. To Wissler he reported: "The material is sufficient to establish a chronological subdivision of Pre Pueblo culture."[18]

In August and September of 1922 Earl returned to the La Plata area to study this early Post Basket Maker material in more detail. His destination was an elevated plateau between Red Horse Gulch and Maverick Gulch where he remembered an extensive grouping of mounds visited eight years previously. There he hoped to recover a more sizeable series of pots and skeletons to clinch the association noted at Long Hollow. He was unsuccessful. Site 18, scene of these initial 1922 excavations, proved to be later in time, with architecture, pottery, and cranial types being identified as Pre Pueblo.

Still determined to find more long-headed Basket Maker individuals, Earl moved the field camp east to the environs of Red Mesa. On a terrace of the east bank near the confluence of Cherry Creek and the La Plata, fifteen or more low mounds could be counted despite the thick growth of sage which obscured the surface. Near one of them the excavators cleaned out a subterranean house which Earl called a protokiva because it had several features to become customary adjuncts of the Pueblo ceremonial chambers.

The real significance of the kiva-like pit did not impress Earl until a shallow burial ground was examined, the extent of which was so great that time and funds did not permit total clearing. Thirty burials were found; all were dolichocephalic and undeformed. Thirty-three Long Hollow-style pots were recovered from their resting places beside the flexed bodies. Jubilantly Earl knew he had what he came for: the Post Basket Makers to Kidder and Guernsey and early Pre Pueblo to him. As he said, the ribs of the chronological skeleton were slowly being filled out with flesh,[19] even though the names by which they were called varied.

The protokiva was the oldest one yet dug. If Site 19 were Pueblo as he thought, his use of the word "kiva" to describe such a subterranean chamber would be acceptable to his co-workers, even though certain traditional elements were missing. If, however, the site were Basket

Maker, that would be another matter. Kivas had been considered an integral adjunct of the Pueblo culture, but no one had seriously thought of their being present among the Basket Makers also. The whole perplexing question of the origins of various kinds of pithouses and underground structures and their distribution over much of North America was opening up before his eyes.

When Earl drove to town for supplies, he hurriedly wrote a note to Henderson in which he recounted his latest victories. "Our work this summer I regard as some of the most important I have ever done. The collection of pottery is at present somewhat short of one hundred pieces, but these are very rare, and make up in quality what they may lack in number. The wares are wholly of the early and late Pre Pueblo types, each coming from different sites . . . . we will be able to give to the world the first record of the earliest forms of kivas to be found in the San Juan country."[20]

Excavating and exploring as continuously as he did in a number of different places, and making such large collections of artifacts, it was inevitable that Earl would be snowed under by data. When appropriations from the American Museum diminished after withdrawal of Huntington's support and Earl realized work at Aztec would probably never be resumed on the scale of the past, he began to take stock of his future. His reports on much of his work were long overdue. The Gobernador, certain aspects of Aztec, and the comparative study of Chaco and Mesa Verde ceramics were papers he had in mind to complete. Now here he was further burdened with the preparation for publication of four seasons on the La Plata, two (1915 and 1916) dealing with terminal periods and two (1921 and 1922) with early ones. At his home at Aztec Ruins he grimly undertook the tedious task of analysis and writing, vowing that he would not dig again until he had freed himself from some of the backlog. He was helped along by a cold winter when snow followed snow with quiet monotony until drifts virtually barricaded him in his home. By April he was able to inform Kidder that he was well along on a La Plata paper.[21]

There were many blanks which became glaringly obvious as outlines were set on paper. Were the earliest folk on the La Plata really a faltering last step of Basket Makers rather than a youthful crawl of Pueblos? Only painstaking work in the crude, ill-defined and superficially unpromising sites would supply proof. He felt the pressing need of better definitions of these stages for they must be the key to understanding the impetus which led to Pueblo achievement at such places as Aztec and was still carried on at Walpi or Oraibi or Zuñi or

Acoma. As yet he could say nothing of their homes, little of their kivas, and still less of items of manufacture other than pottery and stone. Did the gracelessness of form and crudity of design in their pots represent an embryonic stage of development? Was there anything in pottery derived from basketry—shape, techniques of manufacture, stylistic patterns? Was it probable that caves of the area, concentrated in canyon gashes near the broken lands of Mesa Verde, had perishables which could positively link Long Hollow to Cave 1, Tsegi Canyon? He had said, with Kidder, that they were getting at things. Yet how much unraveling remained!

A climax to the research on the Post Basket Maker horizon came in 1927 when Frank H. H. Roberts, son of a college president and then working for the Bureau of American Ethnology, undertook excavations of the first village of pure Post Basket Maker age ever dug. Shabik'eshchee Village, on a barren mesa top nine miles east of the Pueblo Bonito ruins of Chaco Canyon, consisted of eighteen houses, a plaza of sorts, forty-eight storage bins, and a Great Kiva. The houses were not contiguous rooms like Earl's Pre Pueblo dwellings in the La Plata. They were isolated pithouses strikingly similar to the Morris protokivas and presumably were placed upon the elevated mesa crest for better drainage rather than for defense. Some were circular; others were progressing towards being rectangular; some had a ventilator-entryway on their southern margins; some had abandoned the use of the passage for entrance and used it solely for obtaining fresh air. These pithouses were plastered with adobe which had been patted over the undulating pit surface, leaving finger impressions in the mortar. Occasional stone slabs encircle the interior of the pit. Floor features were practically identical to those of houses to the north except for the universal presence of a sipapu (or round hole in the floor), thought by the modern Indians to lead to the spirit world underground. Superstructures were of pole, brush, and mud. The storage cists were of similar construction.

Of outstanding importance was the unearthing of a large pit chamber in which Roberts saw the genesis of the classic Pueblo Great Kiva. Its discovery illustrated the element of chance which surrounds every archaeological undertaking. There were no sinks or depressions to indicate a former structure, no slab edges projecting from the soil. Only through routine trenching were its walls revealed. It was nearly as large as the type specimen at Aztec, forty feet across, four-feet two-inches deep when found, and its fill suggested two definite periods of deposition, as though the village might have been unoccupied for some time during its middle period. In the reddened plaster and floor were indications of a conflagration which had caused almost total destruction.

This subterranean building apparently represented a beginning of the religious architecture which evolved into the massive sanctuaries found down canyon at Rinconada, Pueblo Bonito, and Chetro Ketl. The structure suggested that there might have been two strains of kiva ancestry, one the community Great Kiva such as was being sired in Post Basket Maker villages like Shabik'eshchee, and the other clan-sized kiva which issued from the old fashioned pithouse family homes. The latter retained features peculiar to that structure, including an offshoot shaft, which no longer served as entrance but did allow fresh air to reach the stuffy underground rooms, and a sipapu.

There was no doubt that this cluster of dwellings called Shabik'eshchee, Navajo term for the sun symbol pecked on a nearby rock, was of an age nearly identical to that variously called Post Basket Maker or Pre Pueblo. Not only was the architectural complex about what investigators had expected to find and the few skulls obtained dolichocephalic, but the pottery, which amounted to only five complete specimens, was so similar it was almost indistinguishable from that of sites on the La Plata and in the Kayenta yielding long-headed skulls.

Roberts' findings in this first pure Post Basket Maker excavation corroborated those of Kidder, Guernsey, and Morris. They suggested an unbroken, orderly progression from Basket Maker to Pueblo. In this presentation of data Roberts pointed to a further riddle: "There was nothing to indicate, however, the correct answer to the question as to what actually became of the Basket Makers. Whether . . . they were completely absorbed by the newer group or whether they were finally driven out to locate elsewhere is still to be determined."[22]

Earl was one of the visitors to Shabik'eshchee that summer of 1927, and one of the most keenly interested. He had taken Harry Shapiro, a physical anthropologist at the American Museum of Natural History who was west to collect skeletal material, on a tour of the Chaco. What he observed at Chacra Mesa fired him with new enthusiasm to get back to the La Plata to see if he could discover anything similar to Roberts' site. As soon as he returned to Aztec he wrote Wissler: "I brought Shapiro here via Pueblo Bonito, and while at the latter place saw a maze of Post Basket Maker pit houses excavated by Frank Roberts. These moved me to return to the La Plata valley to dig out some of the Post Basket Maker structures there. As you know, the Post B.M. remains in that area are very productive of specimens, highly evolved, and singularly unmixed with later remains. From the La Plata sites I have taken some skeletal remains and much pottery, of which you have some, the major portion being in Boulder. Having rather slighted house digging, I would like to excavate a few dwellings and the prekivas which accompany them in order to round out a paper that I have practically completed on the La Plata work to date."[23]

He selected Site 23 in the upper La Plata where he had made the original long-skull finds in 1913 and had reconfirmed them again in 1921. Purposefully picking out a building which had burned, in hopes that its hard-to-determine features would be more distinguishable because of hardening or alteration of color, the crew started initial clearing with a scraper, cutting down to the top of the occupation level in the house mound, and with a plow in the refuse mound. No burial pits were observed, but the house outlines readily took form. Again it proved to be a crescent-shaped affair composed of two rows of rooms with three protokivas lying out in front. A second and third structure were of the same type and plan. From the crawl entrance of one protokiva came the only charred wisps of Basket Maker coiled basketry found in the La Plata sites, and they were of a single-rod foundation type rare in Basket Maker times. Earl preserved and hardened the fragments, which were all a part of one bowl-shaped container, with diluted ambroid, a standard preservative carried in every archaeologist's kit. There were clear-cut distinctions between subterranean and above-ground units, though household furnishings implied some everyday living still being continued in those of kiva-like character.

Because of this established dichotomy and the large size of villages whose individual units were in contiguity, Earl felt that there was proof that the Basket Makers had reached a greater degree of advancement in the La Plata district than elsewhere.[24] This represented a complete shift in thought from his views of 1922 when a similar site (No. 18) was placed in a Pre Pueblo horizon. It was, therefore, all the more ironical that other fieldworkers would have preferred to consider Site 23 an early Pueblo village insofar as architecture was concerned. In his La Plata report he wrote: "In fact some may contend that these remains are Pueblo I. Architecturally they are in advance of Roberts' Pueblo I settlement on the Piedra, ceramically they are on the border line, obviously late, but I cannot bring myself to class as Pueblo I the long-skulled population of the upper La Plata towns."[25] This structure gave inspiration for one of the later dioramas of the stages of Pueblo life installed in the Mesa Verde National Park museum.

Meanwhile, in Chaco Canyon, Neil Judd was having great success working out periods later than Post Basket Maker which unintentionally focused upon the La Plata. He had encountered the Full Pueblos and the patriarchs of the family tree, the Pre Pueblos.[26] From what he had learned from Earl, he was coming to the conclusion that the seed from which Pueblo Bonito had come, if not its actual origin, was somewhere in southern Colorado.

Pueblo Bonito had been constructed over an abandoned pit-house village which Earl would have classified as early Pre Pueblo, Kidder as Pueblo I. A slab-lined floor of one of these houses was met at a depth of twelve feet below Old Bonito refuse. Since only few instances of the next architectural step were present, that is an above-ground, pole-and-mud structure, Judd felt the site on which the town of Bonito would be erected had been unoccupied during that interval. When men again sought to create a settlement on the spot, they built of crude, single-coursed masonry heavily bedded in mud in which spalls were placed to retard surface washing and to aid in load carrying by giving stone-to-stone contact. Rooms, two deep, were rectangular, arranged in a crescentic arc, and faced southeast. Front-row rooms were obvious living quarters; back rows were storehouses. Subterranean kivas with flaring sides, low pilasters, and benches, were embraced within the half-moon of houses. Here was duplicated in style and form the architecture of Site 18 near Red Horse Gulch excavated by Morris in 1922 which he had called late Pre Pueblo. Judd named his variant Old Bonito.

The period which the mass of the ruined city represents was called Late Bonitian. It was separated from the Old Bonito period by drifts of sands which had banked against exterior walls and had blown through rooms. As the picture was reconstructed by Judd, Late Bonitians had moved into the canyon from Earl's north country and had continued their already established architectural traditions (studied in 1916 at Site 39) but gradually improving upon them. They encroached upon the Old Bonitians just as they swallowed up some of the smaller communities along the south wall of the bony defile. The availability of large deposits of laminated sandstone allowed them to create the most handsome and most skillfully executed masonry in the pre-white Southwest. Judd saw three types, various combinations of thin tabular stone and larger blocks, but all facing on a rubble core. Doors, windows, and ceilings were of a style already noted by Earl in the clearing of the West Ruin at Aztec. The town's shape, that of a capital D and covering an area greater than the United States capitol building, seemed to have been preplanned, but largescale remodeling of the units within it occurred at least twice. As time went on, all exterior doors were sealed until the only means of entrance was a ladder which led one up and over first floor roofs, another feature present at Aztec. In its highest section the dwelling rose to five stories.

Two Great Kivas were incorporated within Bonito's large courts. Neither had been explored by the Hyde party. Judd commenced immediate clearing of the one situated in the northern section of the west plaza. Earl shrewdly had seen to it that his at Aztec would be the first one scientifically probed and published, and he was pleased to note that in most respects that of Bonito was little different except for the absence of a line of encircling rooms. Roberts uncovered part of a third Great Kiva while working fill in the west court, but this remained uncleared.

Judd then turned to another tool of age determination coming into wide usage by Southwestern archaeologists, namely pottery. Sherds by the hundreds of thousands were pouring from the trenches at Bonito. They indicated, as Nelson and Earl had said, that the refuse mounds had been so badly mixed in aboriginal times that they were stratigraphically unusable. If this abundant ceramic material could be placed in a framework of technological and stylistic sequence, and cross-checked by stratigraphic trenches at other Chaco sites, it would be of invaluable aid in determining the progression of events in prehistoric Bonito. Roberts was assigned this demanding task. With marked success he accomplished the mission, the results being written up as his dissertation at Harvard.

Together with Earl's fellow Farmingtonian, Monroe Amsden, Roberts pawed through shifting mountains of sherds from deposits at Bonito, del Arroyo, Peñasco Blanco, Pueblo Alto and numerous smaller houses, sorting them into distinct piles on basis of slip, paint, design, characteristics of core, and some intangibles just called "pottery sense." He found an undisturbed refuse area at Bonito beneath the living surface of the west court which allowed him cross-references *in situ*. As a result of these exacting efforts, he and Amsden separated black-on-white pottery at Chaco Canyon into fourteen headings. Of the eight principal types, one was thought to be Post Basket Maker in time, one Pre Pueblo, three late Pre Pueblo, and three Full or classic Pueblo.

Another illuminating bit of information came from sherds. Just as Mesa Verdians had taken over Aztec in its final days, so had they penetrated as far southward as the Chaco Canyon. Some pottery seemed to be proto-Mesa Verde of the sort reclaimed from Montezuma Valley and the La Plata and some could have come directly out of Cliff Palace at its peak period. These Mesa Verde sherds lay stratigraphically above those of true Chaco wares in many instances, showing them to be of more recent vintage.

Digging at the neighboring jumble of fallen walls known as Pueblo del Arroyo was under the direction of Karl Ruppert, who after three seasons of work decided that the structure was in general contemporaneous with the later occupation of Bonito. In addition, it showed many non-Chaco northern features such as an occasional room of different and cruder masonry style, kivas with an above floor ventilator, and the beginnings of a triple walled tower just to the west of the site. Additional evidence for influence, or real occupants, from north of the San Juan was seen in the intramural burials which came to light, not a characteristic method of disposal of the Chaco dead but one which Earl had reported at Aztec as being highly typical of the Mesa Verde tenancy. To substiantiate the mounting evidence that northern peoples had reached down into Chaco was the great amount of pottery which, being painted in carbon rather than mineral paint, seemed more Mesa Verde than Chaco. This was a group which Roberts called Chaco-San Juan to indicate its extensive distribution. Much later research would seem to indicate considerable northern influence but a relatively small Chaco occupation by Mesa Verdians themselves.

To record the riches hidden in the dirt of ages within Bonito's walls would repeat a tabulation from its smaller sister site of Aztec. In many respects finds were richer, although the best materials had been removed by Pepper. There was more turquoise and more bizarre pieces of pottery were recovered. There were larger caches of pots, more exotic trade goods like copper bells, macaw feathers, and shells, tall bifurcated baskets and copies of them in clay. In other respects the finds were less numerous. Fewer burials, although Bonito presumably had an aboriginal population of larger proportions, and fewer perishables came from Bonito than from Aztec.

The Chaco graveyard never was found. Probably because of alluviation which has occurred subsequent to occupation by the Indians, it lay deeply buried. Only north of the San Juan where the people were accustomed to put their departed away in unused rooms within their homes were interments of Full Pueblo times encountered in any quantity. Even these nowhere approximate the estimated number of deaths which would have transpired during the lifetime of the villages. Judd guessed that fifty-four hundred persons must have died during the two hundred fifty year tenancy of Bonito; less than one hundred bodies were recovered by his and Pepper's explorations; a mere three hundred are known to have come from one hundred years of looting and excavating within the confines of the canyon.

And how could a group numbering in the thousands, to judge from the prevalence of their architectural remains, have survived in the bitter silent wasteland that is now Chaco Canyon? Estimates of twelve hundred people at Pueblo Bonito seemed realistic, an impressive figure when one realizes that in modern New Mexico there are not two dozen towns of larger population than this single Pueblo house. The answer obviously is that favorable living conditions must have shifted unsatisfactorily because of some natural disaster such as a lowering of the water table; an incipient cycle of degradation and arroyo cutting which made customary flood farming impossible since tillable lands lay above the level of the arroyo; denudation through careless destruction of sparse forests for firewood and constructional purposes. There is ample evidence for such changes. A stump of a huge evergreen was found in Bonito's enclosed sunbaked courtyard; another still stood in a neighboring rincon. Men who study biotic upheavals believe that forests once might have pushed over the mesa declivities and into the now desolate canyon bottom itself. Geologists like the late Kirk Bryan of Harvard, who conducted extensive researches at Chaco in 1924 and 1925, know that rhythmic periods of alluviation and degradation have taken place over the Southwest during its whole history, that there is evidence for three cycles of dissection and two of deposition in Chaco Canyon. Bryan affirms that a slight shift in climate and the resulting channel cutting underlay the disruption of ancient life there.[27]

It has to be remembered, too, that because the Indian had no livestock to eat into his supplies or no need to accumulate large hoards for trade, he did not demand the acreages of white farmers. In their limited types of crops—corn, beans, squash, and cotton—the Indians could have survived in more marginal areas. Thus Chaco might not have been a luxuriant paradise in order to attract Indian farmers. A few acres could adequately support a family, if the gods brought rain.

Environmental changes were considered by Judd to lay behind Chaco's abandonment a hundred or more years before the migration of population out of the basin of the San Juan occurred. Of late, other factors are being considered, an erosion of the spirit which has brought doom to other civilizations.[28] Marked strife with outsiders seemed unlikely. In that event there would be seen signs of fire and pillage and violent death. There were none. A general state of tidiness marked the condition in which the Late Bonitians left their homes. The people had apparently packed up and moved away.

Exactly twenty years had passed since Hewett had begun his Puye field school and Cummings had explored the wilderness of southeast Utah; fifteen years since Nelson had set out upon his chronological studies in the Rio Grande valley and the partnership of Kidder and Guernsey had studied the Kayenta caves. In that time the number of men and women engaged in attempts at understanding the unwritten history of the Southwest had grown rapidly. The amount of work accomplished, the data obtained and digested, had been impressive. It was time for taking stock. Investigators needed to know not only where they had been but where they were bound. A meeting of interested persons was called.

In March 1927, Earl received his invitation from Ted Kidder. "This is a little premature, but I want to get a bid for your time in as early as possible. Roberts and Judd and I are planning to have a get-together of as many field workers in Southwestern archaeology as possible at Pecos for two or three days, beginning August 29th, in order to thrash out at leisure the various questions of problems, method, and nomenclature which we discussed in a preliminary way in Judd's office this autumn. I hope very much that you can arrange your affairs in such a way as to be there, as the whole project could hardly be a success in your absence."[29]

Along with about forty workers from widely separated digs all over the four states comprising the Southwest, Earl and his party arrived at the rocky Pecos mesa. In its shadow, after evaluating past accomplishments, they set about charting the future course of Southwestern archaeology. Their names were the cornerstones upon which the discipline had been founded, and their endeavors, completed and yet to be begun, would bring them honor among American scholars.*

Three days had been set aside, as an account in *Science* stated, "to bring about contacts between workers in the Southwestern field; to discuss fundamental problems of Southwestern history, and to formulate plans for coordinated attack upon them; to pool knowledge of facts and techniques, and to lay foundations for a unified system of nomenclature."[30] During long sessions held at Kidder's field camp and in informal evening gatherings in the various tents of the conferees, these were matters talked over with earnestness of purpose. Out of

* (See Appendix.)

these discussions came a historical chronology listing three stages of Basket Maker development and five stages of Pueblo development. Of these phases, several were singled out as targets for future research.

The reconstruction of Southwestern prehistory began at midstream. It was conceded that the first Basket Makers had not been found and perhaps might never be, as surely their array of possessions which would have survived would be small. It was obvious to the most casual observer that the Basket Maker II were well up on the ladder of culture. The finely made coiled baskets in a variety of forms, the sturdy square-toed sandals, the twinged bags of apocynum or yucca fiber which once must have been soft as cotton cloth, the ingenious creation of blankets from strips of rabbit fur wound around a yucca-fiber base, and many other items attested to a skill and technology beyond what might be considered an archaic or initial stage of civilization. The numbers of their dead uncovered by 1927 implied either a large, widely dispersed population or lengthy time of residence or both, certainly leading to the conclusion that a successful adjustment had been made to the harsh environment, but only after prolonged experimentation. The exact definition of Basket Maker I was pointed out as a particularly important problem yet to be solved.

Another question as yet not satisfactorily answered was how the Basket Maker horizon related to the later Pueblo. The conferees thought that probably at about the time of Christ something of tremendous importance had transpired which brought about a new era, that of the Pueblos. "The majority of those present at the conference believe that a new broadheaded strain supplanted the ancient long heads."[31] The newcomers used a hard cradleboard for infants which marked them for life. It became so universal a characteristic that anyone with the occipital portion of his skull undeformed would have been regarded as a freak. Several new additions to the cultural pattern were the use of cotton in making cloth and domesticated turkeys whose feathers were used primarily in the manufacture of robes. Pottery became the dominant type of container. Basketry declined, or so it seemed, though few dry sites of the period had been found. Architecture assumed greater importance. This was Pueblo I; the term Pre Pueblo was dropped.

Pueblo II, formerly late Pre Pueblo to Earl, little understood although more ruins seemed to be of this horizon than any other, was the period of greatest territorial expansion known for the Pueblos. They pushed to the Colorado River on the west, the Mogollon Rim on the south, the Rio Grande on the east. The Pecos Conference recognized the study of Pueblo II to be of prime importance in understanding the crystalization of culture which occurred in Pueblo III in the several centuries prior to the abandonment of the San Juan. Pueblo III replaced the Full Pueblo or Cliff Dweller of earlier classifications.

The period following the abandonment of the San Juan was known to have been one of withdrawal, physical and psychological, when culture degenerated. In pottery the manufacture of orange and polychrome types, sometimes decorated in glaze paints, completely replaced the black-on-white styles of the past. Houses were sprawling affairs, lacking the defensive features of Pueblo III. This period was divided by the archaeologists into two phases, one extending from the abandonment of the San Juan to the arrival of the Spaniards in 1540, and a second of further decline up to Spanish resumption of power in 1700. This was Pueblo IV, the low ebb of a once vigorous people, a stage in Pueblo history neglected by the archaeologists but which needed much study. Pueblo V was the historic period.

The importance of this first Pecos Conference, which found inspiration in the earlier symposia held by Judd at Pueblo Bonito, cannot be overestimated. It set the guidelines for the future, the Pecos Classification which became the chart every Southwesterner consulted in assigning his ruin a place. There were faults in its rigidity, as future work revealed, and a decided overestimation of time involved which would be corrected by dendrochronological evidence. There was danger in the use of a system because it inadvertently would force the fitting of sites into a framework, sometimes without much evidence beyond one or two elements called "diagnostic." But it was a giant step forward. It did much to wipe out a terminological muddle in which more than one worker had been mired. Additionally, it told the world of an impressive record achieved in twenty years, an enlightenment gained through painstaking and laborious study of the small precipitate of life—a few bits of pottery, a hank of yucca-fiber cord, a broken fire drill, or a one-room house made of sticks and stones. It was a series of astute surmises based upon a surprisingly small number of excavations, many of which were unpublished.

From that time until World War II the group met only sporadically, most often at the University of New Mexico Chaco Canyon field school. Since the war, the symposium has become an annual affair, formally named the Pecos Conference though only once held at Pecos, and is attended by several hundred persons who are currently concerned with archaeology of the area.

In 1923 the National Geographic Society, through the vision of its adviser, Neil Judd, decided to sponsor A. E. Douglass in his continuing drive toward the hazy world of the unrecorded date, hoping that in the wake of such research Pueblo Bonito itself might be hung upon the Christian calendar. Two men were engaged for the summer of that year to gather specimens of wood used in the construction of ancient domiciles throughout the San Juan. J. A. Jeancon, of the Colorado State Museum, and Oliver Ricketson, of the Carnegie Institution, took on the assignment. They made a whirlwind tour, collecting over a hundred specimens which once had been part of beams of ceilings in such classic sites as Betatakin in the Kayenta, Mummy Cave in Canyon del Muerto, and Cliff Palace in its shelter on an escarpment of the Mesa Verde. Careful analysis in the laboratory at the University of Arizona built up a prehistoric chronology for these ruins of one hundred eighty years' length, and subsequently this series could be hooked on to the top of a Chaco-Aztec relative sequence arrived at earlier. Five hundred eighty-five years of tree life were represented, an indelible graph which told of the vicissitudes of weather, pest infestations, and utilization by a stone-ax-wielding group of men. But the chart was as yet unanchored at either end.

By 1928, Douglass was ready to attempt to bridge the gap between history and prehistory. He decided there was no better place to look for wood which might straddle the chasm between known and unknown, called The Gap, than the Hopi towns in northern Arizona. These settlements had been in use at the time of Spanish arrival from Mexico and presumably had been thriving upon the same spot for considerable time previously.

Douglass proved himself a diplomat in dealing with the Hopi, who were far from eager to have the white men snooping through their houses and drilling holes in their roof beams. He won them over with bolts of regal purple velvet, turtle shells to be used in the creation of ceremonial rattles, and old discarded felt hats from which they contrived dance masks. But it was no use. The earliest cutting date read A.D. 1400, too late to connect on to the ruin dates obtained.[32]

Then Douglass turned to archaeological sites of the area, knowing that some immediately preceded the establishment of the modern towns. Earl agreed to look for promising dendrochronological samples while engaged in excavations for the University of Colorado at the enormous ruin of Kawaikuh (named Mishiptonga by Mindeleff) located on eleven acres of rocky mesa tongue overlooking the Jeddito valley nine miles from the Keams Canyon Agency.

However, Earl failed to find the tree rings which would bridge The Gap, a fact which in its very negative character reassured other field men that Earl was after all human and not equipped with some super-sensitivity which they lacked. Looking particularly for charcoal, which dendrochronologists had learned to use (because unburned wood, except in rare instances, would have rotted in open sites such as these at Jeddito), he had probed portions of Kawaikuh which might have burned. To Douglass he wrote: "We combed Kawaikuh for other burned areas but failed to find another. It is altogether probable that buried somewhere beneath the refuse fill there are chambers which were fired and subsequently covered over, but there certainly is no way of locating them from conditions within a few feet of the surface."[33] The charred fragments submitted were treated by a method Earl devised to forestall their disintegration in shipment. Each one was bound with cheese-cloth and string and dipped in paraffin dissolved in gasoline. They gave dates from A.D. 1300 to A.D. 1495. Then he moved to Chacpahu where fire-hardened walls were discernible. The burned material within them was brush and grass, unsuitable for dating. A third site, Kokopneama, built of pinkish stone appeared to have been fired but had not. "I know that the gap material that we so much crave once existed in the Jeddito ruins, and I fully believe that some of it is still there in the form of charcoal . . . I sincerely regret that we were not able to secure the bridge for the gap this fall. But it can and will be done, and I hope that when the time comes, it will be my privilege to be a participating agent."[34]

That honor went to two Arizonans, Lyndon Hargrave and Emil Haury, who set about in what was formally called the Third Beam Expedition during the summer of 1929 to nail down the floating chronology. They had moved south of the Jeddito sand dunes, south of the scorching heat of the Painted Desert and the Petrified Forest, to the breaks leading to forest lands by the Mogollon Rim. At a place with a hold-over name of Wild West gambling days—Showlow, Arizona—they worked in one of the most unglamorous sites in the Southwest.

It was the cluttered barnyard of a Mormon farm. But underneath the barns and outbuildings, the piles of outdated machinery and tin cans, and areas of chicken scratchings and droppings was a sizeable ruin which seemed like many of that area to have been established during the troubled years following the breakup of San Juan culture. Less than a foot beneath the modern stratum, the diggers encountered a large log, its crust preserved by charring but its center consumed by decay. It was bound with twine, bathed in preservative, numbered

HH39, and set aside. When it was studied that evening, Douglass counted back to the year A.D. 1237 at the log's core.

This was too promising a matter to be delayed. Quickly, by the light of a lantern, the excavators got out the charts of the prehistoric sequence in an effort to match them with HH39. Whether the prehistoric would coincide with the modern or whether there would be a break of several centuries was the question. At Showlow on the night of June 22, 1929, it was seen that the relative date of 551 (twenty three years beyond the last ring from Aztec Ruins) was identical to the modern ring for A.D. 1251; the two series overlapped by twenty-six years! This was a major archaeological breakthrough.

Within a month, over forty ruins could be dated through an analysis of the wood used in their construction. Earl had been skeptical in 1919, but a decade later he was enabled to place a specific time upon his sites with as much positiveness as if those dates had been engraved upon a cornerstone.

Just what the actual dates were was to be kept a secret until formal announcement of this tremendous achievement by the National Geographic Society. However, three weeks after the find at Showlow, Douglass gave Earl a broad hint that he had at last secured the key to the doors of the past. "Of course anything I say about the gap, even between the lines, is strictly confidential, but I believe that by the time I have looked over all the many hundreds of pieces collected this summer I shall be able to give the true dates of the various ruins tied in."[35] Again in the fall he let his young friend know that the big announcement was coming. "I remember very well the matter we were speaking of out at Jeddito. The decks will soon be cleared for making an extension of the prehistoric series, now happily historic, into the unknown again. I would like exceedingly to see enough material to carry dating back into the B.C.'s."[36]

If anyone had a right to be curious it was Earl. Yet because of the commitments under which the beam project had been done, he could not be informed of the results prior to their publication. He jokingly commented, "I shall do my best to worm the gap dates out of Judd, but I fear it will be much like trying to elicit information from the Sphinx."[37] Douglass, feeling rather badly that Earl should have been left out in this manner, responded: "The one thing which has seemed wrong to me about that dating business is that I did not have you nearby to talk it over, for you deserve it first of all. If I had been running this show you would have known but this has been a game in which I have been under obligations to cooperate."[38]

With the long awaited statement, the astounded world learned that portions of Pueblo Bonito covered a range of time from the 900's to A.D. 1130. It seemed impossible that a mere two hundred years had witnessed the architectural and artistic advancement apparent there, but it was so. The colonies from Chaco such as were represented at Aztec Ruins dated at a time corresponding to the final cultural resurgence in the canyon.

The Mesa Verde cliff dwellings, it was learned, were more recent, having been begun at the peak years of Chaco bloom but having been utilized and added to at least a century and a quarter longer. At a later time and through the efforts of another dendrochronologist, Earl learned that the Mesa Verde occupation of Aztec was placed at A.D. 1252 from tree-ring specimens obtained in the East Ruin.

Moving over into Arizona, beams from the tower at Mummy Cave in Canyon del Muerto and from Kiet Siel in the Tsegi Canyon area of the Kayenta were dated in the twelfth and thirteenth centuries. These two separated sites south of the San Juan River also proved to have the most recent dates (A.D. 1284) found in the drainage.

South of the Little Colorado River, ruins classed as Pueblo IV by the scholars were of still more recent times, reaching into the late 1300's. The straggling Jeddito ruins Earl had tested the year before occupied a span between A.D. 1254 and A.D. 1495, with the Hopi towns on their First, Second, and Third mesas picking up at the middle 1300's and carrying up through Pueblo V and the present year.

Dating of ruins was not the only result of the new science. There was a corrollary dating of climatic fluctuations. In the rings were records of periods of excessive dryness which seemed to recur about every hundred years. One such drought might have had overtones of disaster. It lasted twenty-three years, from A.D. 1276 to A.D. 1299. There were no evidences of building anywhere in the San Juan after A.D. 1284. To a person dependent upon rains which came in the summer, or streams fed by melting winter snow pack, a prolonged cycle of drought could only have meant defeat.

The picture thus sketched was one of the growth of the Pueblo culture in the San Juan, its progress through the centuries to a zenith in Chaco Canyon sometime during the twelfth century and then being dissipated; a similar rise and fall in the Mesa Verde district until the thirteenth century when, in an outward movement, it swept toward the Rio Grande (as discovered at Pecos and Galisteo) and into the Kayenta. At the latter place it took over, or greatly influenced, a local variation of the same basic culture.

If Douglass's accomplishments were great, equally so were those of the archaeologists. Through their deductions, arrived at from season after season of digging and analyzing, they had plotted the route of human development in the northern Southwest with amazing accuracy. Tree rings and their confirming records, while tremendously gratifying, merely added definitiveness to the testimony of the ruins.

With characteristic desire to push on toward a total reconstruction, in the same letter in which he sent congratulations to Douglass on the job just completed, Earl handed him a new problem. What of times before Pueblo III? When did Pueblo II, Pueblo I, and Basket Maker III come into the chronological skeleton? What lay back of A.D. 700, the earliest date the dendrochronological experts could read? At the time deeply involved with Canyon del Muerto and the La Plata, where he was attempting to unravel threads of origin, he said: "My every effort will be spent to see that material is found to carry the sequence back to the Post Basket Maker. Already we have considerable material toward that end."[39]

From the La Plata, two years earlier, Earl had shipped to the laboratory a number of tree-ring specimens from the crescentic Basket Maker III village numbered 23 in his series. This was, of course, before the closing of The Gap, and the wood, like that he had submitted from del Muerto, had been stored away in a dusty corner.

In 1929, at the very time when Douglass was close to bridging The Gap, Earl was camped on a mesa near Johnson Canyon about eight air miles southeast of the Mesa Verde headquarters, again on the trail of the early Indians of the La Plata. His men had slashed a ten-mile road through the dense stands of low timber, had located some potholes along the rimrock which held rainwater suitable for camp use, and had pitched their tents beside an old Indian trail which, worn to a depth of over four feet in places, ran from the La Plata Mountains to the San Juan Valley. The village they attacked with their shovels was a mammoth one Earl had first seen under a blanket of November snow four years before.

It was bigger and better than others so far dug, though after tiresome days of trenching and plowing no burial grounds could be found, only eight skeletons being recovered during the entire summer. The house layout was new moon in contour with two rows of contiguous, misshapen rooms made of a variety of materials including sand, mud, poles, and upright slabs of stone. Within the partial enclosure of its wings were the familiar protokivas, six in number, and not at all dissimilar to others already studied. There were some differences at this Site 33 not observed in the settlements previously dug. For one thing, there was erected directly over the snake-like line of pole-and-mud chambers a massive, walled, D-shaped house of thirteen rooms and a central kiva of late Pueblo III age, termed "the Mesa Verde variant" by Earl. Here the crew again came across the paths of the Wetherill brothers; in the crotch of an adjacent gnarled cedar was a rusty shovel which once had belonged to them.

Most exciting to Earl was the presence of a vast bowl in the ground beyond the area of the protokivas. As he stepped off its sixty-three foot diameter, he recalled the Great Kiva at Shabik'eshchee. Would he be able to match that one in a town of different composition? The vegetation covering this expanse was so dense that an untrained observer might have disregarded the depression, believing it to be a natural phenomenon. To Earl, however, here was a challenging problem. The probable size of the structure, the efforts involved in its clearing, and the volume of fill dirt were obstacles to be surmounted.

When approximately one-third of the chamber had been exposed, Earl saw that it was what he had hoped for—a Great Kiva, like Roberts' in all respects except for being larger and having a narrow ventilator which made the outline of the building appear like a stemmed apple.

The Great Kiva of Site 33 was to have particular significance for the tree-ring timetable because it produced one of the two dates ultimately determined for the La Plata. Four huge posts had been raised in a quadrangular pattern from the earth floor of the kiva to support a roof of timbers and dirt. In 1929 Earl secured the two stumps in the southern half of the kiva; one was thought to be of little value because of its badly weathered condition but the other Earl judged to be worthy of extreme care since approximately three hundred rings were apparent on its surface.

Pressed with work, it was several years before Douglass got to work on these specimens. In early 1931, with the assignment of a workshop under the grandstand of a new stadium at the University of Arizona, and with the assistance of Haury, he turned to the Site 33 log, now called M200.

Douglass found a cutting date for M200 at A.D. 831. Earl was aghast at its recentness, having convinced himself that as much as three centuries must have intervened between the nether historic date of A.D. 700 and the upper limits of M200. He urged a restudy. Then he arranged to return to the Great Kiva in the fall of 1931, after fieldwork in the Chuskas, to take out the other two stubs of roof supports which he assumed would be present in the unexcavated northern section. The weather caused a change in his plans for record rainfall drenched the La Plata watershed. As a result, roads, normally bad, became impassable. After a day of sliding uncontrollably on a slick film of clay and of chopping brush to permit traction in soupy tire tracks, Earl gave up for the time being. When he had succeeded later, it was seen that all four of the roof-supporting beams from the Great Kiva had been felled in the same year, A.D. 831, leaving no doubt of the chamber's age.

Still dissatisfied with the date Douglass had given for the La Plata site, which in all respects seemed to be transitional between Basket Maker III and Pueblo I, Earl sought to attain more proof through an outflanking maneuver. He would come at it from the reservation. In the fall of 1932 he brought a party of excavators to Bennett's Peak. They set up tents on the same spot where Earl and Oley had camped in 1920, at the time of the original reservation trip. Winds of great intensity bearing skiffs of snow made life in the open miserable for several days. Digging through the dry earth of the ruins was nearly impossible, and, at its best, fruitless. Nineteen mounds were pitted and were found to contain no charcoal. Earl wryly wondered about the fate which had kept flames from these sites when nearly every other ruin he had ever dug had been burned during the course of its use.

When he was about to abandon the search, three miles west of Bennett's Peak he found a crescentic-shaped Pueblo I house of considerable size. It seemed to have burned. Pottery observed on the surface was the same as that at Site 23 in the La Plata. Two hundred ninety-five wood samples were collected from trenches. Earl wrote to Douglass: "The pueblo I site must inevitably cross date with Johnson Canyon, since architectural plans and pottery were identical."[40] It did, exactly at A.D. 830. Work upon this Pueblo house was reported upon after Earl's death by his eldest daughter.[41]

The A.D. 830 date from Bennett's Peak correlated with material being collected by Roberts from the Puerco River to the southwest. There Roberts had a transitional Basket Maker-Pueblo village with dates in the late 700's and early 800's, which as the Associated Press reminded its readers (July 21, 1931), was the era of Charlemagne's youth and the Danes' warlike arrival on the shores of England.

Gradually the early Pueblos were being pinned down to the eighth and ninth centuries. Archaeologists had to accept the fact that Pueblo development had been far more rapid than originally thought, but Earl still believed that the "Posty," or Basket Maker III, sites would take history back to near the time of Christ. He would continue to attempt to supply Douglass with the necessary resources to prove or disprove his notion. Meantime he expressed the debt all regional students owed Douglass: "It is tremendously gratifying that so many dates are coming forth. I often feel that those of us whose interest is primarily in archaeology make life a burden for you because of our insistence, and distract your thoughts from the more fundamental problems which are your central interest. If such be the case, I hope that our unending gratitude will to a slight degree balance our indebtedness."[42]

During the winter of 1930 Earl was at the museum in Boulder where he was attempting a scientific report on the years of digging in the La Plata district. It seemed a goal which took on larger proportions as each year passed. To Kidder, now Chairman of the Historical Division of the Carnegie Institution, he reported: "The La Plata job doesn't shrink a bit with familiarity. I cannot as yet form any estimate of the length of time that it will take to finish it, but whether it be three months or six I will just keep pegging until it is done."[43] Furthermore, he soon discovered that so many questions about cultural sequences remained unanswered that it was necessary to do further digging.

As always, Earl not only got Kidder's blessings but a sum of twenty-five hundred dollars for the work. Additionally, the University of Colorado regents gave him, through the University Museum, its annual appropriation of one thousand dollars. Because the Carnegie Institution had no museum, all the artifacts collected were to go to the university in order to keep the La Plata collection intact.

The size of the field party swelled beyond Earl's expectations as five friends of Carnegie came West. One was Dwight Morrow, Jr., son of an illustrious American ambassador to Mexico and then a freshman at Amherst, who arrived accompanied by a friend and a tutor. Rodgers Johnson, from the Carnegie Washington office, came to help with the mapping and stenographic detail. And finally there was Marjorie Trumbull, wife of a newspaper sportswriter, a lady who had taken up archaeology as a hobby and had prevailed upon Kidder to allow her to participate in this expedition. Of her Earl remarked, "By the time I have answered all the questions she will ask, I expect to have learned a lot more than I now know about Southwestern archaeology."[44] This unexpected addition of more people required the acquisition of more dishes, another stove, and a camp roustabout, items which cut into the budget but at the same time allowed further work to be accomplished. Because of the distinguished background of his helpers, Earl took unusual pains in arranging camp on a low terrace by the bank of the La Plata. Planning to stay in the field for as long as the money lasted, he hired local Mormon boys as diggers and Willard Fraser, a college lad whom he had met during lunches at Marshall's Cafeteria in Boulder, as cook. Then he secured permission from a rancher to clear out a ruin area of the desired age.

From July to October the group worked at Site 41 on a promontory above the west side of the La Plata just south of the New Mexico-Colorado line. It was a generally hot dry summer but was to be remembered for a flash flood which could have brought calamity. Storm clouds had been observed one afternoon rolling swiftly in over the La Plata Mountains on the northern skyline. Although Earl had commented that the river by camp would be running high by nightfall, there was no sign of a rise in its level by bedtime. There was instead a rare phenomenon, a night rainbow which glowed off toward the high country. Several hours after everyone had retired, assured that all was well on the La Plata, a distant rumble of oncoming water awakened the camp. Huge boulders were snatched off balance, trees were uprooted, and gallons of gravel and mud churned before a twenty-foot-high wall of water. In a state of pandemonium tents were quickly lowered, duffle bags were stuffed with clothes snatched from tent poles, and assorted cameras and supplies were dragged to higher ground. Still the heavy waters pushed upward along the cliff walls, eating hungrily into dry earth. Gear was moved a second time before unassailable dryness was assured. The breathless adventurers sat on their tumbled possessions watching. By morning the crest had lost itself in the San Juan, but the soggy debris windrowed along the valley bottom reminded the diggers of a night which might have ended tragically.

The largest masonry structure of the La Plata valley stood at the tip of the bluff whose entire surface was artificial. Because of lack of sufficient money, its excavation was not undertaken. Instead Earl spent the four months working through sixteen sprawling mounds (one hundred seventy rooms and ten kivas) lumped together as Site 41 which lay behind the big cluster on the point. This was a zone of intensive usage by a sizable pre-white population. Some forty mounds were grouped within three-eighths of a mile. Building stones were so abundant that Earl later used this area as a quarry for the Aztec Great Kiva reconstruction. Results were about as expected—multi-roomed, multi-kiva structures, some of bizarre form, and all of late Pueblo III age, Mesa Verde variant. There was a depth of underlying cultural material which extended back through a Chaco tenancy to weak Pueblo II and Pueblo I and Basket Maker III. Perhaps fifteen hundred years were represented, a cycle in which there were no cataclysms or no invasions. The history of this site and others along the La Plata was wholly one of response to a rigid and exacting environment.

The prodigious amount of muscle-hardening excavation of 1930 almost brought to a close the arduous field campaign in the La Plata district. Two years later Earl returned alone to do a bit of digging around in a contemporaneous ruin across canyon to get wood for dating. Douglass returned him a date of A.D. 1158, one which Earl considered to jibe perfectly with the archaeological evidence. The tedium of getting a report assembled and through the hands of editors consumed another nine years, which even though an exasperating delay, allowed him opportunity to incorporate later ideas and systems.

So many expeditions had bivouaced upon the Colorado Plateau by the 1930's that to tell of their findings would lead far beyond the world and work of Earl Morris. Some, however, had a direct bearing upon his research in the north country. Earliest to contribute in a collateral study was Frank Roberts who was turning out reports with piston-like regularity. Kiatuthlanna and Allantown in north central Arizona, and the Village of the Great Kivas in New Mexico near the pueblo of Zuñi, were excavated and promptly described. These sites, situated at the southern periphery of the San Juan, showed cross-currents of influence from both north and south, but Chaco patterns seemed dominant. They also produced further bits of evidence for the widespread and superficially homogeneous early phases—Basket Maker III and Pueblo I—with early Chaco and Kayenta pottery and pithouses exhibiting regional variations.

Of particular interest to Earl was work done in 1928 by Roberts on the Piedra River, some miles north and east of Aztec on the Animas, where, with the aid of a crew composed mostly of Ute Indians from the Ignacio Agency, he examined eighty houses, two kivas, six circular depressions, and seven burial mounds. Pottery recovered from these excavations was similar to Basket Maker III-La Plata pottery, but a jacal type of architecture differed from that known to the west. Roberts considered the Piedra houses representative of the early eras of the northeastern San Juan, though he saw slight similarities as far away as central Utah and southeast Nevada, and he called them Pueblo I. A tree-ring date was obtained which read A.D. 774.

Earl's judgment was: "I find there are many interesting parallels on the ceramic side between Frank's district and the La Plata, but almost no parallelism in architecture. The people in the La Plata district had gone a great deal farther toward the eventual acquisition of pueblo structures than had the residents of the Piedra district, although they were about on the same horizon as far as pottery is concerned."[45]

Many problems demanding answers were emerging from fieldwork such as that done in southern Colorado by Roberts and Morris. There was a growing feeling among researchers that uninterrupted streams of development existed throughout the long circuit of aboriginal life. No spectacular introduction or changes could be credited to the Pueblo because practically everything—architecture, pottery, feather cloth, cultivated plants (with the exception of cotton), and weapons—was firmly established in the Basket Maker age. The Pueblos seemed to have been improvers, not innovators. Almost missing, unless one were to read between the lines, were indications of turmoil or disruption which might have occurred had one group forced itself upon another. True, some students postulated such events, but this was science fiction. Also there was a diminution of what had appeared a rigidulous split between long- and short-head forms. Newly uncovered graves yielded skulls of both types in positive cultural association. In fact, some skulls originally described by archaeologists as long were in truth medium. It was a possibility that the Basket Maker strain had not been something diametrically opposed to the Pueblo strain, that both might have been variations of the same type with divergence overemphasized because of deformation; that the predominance of brachycephals at later dates did not necessarily signify wholesale invasion but might have been the result of prolonged infiltration. It was being realized that many pitfalls lay in connecting physical with cultural characteristics and that the digger was not usually equipped by training to judge cranial types.

Other finds were at the same time showing that there were numerous cultural lags in terms of time across the central Pueblo area. Not every district had witnessed development at the same rate, nor had all the model Pecos Classification steps been taken. One group appeared progressive and quick to embrace new ideas and elements while its neighbors became reactionary. It might have adopted a complex of traits which had evolved elsewhere, without itself undergoing the procedural trial and error. Might not peoples along the peripheries of the Pueblo distribution have moved more slowly than those in the centers of largest population, the old condition of the backwoods versus the metropolis? For example, in the Flagstaff region, ruins showing traditional Pueblo II culture dated from the 1100's; in Chaco Canyon the 1100's had been the Golden Age of Pueblo III.

At this confused period J. O. "Jo" Brew, of Harvard University, for three seasons (from 1931 through 1933) in a most businesslike fashion took up the work where Earl had left it. His project directed at one thing: definition of Pueblo II. Paradoxically the Pecos Conference had stated that this was the most widely spread period of the entire sequence, that the hundreds of small masonry houses to be seen on almost every swale from Pagosa Springs to the Colorado River had pertained to that horizon, that the unique corrugated pottery which was to be found in abundance was a characteristic sign of the times. Yet no pure Pueblo II site had been dug. Earl was inclined to believe that such a period had not existed in the northern drainage of the San Juan. However, Brew planned to engage the Pueblo II in the cedar breaks of Alkali Ridge south of Monticello, Utah, where the archaeological triumvirate of Kidder, Nusbaum, and Judd had carried out their first archaeological work in 1908.

The Pueblo II had been an Alkali Ridge all right, but they did not fit the preconceived notions about them. As early as 1903 Prudden wrote of the small houses of shaped stone left abandoned in some long-forgotten day which were so commonly met in his pack trips with Clayton Wetherill through the San Juan basin. These ruins he called "unit houses" because they were constructed in a simple block of rarely more than six to eight rooms, usually in a double row, with a kiva for ceremonies nearby and a dump beyond that. Limited excavation showed that a tunnel connected house to kiva. The type of structure became linked with the author. Subsequent anthropological literature of the region was filled with references to Prudden's unit house. He, and those who came after him, for many years thought that herein lay the idea of later large houses. The Pecos Conference called the unit house Pueblo II.

Brew, in his growing belief that Prudden houses were more recent than Pueblo II, was looking for masonry structures older than the unit house. He was successful. At Alkali Ridge there were coursed-masonry buildings of very small size associated with Pueblo II pottery. Furthermore, in several instances they overlay jacal houses which also had Pueblo II pottery. Both types had associated kivas.

The four months' work of the 1933 season brought attention to another matter which was of vital concern to Earl, the crescentic, pole-and-mud-type of settlement which he alone had thus far discovered. In Brew's voluminous report upon the Alkali Ridge project, published thirteen years after fieldwork and dedicated to Al Lancaster, his foreman and friend, he summarized the architectural findings at his Site 13. "The discovery of this site holds many significant implications for the history of Pueblo architecture. Perhaps the most important of these is the appearance of large accumulations of contiguous rooms assembled around open plazas in which were placed subterranean structures, all of this antedating the small "unit-type" dwelling supposed to have been the "germ" of Pueblo village form. The few tree-ring dates obtained place the buildings in the eighth century A.D. . . . The wall construction included all of the major types previously described for the San Juan: Walls of upright slabs, of post-mud-adobe (jacal), of horizontal coursed masonry, and of simple adobe. Fortunately, minor details in the fabrication of these walls distinguished them from walls of other times and in other localities which otherwise may be classified in the same broad types."[46]

The architecture represented had been studied also by Earl, but in a village of lesser size that was not totally cleared. On the other hand, the painted pottery was something vastly different. In a region considered a stronghold of the black-on-white tradition, this pottery was sometimes as red as the bluffs near the goosenecks of the San Juan. The designs upon it were painted in red which ranged from dark to light and even had purplish tones. Sometimes the paint was black; occasionally both black and red were used. In many cases designs were taken directly from Basket Maker III baskets. This pottery's location in a pole-and-mud house fixed its period of manufacture as probably Pueblo I.

Red ware was not unknown in the San Juan and, except for the Kayenta in Pueblo II and Pueblo III, it never comprised more than an insignificant fraction of the total ceramic yield at any one site. Only at Alkali Ridge was there evidence for a center of manufacture where red pottery dominated black-on-white. Its source of inspiration might have been far to the south where reddish-brown pottery was the normal type. It might have given birth to Kayenta black-on-reds and polychromes. These were mere speculations at the time of Brew's report, and they will remain so until a great deal more earth has been moved.

Five years later Paul Martin of the Field Museum of Natural History dug several sites in an area twenty-five miles to the east of Alkali Ridge which revealed striking similarities in architecture and ceramics.

Alkali Ridge Site 13 houses and the Piedra houses were contemporaneous in the 770's; the former were called Basket Maker III-Pueblo I, the latter Pueblo I. Jacal and slab-walled houses in the Ackmen-

Lowry area of southwestern Colorado, excavated by Paul Martin, were dated A.D. 747-68; crude coursed-masonry houses in the same region were dated A.D. 855-72. Both settlements were considered Basket Maker III by Martin. Johnson Canyon Site 33 was fifty years younger than these other jacal types; it was pegged as Pueblo I. Its closest parallels were the sites in Utah and Martin's Site 2, but in some respects it was less advanced toward the rectangular plan of later times.

The uncomfortable fact of nonconformity was being highlighted. It was undeniable that cultural lags and overlaps were the normal condition rather than the atypical, some of them being the result of geographical position and some not. In the conceptual scheme devised at Pecos there was inflexibility and a complex state of affairs was oversimplified. One house type or one style of pottery could not be the only standard for a given period.

The weather-worn face of the Mesa Verde cuesta had been on Earl's distant northwest horizon for most of his life. Yet not until after the completion of the La Plata project did he ever work there. Then he was called to duty because of his high reputation in regard to matters of repair.

Care was imperative if the ruins were to remain intact. The debris which drifted over ancient walls actually had saved them for our time. Once this detritus was removed, the ruins were thrust out to wind erosion, which ate away rocks and mortar a grain at a time, and to the quiet attrition of drops of water, which in many caves seeped from beneath sandstone layers at the rear of the ruins. Cracks in walls became wider and longer with each passing year. Slabs of sandstone scaled from the cliffs as they had for eons but now they could fall on the very unprotected stuff of which American history was made. The traveler was prevented from carving his initials on door lintels or pocketing grimy souvenirs by watchful rangers, but by the tread of his feet he unknowingly caused deterioration. Walls weakened by the ages were not meant to be climbed and constant shuffle of shoes wore down mud and stone with sandpaper efficiency. In some cases the vibration of movement itself was destructive. Furthermore, old reconstruction done in the Fewkes period was glaringly obvious and needed to be replaced.

With the aid of Al Lancaster from Alkali Ridge and Gustav Stromsvik from Guatemala, Earl undertook extensive repairs at Cliff Palace, Spruce Tree House, Balcony House, and Far View. Although at one crucial point in the work a fire raged across the southwest corner of the Park which required the help of all available manpower, work was successfully completed and Mesa Verde remains secured for future years.

In keeping with a new approach being tried in the Southwest—archaeological surveys and the collection of surface sherd assortments to delimit definite culture phases—the next year Mesa Verde Superintendent Nusbaum sought permission for Earl to make an archaeological reconnaissance of the Park. This plan did not materialize. However, Nusbaum's stepson, Deric, was engaged to survey the La Plata under Earl's guidance. He reported a total of a thousand sites within that region, many being very small; all periods following Basket Maker II were present. The Mesa Verde survey was accomplished for Chapin Mesa years later. Here Lancaster and Arthur Rohn tabulated nineteen hundred fifty eight sites which included one hundred ninety one cliff dwellings, seven hundred eight mesa top sites, forty six groups of farming terraces, five groups of pictographs, six shrines, and two Navajo sweat houses. Everything from Basket Maker III on was represented. To consider the Mesa Verde culture area as extending over the broad valleys west of the mesa, where no systematic surveys had been attempted but where hundreds of ruins were obvious even to unschooled eyes, was to realize the teeming numbers of the ancient Pueblo who had made this land their home.

When at last Earl sat down to writing of the Old People of the La Plata how could he characterize their culture on the basis of his excavations or the inanimate objects he had piled up in barrels and boxes around him? Their means of subsistence and their style of architecture he now understood but what about artistic achievements? What were these and what part did they play in La Plata life? Aside from the examples of fine masonry to be noted in some of the Pueblo III structures, pottery was the principal surviving craft in which there was artistic creativity expressed as embellishment of utilitarian objects. In order to understand pottery's development and growth, the sources of its inspirations and the unconscious controls placed upon its variability, Earl knew he had to work out both temporal and technological order. Although he had known this kind of pottery since the age of three, he found the description of it through the course of subtle transitions very taxing. A common dilemma to all ceramic taxonomists, Earl expressed it more eloquently than most. "The extremes of the series and certain stages between are obvious enough, but adequately to segregate the distinguishing characteristics of wares of the intermediate phases through which one ceramic complex slipped into the next has seemed as perplexing as an attempt to express in words the color changes of a clear sky between two and three o'clock in the afternoon. Differences there are, that, as a result of long familiarity, one feels clearly enough. They may rest upon a blend of numerous features, each in itself intangible yet contributing to an ensemble of individuality, valid beyond question but recognizable subliminally more than consciously, hence so nebulous that it tends to slip through even a finely drawn descriptive mesh. Here one is immediately confronted by the lack of words of positively delimited and accepted meaning. Paste, temper, slip, rough or smooth finish, matt or glossy pigment—valuable tools all of them, but too crude and clumsy for truly detailed work."[47]

In an effort to more fully understand the physical composition of this La Plata pottery, Earl sought the aid of Anna O. Shepard, a fellow employee of the Carnegie Institution, who possessed an astonishing breadth of knowledge in three areas—archaeology, chemistry, and geology. In seeking such technical aid, Earl was reflecting the awakening of archaeologists to the realization that if they were going to recapture a total picture of prehistoric life, they were going to have to turn to allied sciences, however reluctantly. Miss Shepard was able through a meticulous study of temper particles incorporated in the pottery clay to point out an interesting fact about the La Plata pottery. Several pieces, although having typical La Plata surface finish and design, may have been made at settlements bordering the Chuska Mountains. Was there a stamp on the bottom of the vessels which read "Made at Chuska by Chuskans?" Unfortunately, no. But there were bits of a rare type of basalt which had been crushed and thrown into the batter to serve as temper. The La Plata women would hardly have had access to this rock which occurred only along the feet of the mountains to the south. Miss Shepard had also observed this peculiar rock in pottery from Pueblo Bonito. She suggested that there may have been a thriving trade in either finished pots or in temper agents from that portion of the reservation which Earl had explored in the 1920's to Chaco Canyon and/or the La Plata. Chaco influence in the La Plata region already was an established fact. This further substantiation was of added interest because of the method by which it had been obtained.

When Earl had talked of their houses, diet, clothing, tools, and crafts, what conclusions could he have drawn about the La Platans themselves? Physically he saw them as a mixed group, long-headed in early horizons and predominately round-headed in Pueblo times. He felt they must have looked much like their modern descendants—short in stature, stocky in build, possessed of straight black hair and bronzed skin—but because of the flattening of the back of the head, their facial features may have been somewhat different.

What of the group personality? Could an archaeologist, a dealer in lifeless material objects, make valid conclusions about such a thing? Earl thought so.

His first thought would have been of the communal nature of La Plata homes, an aspect of their culture which must suggest a great deal about the occupants and the breadth of their democracy. The structures unquestionably had been erected by shared efforts and skills, the product of voluntary labor. Occupying them would have meant complete submergence of the individual to the group. It was no place for the rugged individualist. The house type also revealed the gregariousness of the Pueblo as opposed to the Navajo who prefer to live isolated from each other. Nor was any house outstandingly better than its neighbors. There were no Jones with whom one had to keep pace, nor were there rulers who had to have something better or more lavish than their subjects.

From the kiva Earl could have seen first of all the powerful hand of tradition and secondly the great force of religion. In the Great Kiva complex, where such enormous amounts of labor would have been demanded of everyone, perhaps he could have inferred an incipient theocracy. The belief in an afterlife was obvious in the burial practices for who would sacrifice his best possessions if they were not to be put to some better use?

From his rapid transfiguration from a homeless savage dependent upon the vagaries of hunting and gathering to a sedentary individual making his environment work for him, all achieved within the space of fifteen hundred years, Earl judged these Indians to have been men of intelligence, fortitude, and courage. Their resourcefulness and ingenuity in obtaining a rich vital life in a restrictive environment were unquestioned. The work of their hands showed a capacity for controlled technical excellence. Uppermost in any list of their attributes would have been originality, expressed in ceramics, architecture, and the type of society in which they functioned, all of them being entirely unique for the Western Hemisphere. They were men who had pride in their craftsmanship, whether it was weaving a Basket Maker pannier, molding a Pueblo pot, or building a tower of sandstone blocks, but within these crafts could also be seen the seeds of decay. In their unfaltering adherence to convention, their denial of any artistic exuberance of spirit which promoted free expression, they, like older and younger civilizations in the history of the world, while still at full flower were drifting toward decadence.

Most impressive perhaps to anyone of Western European background was the fact that these men had been able to live at peace for hundreds of years if not a full millenium. Many had been the statements of intertribal warfare to account for otherwise unexplainable events such as their quitting the San Juan. Along with his associates Earl had accepted this theory. With the volume of data being collected by the 1930's, he saw that such a position was untenable. There was only one hint of troubled times which was met frequently. That was fire. In the La Plata and at nearly every other early site in the north country there had been conflagrations which had wiped out entire villages. There was no proof that this fact related to warfare but there was no escaping its possibility. If there had been war, by rules there must have been victims. However, no bodies were found sprawled about the ruins rammed with arrows or shattered by clubs, much as those calamitous occurrences would have enlivened research. Archaeologists found only possessions and those were sprinkled throughout the rubble of the burned dwellings, a fact which could have been interpreted as evidence for sudden firing of either accidental derivation or a scorched-earth policy instigated by the town's occupants who made the hard choice of destroying their homes rather than allowing enemies to take them. Not until late Pueblo III were fires once more seen to have raged through Indian villages, but here again no victims of war were encountered. Some towns were unmistakable fortresses built to withstand shadowy enemies who never came. The Athabascans, being both warlike and predatory in historic periods, at one interval in the course of reconstruction of Southwest prehistory were held responsible for the abandonment of the San Juan. By the time Earl had cut off his La Plata work, it was known that they had not arrived at the scene until perhaps several hundred years later. But just because human nature is what it is and probably always has been, Earl felt that there must have been feuds between groups of the same stripe. Yet where was the proof?

When he added up all the diverse views of the Old People, Earl liked the results. He knew he was forever in their debt. Through study of their past, they had provided him with deep-reaching pleasure and stimulation which had given color and goals to his own life. "Given the same opportunity, some other might well have done a better job than I, but that opportunity will come to no man again because archaeological sites, once excavated are pied type thenceforward."[48]

IV.
Basket Maker

Del Muerto

"Mummy Cave offers an unusual opportunity for a striking and highly constructive piece of work."[1]

The patron has long been a familiar adjunct in the worlds of arts and letters. In Southwestern archaeology too the wealthy dilettante has played a role, although in the current tax-burdened period patronage has passed largely from private to institutional hands. Earl came of age in an era of archaeology prescribed and paid for by the very rich. The Hydes, Morgans, Huntingtons, Hemenways, Claflins, and others had made many a dig a possibility. As an employee of a research institution constantly seeking such outside support, Earl knew the value of the well placed hint and the gracious gesture. He was amazingly adept because of his innate gentlemanliness and undiverted dedication to his chosen field at winning friends and influencing proper pocketbooks. In Charles L. Bernheimer he found a patron who paid for some of his most fascinating research.

Bernheimer was a man who in middle age developed a passion for the scenic wonders of the Southwest. Being a wealthy cottonbroker in the Bear Mill Manufacturing Company of New York, he could indulge himself in this expensive hobby. For over a decade, beginning in 1920, he made fourteen pack trips through remote districts of the

Four Corners. He published a few popular articles and a book on his great experiences in the West, donated artifacts purchased or found along the way to scientific bodies, and in general enjoyed his role as a man of action for at least three weeks out of the year.

In 1921, with one trek to Rainbow Bridge behind him, Bernheimer called on Clark Wissler of the American Museum of Natural History. He wished to have a scientist accompany him on another ride to the Bridge in order to explain to him the ruins which he had seen at Kiet Siel and Betatakin. It was altogether possible that new archaeological discoveries might be made because the region was still relatively unexplored. Wissler immediately suggested Earl, the only museum employee resident in the Southwest and a person interested in the Kayenta prehistory. So it was that Earl became Bernheimer's guest for five different trips which were known as the Bernheimer Expeditions under the auspices of the American Museum.

The plan was for Earl to meet with Bernheimer at Flagstaff in mid-June and from there proceed to Kayenta where John Wetherill, Zeke Johnson, and Al Smith were to have a pack outfit in readiness. On June 1, Earl wired Bernheimer concerning a typhus epidemic on the Navajo Reservation southwest of Shiprock which had taken the lives of two white doctors, a number of white settlers, and many Indians. He pointed out that although the disease had not spread westward, the Navajo traveled about a good bit and were infected with lice. The danger could not be ignored. Bernheimer cancelled the trip, and Earl went off to join Judd's field camp at Chaco.

Two weeks later, on advice from Wetherill, Bernheimer decided to continue with his original plans and so notified Earl at Aztec. Earl's mother had the message relayed to the Agency at Crownpoint, south of the canyon, and a rider brought word to Earl.

On June 26 the two men started toward the trading post at Kayenta. For the next several weeks their party moved through the wilderness toward the Rainbow Bridge and the Colorado River. The rides were short for the first several days to allow Bernheimer to become hardened to the unusual exercise, but before the circuit back to the group of rock buildings at Kayenta had been completed, an eighteen- or twenty-hour day on horseback had become routine. From Betatakin to Shato Spring, to Nitsi Canyon and Jayi, to Navajo Canyon and up to Navajo Mountain the party and their train of pack mules made a winding path.

The group was a congenial one. Johnson, an affable Mormon from Blanding, Utah, and later the first Custodian of Natural Bridges National Monument, had spent years guiding visitors through the uncharted clay hills and rugged mesas north of the San Juan. He was one of that group of native frontiersmen who met the test of camp with consummate skill, fathomless calm, and, Earl thought, lack of organization. He was undisturbed by sand dunes or rock ledges for a bed, a grimy gunnysack or bandana for a dish towel, an interminable diet of beans and Mormon tea. Johnson made it his job to see to Bernheimer's personal comforts and to keep things enlivened with jokes, songs, and tales of pioneering. Wetherill, intimately familiar with the Navajo deserts from having operated a store for the Indians of that area for fifteen years, had made a lucrative business of leading such prominent figures as Byron Cummings, Sam Guernsey, Neil Judd, Zane Grey, and Teddy Roosevelt through the canyon fastnesses. Hosteen John, as the Navajos called Wetherill, knew more of the region's antiquities than any other man. His brothers had discovered the largest cliff houses such as Poncho House, Kiet Siel, and Inscription House. Bernheimer was impressed with Wetherill's firsthand knowledge of the geology, anthropology, and geography of the Kayenta district. Everyone enjoyed his modest competence.

To Earl the archaeological aspects of the trip were disappointing. There were the classic cliff dwellings he had expected and here and there a few small rooms crowded along a cranny. All the stages of Pueblo sequence were recognizable in the shelters and in the open including those of the Pre Pueblos he was coming to know so well at the San Juan's eastern limits. There were other caves which looked promising for Basket Maker remains, but time did not permit excavation. Since he had never dug a site pertaining to that age, he longed to do so.

As day followed day devoid of archaeological discoveries other than a few chance sherds or a discarded mano, Earl abandoned suspicions that Wetherill was deliberately bypassing ruins in order to keep them inviolate for Cummings and Guernsey and began to realize that much of the region had been too rough for human occupation at any period. But he kept looking. While the others escaped noontime heat under brush ramadas built by the wranglers, Earl was scouting the canyon rims and arches for signs of former habitation, sometimes hiking three or four hours from base camp and returning with his clothing completely soaked with sweat.

The sand deltas of the Colorado River and what Wetherill then thought was the Crossing of the Fathers, (where Escalante's party in 1776 had forded the river on the return loop in a march from Santa Fe), were reached by the Fourth of July. Six days later the men made camp under majestic Nonnezoshe or Rainbow Bridge. They signed a register which had been placed at the north end of the arch, among the first entries which began at the rear of the book and moved toward the front. Bernheimer succeeded in taking the most comprehensive photographic coverage of that gem of nature made to that time.

Despite Bernheimer's effusive conversations drawn from *The Riders of the Purple Sage,* which he could quote by heart, his dietary idiosyncracies, and the red skating cap he wore to bed, he was admired by the men in his employ for his nerve and for his willingness to endure the hardships of the trail. Earl found him a man of rare qualities and was glad to accept another invitation to join the expedition the next summer.

However, a return to Rainbow Bridge was not Earl's idea of an archaeologically profitable enterprise. He wrote Wissler he would go, if necessary, to keep alive Bernheimer's interest in archaeology for he was sure that the old man would succumb to its lure if he once witnessed relics being removed from the ground. But to work the Kayenta would encroach upon the preserve already claimed by other colleagues.

Instead he proposed a pack trip through a region new to Bernheimer, a strip of land along the New Mexico-Arizona border one hundred miles long and fifteen miles wide to include the canyons draining Carriso Mountain, the Red Rock Valley lying between Carriso Mountain and the Lukachukais, the eastern side of the Tunicha range as far south as Toadlena. Such exploration could be begun either from Newcomb's trading post in the south or the Tisnaspas trading post in the north. It would dovetail with the fabulous reservation finds just coming to light and, Earl hoped, would lead to the study of the transitional phases between Basket Maker and Pre Pueblo in which he was absorbed. He was sure that ruins of the desired age were to be found there upon no less an authority than Clayton Wetherill who had said that there was no unexplored area in the Southwest so rich in ruins. But Bernheimer turned a deaf ear to the suggestion. He wanted to attempt to blaze a new trail to Rainbow Bridge around the west end of Navajo Mountain.

So for twenty-one days in midsummer of 1922 the same group of men who had traveled together the previous season rode from Kayenta southwestward to Marsh Pass, then in a westerly direction across the plateau south of Tsegi Canyon to the east side of Navajo Mountain which ultimately was completely circumscribed. Earl's report to Wissler recounted the experience.

The territory both north and south of Navajo Mountain was previously known so that our contribution in the way of actual exploration consisted of traversing the region between a spring called Segi-to in a canyon draining southwest from Navajo Mountain, and the Rainbow Bridge. From Segi-to we worked our way along the western skirt of the mountain crossing the heads of several deep and rough canyons, and finally ascending to a notch separating Nameless Mesa from Navajo Mountain. From the notch an abrupt descent of 1500 feet brought us to the bottom of a tributary of West Canyon which we named Cliff Canyon. The lower reaches of this sheer walled drainage course lie some three miles southward of, and nearly parallel to the western portion of Bridge Canyon, to which it was our desire to gain access. After considerable reconnaissance John Wetherill found a crack which offered a possible route for a trail cutting through the towering rock mass which separates the two canyons. Six members of our party spent four days cutting timber, and grading and blasting a way through this pass. On the morning of the fifth of July, we passed over the trail thus made and on into Bridge Canyon. Never before had the Rainbow Natural Bridge been reached except over the trail northward of Navajo Mountain opened by John Wetherill in 1909. In making passable a second trail to the Bridge by way of the south and west sides of the mountain, the principal object of the expedition was accomplished.

From the base camp in Cliff Canyon the lower reaches of this drainage course were explored as well as the portion of West Canyon northward from the mouth of Cliff to the mouth of Bridge Canyon, and southward toward Clematis Camp of the previous year as far as animals could travel. In addition Nameless Mesa and a high mesa lying south of the Rainbow Bridge were climbed. Contrary to expectations no ruins were found on these mesas. However, numerous traces of aboriginal occupation were observed elsewhere.

On a soil-covered bench between Cliff and Bridge Canyons there were extensive camp sites of a non-pottery making people. These were marked by slab-lined fire boxes, quantities of flint chips, and black earth, but no signs of dwellings. On the walls of Cliff Canyon pictographs were seen in several places. The most notable group was in a cave on the north side just westward of the point where there were incised Cliff Dweller designs and painted Basket Maker figures, the latter being characterized by large triangular human forms done in yellow, red, and black. Doubtless there was much frequentation of this cave, but floods had swept the floor clean, removing all traces but the pictographs. In a tremendous cave in the wall of Cliff Canyon there were large quantities of charcoal

Johnson Canyon cliff-dweller ruins.

The ruins of Johnson Canyon were explored by Morris in 1913. (Illustrated in Morris, 1919, Pl. 33)

Above: Aztec as it appeared about the end of the 1918 season when the exploration and repair was about half completed.

Opposite page:
Top: Portion of La Bajada ruin, New Mexico.

Middle: In the fall of 1915 a trip through the Gobernador region of northern New Mexico revealed sandstone masonry dwellings.

Bottom: Corner fireplaces and timbers obviously cut with metal tools indicated the Gobernador settlements had been constructed and occupied after the coming of the Spaniards. Tree-ring dates ranged from A.D 1625 to A.D. 1745.

Above: Aztec Ruins in the late nineteenth century.

The Warrior's Grave. A doorway in the rear wall had been sealed by the aboriginal masons.

View of the Great Kiva looking toward the North Wing, after excavation of 1921. The altar, upper center, is covered with canvas.

The roof of the Great Kiva exemplified the immense skill of the aboriginal engineers. The wooden framework had to support not only its own weight but a covering of at least a foot of earth, or a direct load of an estimated ninety tons.

When restored, the Aztec Great Kiva became a shrine, not only for the men of the past but for Morris himself.

Aerial view of Aztec Ruins, 1934. The Hubbard Mound is located at the tip of the triangle of road and ditch, center left. Mound F is at the top of picture.

Digging carried on in 1921 and 1922 on the Navajo Reservation south of Shiprock produced hundreds of ceramic specimens in a few days.

In the La Plata district of northern New Mexico the typical house of early Pueblo culture was a pithouse.

Site 41, the largest masonry structure of the La Plata area. In 1930, Morris excavated 170 rooms and 10 kivas. Those viewed here are of Pueblo III age, but successively early strata lay below. Stones from this site were later used in the reconstruction of the Great Kiva at Aztec Ruins. (Illustrated in Morris, 1939, Pl. 84)

Opposite page:
Top: One interment from Site 23 in the La Plata Drainage suggested cannibalism.
Middle: The deep ceremonial structures indicate the pervading power of religion for the Anasazi of the La Plata district. Masonry benches encircle the interior, upon which are pilasters which once supported a wooden roof.
Bottom: Pottery in various conditions was plentiful at La Plata Site 33. (Illustrated in Morris, 1939, Pl. 41)

A Great Kiva at La Plata Site 33 was the second one known of Post Basket Maker age. The holes for, and remains of, two huge logs which served as roof supports can be seen. Analysis showed the trees had been felled in A.D. 831. (Illustrated in Morris, 1939, Pl. 47)

Basket Maker II dwellings near Durango were the first of that horizon known, and yielded tree-ring dates which are still the oldest.

A cliff wall in the Red Rocks district.

Left: The Bernheimer party examined finds made in preliminary testing of Broken Flute Cave in 1931. Left to right; Morris, Bernheimer, Wetherill, Johnson.

Right: The floor of Pocket Cave in the Red Rocks district.

Some architectural units in Broken Flute Cave.

Above: A thirty-five-foot vertical wall separates the two structures comprising White House in Canyon de Chelly National Monument. In 1926, Morris constructed two wing dams across the canyon floor to protect the lower unit from flood waters which occasionally pour down canyon.

Opposite: Repair of the House of the Tower at Mummy Cave was undertaken in 1932 when the area was declared a national monument.

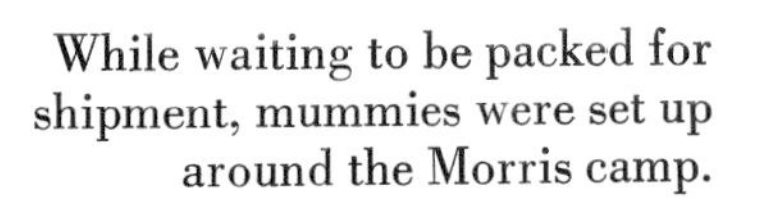

While waiting to be packed for shipment, mummies were set up around the Morris camp.

The Tomb of the Weaver.

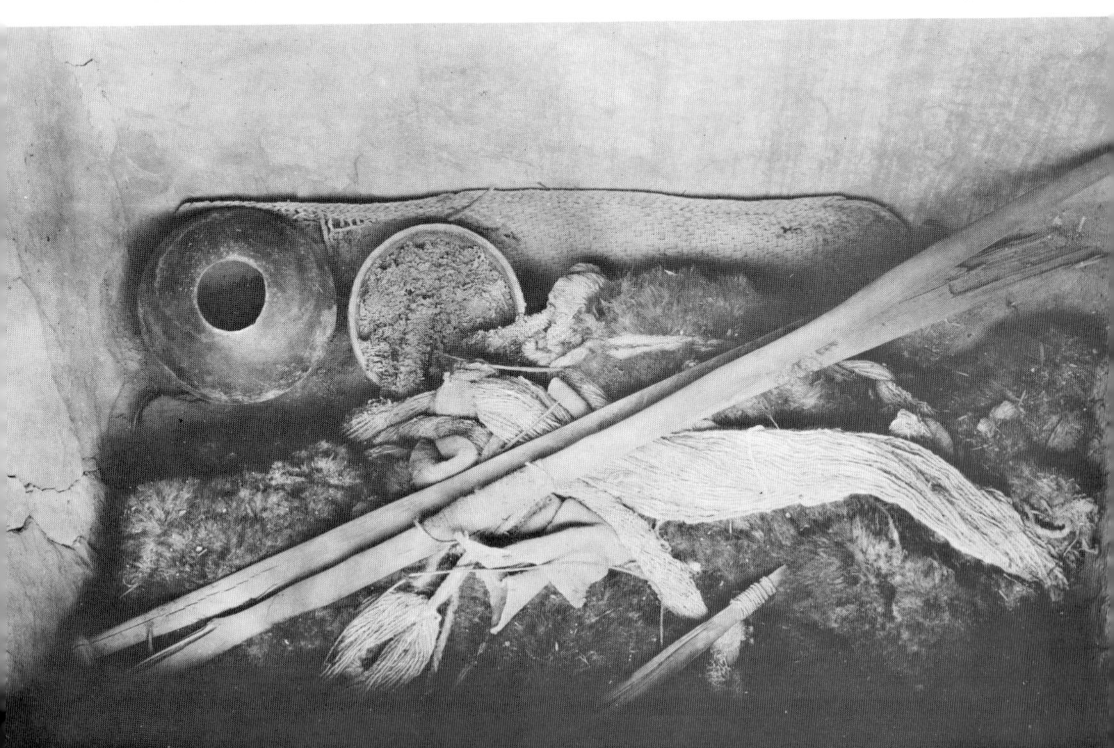

A typical Basket Maker grave in a slab cist.

John Wetherill, brother of the discoverer of the Mesa Verde cliff dwellings and the Basket Makers of Grand Gulch. In 1923 he led Morris and Bernheimer to Canyon del Muerto.

Mummy Cave, Canyon del Muerto, introduced Morris to the Basket Makers.

and ashes but no house walls. Here was found one Basket Maker grave containing the skeleton of a child with typical dolichocephalic undeformed cranium, wrapped in a fur string blanket, covered with a basket, and accompanied by a strand of beads and eight chipped blades. Elsewhere in the cave were found a few Cliff Dweller potsherds, and some sandals, corn refuse, and yucca leaves. As a generalization it may be stated that this cave and practically all others in this region were frequented by the Cliff Dwellers, and more recently by the Piute and Navajo. Many of the latter tribe found refuge in the extremely rough country westward of Navajo Mountain during the expedition led against them by Kit Carson.[2]

These had been two trips cutting through the core of Basket Maker domain. Earl dug only one Basket Maker burial, that an isolated find.

After three trips to the Rainbow Bridge, Bernheimer was ready to carry his explorations elsewhere. The first plan was to move over into Zeke Johnson's territory north of the San Juan, but Mrs. Bernheimer protested the strenuousness of that undertaking for her husband. Earl then suggested that maybe the Easterner would enjoy seeing archaeologists at work.

He reasoned that everyone adored a treasure hunt. That was part of the universal appeal of archaeology to small boys and mature men alike. So he selected his most specimen-producing sites, those along Cemetery Ridge explored the summer before, put Owens and a helper to work, and arranged for Bernheimer to be on hand at the right time. From the day of his first visit to an actual dig, Bernheimer became an avid fan. Pleased to see his guest's excited reaction as the clutter was salvaged from the shallow burial grounds, Earl tactfully mentioned the need of funds and prompt action. He was assured of aid.

From the diggings near Newcomb's, Earl, Wetherill, Johnson, and Bernheimer rode in the Ford to Canyon de Chelly on the west side of the Lukachukais traveling via Tse-a-chong and Round Rock. At Chinle, a name which sounded like a chop suey parlor set down in the middle of the Navajo Reservation, they secured supplies and horses at Cozy McSparron's trading post. If Earl was on the threshold of an epic period in his life, at the time he was totally unimpressed, thinking that the sites had been so badly mutilated by the Days, father and sons, who once operated the trading post that there was little to be salvaged.

The men jogged along through the deep sands of the arroyo, riding in single file up into the narrow constriction of a gash called Canyon del Muerto, Canyon of Death, at that time believed to have been named from a massacre of a group of Navajos by Mexican soldiers. Members of the party found it as awe inspiring an experience as entering a cathedral as from the canyon floor they gazed upward at sheer cliffs, streaked and dark from years of rain.

Naturally it was the ancient ones who had lived along the canyon walls who appealed to Earl. In overhangs and at the bases of many cliffs he saw evidence of their occupation, sometimes in the form of masonry structures set along a ledge; sometimes as the tips of up-ended slabs, which experience had taught him were the rims of cists; sometimes as artifacts weathering from deeply-laid, compacted trash. So electrified was he by an entire canyon crammed with loot and corroborative data that he could scarcely sleep. In a magazine article he described his reaction to this exploratory trip. "One day we brought our pack train down a difficult trail that scales the north wall of del Muerto and turned up canyon toward Mummy Cave. For days John Wetherill, our veteran guide, had told me of the rich archaeological promise the canyons still contained, but I was in no wise prepared for what I saw. Before night I was literally wild over the wealth of specimens and of information that lay snugly tucked away in the dry ledge shelter. I resolved to begin their exploration at the earliest possible date."[3]

Back at Aztec the next day, Earl, bursting with enthusiasm for a new project, described his observations to Wissler, at the same time indicating his great fear that after the ruins had lain undefiled for seven centuries someone else would move in on them in the upcoming several months.

> We spent four days in Canyon del Muerto which I had not previously visited. Judging from the collections in the Brooklyn Museum and from the known activities of the Day brothers and other relic hunters, I had assumed that the ruins in this canyon were gutted or at least so badly messed over that systematic investigations there would be a very discouraging proposition. This is by no means true. Some digging has been done, but the bulk of each ruin is untouched. Never have I seen or expected to see such opportunities for stratigraphic observations. Every cave offers great promise in this respect, but I will confine myself to Mummy Cave wherein conditions are most clearly evident. As indicated by the rough cross section given herewith, near the foot of an enormous refuse talus there are Basket Maker burials. Farther up the slope the walls and roofs of pre-Pueblo slab structures protrude from the refuse. On the surface of the talus were picked up early pre-Pueblo sherds with red-

washed exteriors, and fragments of decorated paste pre-Pueblo ware. In the cave proper is situated the largest cliff house in the de Chelly-del Muerto canyon system. This structure is older than the Mesa Verde cliff ruins, most of it dating from early Chaco time. Judging from differences in masonry the cliff house itself is representative of two periods. Thus in Mummy Cave there exist remains of the first four culture periods which have been identified in the San Juan drainage, and probably a fifth. The relations of these periods I have determined to my own satisfaction in the La Plata country and along Captain Tom's Wash directly eastward of Canyon del Muerto on the opposite side of Tunicha Mountain. However, the work in these localities has been in open sites where no perishable artifacts were obtained. To you I need not emphasize the desirability of securing collections of objects of hide, wood, basketry, and textiles for a delimitation and comparison of the material cultures of the successive time periods. Upwards of twenty sandals, a cradle, matting, fragments of cloth, buckskin, a flute, four pipes, and numerous minor objects secured from four caves with less than a day's digging, indicate the volume of specimens which may be expected.

Mummy Cave offers an unusual opportunity for a striking and highly constructive piece of work. I greatly desire to do this work, and would like to see the American Museum have the credit for it. I would recommend that you endeavor to raise funds at once. Two thousand dollars would be desirable, with $1500 as a minimum. In this matter speed is essential. Kidder and Guernesy, Judd, and Cummings have declined to examine Canyon del Muerto believing the ruins there to have been spoiled by pot hunters. However, by this time Guernsey who is now working in the Chin Lee valley of which the canyon in question is a tributary will have learned from John Wetherill who accompanied us, that there are Basket Maker remains in Mummy Cave. He will be digging there before fall unless we are there first. My observations give us priority, and I hope you will see fit to secure a permit at once for Canyon del Muerto, naming Mummy Cave as the principal objective.[4]

Wissler understood his young protégé's desire to begin work. He wanted Earl and the museum to profit from these new discoveries. But there were problems, not insurmountable but undeniably difficult. Certainly it would be singular for one man of average energy to require three government permits for excavation in diverse places upon federal land in a single year; Earl already had papers authorized by Fewkes for digging on the La Plata and on the reservation in the region of Mitten Rock and Cemetery Ridge. Then, Earl had far more than ordinary vitality and ambition, and Wissler sensed that he would willingly dig year round if weather and money permitted. Fewkes might be won over with the assurance that the new project was merely an extension westward of a research program already under way on the east side of the Tunichas.

But there was also Sam Guernsey. Earl realized that Guernsey, having spent ten or more years on the scent of the Basket Makers and at that very moment being virtually at del Muerto, would come running as soon as he learned of their extensive presence in the talus slopes of the canyon. Wetherill had said, "I am obligated to tell Sam Guernsey what I see."[5] Earl suspected that Wetherill had ridden directly to Guernsey's camp after Earl had departed to put Bernheimer on the train. In his desire to see his friend get this opportunity, Bernheimer wanted to take steps to keep Wetherill quiet. But Earl knew that efforts to silence him would drive the old trader even more firmly into the opposing camp. There was only one recourse—to act as if it were a foregone conclusion that the museum was undertaking immediate excavation in the area. Earl sent a note to Guernsey. "By now I presume you are again hot on the trail of the Old People. I suppose it is unnecessary to express the hope that you will find them in plenty as I know of your propensity for locating the right spots. Probably Wetherill has told you that we found almost certain evidence that the caves in Canyon del Muerto were inhabited by everyone from the Basket Makers to a cliff house people prior to those of the Mesa Verde. This was a pleasing discovery for I have been fired by your cave work, and have been anxious to get into some dry sites in relative proximity to the open sites in which we have done so much digging just across the mountain from the head of del Muerto. Judging from a recent letter from the Museum, unless unforseen complications arise, I shall be out there before the year is over. I do not expect to rival such discoveries as you have made, for instance in White Dog Cave, but I do look for a good series of perishable objects to accompany my several pottery types."[6] Earl had staked his claim as surely as a prospector.

Meanwhile, faithful to his statement that he would intercede, Bernheimer held interviews with Curator Wissler and President Osborne in New York. In just six weeks from the time Earl first requested permission to transfer work to del Muerto, he had the necessary permit and funds to pay for the Cemetery Ridge work as well. With whatever money that could be saved from the museum's physical anthropological expedition under the direction of Dr. Sullivan, Earl was set to plunge into a new chapter of his kaleidoscopic career. This time he was to have a partner.

Earl married in 1923. This was astounding news to his friends and associates because for a long as anyone could remember Earl had had only one interest—his work. Now he had fallen in love with a slim beautiful girl from the midwest, Ann Axtell, daughter of a well-to-do family in Omaha, whom he had met at Shiprock several summers previously when she was visiting her cousin, Bruce M. Barnard, for a number of years operator of a trading post near the Navajo Agency. After being married at Gallup during the annual Intertribal Ceremonial and having an archaeological honeymoon which took them to Hodge's excavations at Hawikuh near Zuñi and then to Judd's diggings at Chaco Canyon, they prepared to go to del Muerto.

The tan-red canyon face housing the ancient structure at Mummy Cave rose from the stream course some six hundred feet, leaning slightly forward to provide a protective overhang for the dwelling. The pueblo had been placed in two pockets about halfway up the cliff, where the ancient residents could have had an unobstructed view of ramparts of spectacular canyon winding down below. Fifty or more stone-coursed rooms, some with a whitewashed wall or two, had been erected within two arches which originally had been connected by a rock ledge, rather like a pair of eye glasses held together by a nose bridge. The ledge had broken away during some period of occupation to crash down the steeply sloped talus drift to the canyon below, leaving exposed a fresh cut of red cliff wall. The indefatigable natives had then constructed a retaining-wall causeway to reunite their divided town. Upon this a beautiful three-story tower and series of seven large rooms had been built. By 1923 the masonry walls were cracking under wear of wind and water. However, because of its comparatively fine condition, Mindeleff thought the tower might have been the work of Spanish priests.[7]

Of over four hundred ruins found wherever the sun could have reached the vault depression of del Muerto to sweep out the chill, Earl thought Mummy Cave offered the most allure for the stratigraphic study of the entire Basket Maker—Pueblo cycle as it had been outlined elsewhere. Undoubtedly in the prevailing dryness of the cave, where germs of decay could not have survived, there would be precious perishable artifacts needed to fortify his ideas of pre-Caucasian life.

The name of the site was indicative and dated from an 1882 discovery of two naturally dessicated mummies by Colonel James Stevenson of the Bureau of Ethnology. Up to this date Earl never had the questionable pleasure of unearthing such a body other than the isolated find during the Bernheimer Expedition of 1922. Within his first hours' digging in Canyon del Muerto he would discover numerous mummies and would say that Mummy Cave had been aptly named.

It was not the roofless house nor the stately Tower that interested Earl the most. Ann could only shake her head in bewilderment at this husband who chose to concentrate his efforts upon the slide of rock, ash, and trash which poured down the steep incline below the house. But Earl and Oley spotted some human bones eroding at one end of the man-made dump. Digging, they quickly learned two things: that the bones in this grave had been placed under the drip from the canyon brink above and hence were no longer accompanied by the fragile offerings which presumably had been buried with them; and that the dust stirred up by the digging was stifling. Pits were sunk higher on the slope, some distance behind an imaginary vertical line from talus to canyon rim. There was Earl's first del Muerto mummy.

With a shout to Ann, who was off wandering through the ancient rooms, Earl began to sweep away the soil with a whisk broom which he habitually carried in his hip pocket. As Ann squatted on her heels beside the pit, watching the strong fingers of her husband feel their way toward the burial package beneath a layer of shredded juniper bark, she was inclined to think that there had been a mistake. What was emerging was a small bundle tightly trussed with cord and capped with a dirty, round basket. An acrid odor was detectable. As Earl carefully unfolded the rabbit-fur robe which had served as a shroud, Ann inadvertently recoiled as she peered down into the ugly shrunken face of an old fellow who had gone to his grave lying on his bony back with his knees jack-knifed up over his abdomen. On his feet were a pair of buckskin moccasins with cushion soles of cedar bark. Around his legs were found leggings of buckskin strips. He wore a buckskin cloak and apron and a shell bracelet. And with him were a Basket Maker's proudest possessions—a spear thrower, a bag of dice, a pipe, and smoking materials.

It became Ann's task to brush the filth of the centuries from the mummy bundles which from then on were encountered with great regularity. Overcoming a natural revulsion to such unladylike occupations, she shooed the nesting mice from their abdominal cavities and arranged some of them around the honeymoon camp like guardian angels who saw all, knew all, but never told. At these moments she had hilarious visions of her mother's horror at her choice of bridal pastimes.

The Basket Maker mummies, gnarled and grotesque, were informative. They testified to peaceful days when men were allowed to live their lives and then depart this earth within the trace of custom. They told of epidemics when infants, unprotected by immunization injections or well-balanced diet, succumbed in frightful numbers and were placed in large baskets and were lowered into the ground. They provided a record of normal Stone Age living and dying, of religious awe, and war. Ann observed that on the mummies male vanity and female sacrifice were shown. Men's black hair was long and carefully knotted, an obvious source of pride for the owner. But the poor woman's often was cropped short in the most unbecoming, inverted-bowl manner and was found tied in skeins ready to be used in the manufacture of belts and textiles. Ears of both sexes on occasion were pierced for suspension of ornaments. Teeth were troughed and worn from a diet containing the grit of many grinding stones. Wedged in one decaying molar was found a cactus seed, causing Earl to wonder if dried cactus apples might not have been eaten by the Basket Makers as they are by the modern Navajos. So lifelike were some mummies that the color of the iris of eyes could be determined. Others had become distorted through cramped conditions in the grave or through pressures of burial accoutrements upon soft body parts. Some, despite their age and exposure, had not completely dried up, being malodorous and foul. These were quickly reburied but not forgotten. Bodies were found torn apart by animals or prehistoric human agents. They were recovered from refuse piles or in the open, usually in individual cists. Occasionally there were numbers of them placed together, like those found in a crevice around the bend from Mummy Cave where perhaps one hundred persons and their funerary offerings had been burned to slag.

Because of the fascination of the human element, mummies were the most arresting relics. But artifacts were equally interesting and far more revealing of the thoughts of these vanished people. They came from burials and trash in numbers vast enough to reach Earl's dearest hopes when he had pleaded with the museum to be allowed this opportunity. Most characteristic were the articles woven of what was thought to be apocynum fiber or the baskets from whom the folk had drawn their modern name. Huge, close-coiled baskets, some as broad as the span of a man's arms and decorated in black and red geometric designs, testified to the technological advancement of the ancient occupants of Mummy Cave. Other baskets were of the deep, pointed-bottom types designed to be carried on a human back and held in place by elaborately woven headbands. There were bowl-shaped, coiled baskets of various sizes and some rarer ones of plaited construction called "ring baskets" by the archaeologists. A few were encrusted with hardened food particles; others were as bright then as at the time of manufacture. There were also a number of mud trays which seemed to have been molded inside of baskets, the impressions of the coils still clearly visible on their lower portions. Among the woven wearing apparel for women were aprons of yucca fiber or cedar bark, consisting of a decorated waistband and a front piece which would have passed between the legs and tied in back. Seamless bags of tightly woven, twined construction were both plain and decorated and must have been a women's handbag or a man's pouch. They were finger woven, there being no evidence of the development of a loom until Pueblo times.

Footgear was of tremendous importance to the Mummy Cave Basket Makers, as it would be to any unmounted people living in a terrain of burning sand and jagged rock. The Basket Makers had been shod with fiber sandals which exhibited the finest craftsmanship of woven things. They were decorated in red and black geometric patterns on the upper surface (which never would have been seen when on the foot) and by seemingly endless variations of intricate knotting on the lower surface (which would have been worn down on the first trip). Surprisingly, these sandals were not of the fringed-toe types found in Basket Maker settlements in Grand Gulch, Tsegi Canyon, or Du Pont Cave in Utah. Winter shoes were unusual, possessing sandal soles but uppers of a cord meshwork and a thick lining of cedar bark.

Ornaments on the mummies consisted of beads of shell of such uniformly diminutive size that, as Earl tried to recover them, he could only marvel at the lapidary skill and patience which had produced them. Upon examination by a conchologist (E. W. Gifford, University of California) the shells were seen to be types characteristic of the Gulf of California with the exception of bits of abalone shell which must have originated along the California coast. Other beads were made from seeds of various wild plants or ground bits of stone. Several mosaic pendants of shaped and polished turquoise, mounted on wooden forms and held in place with pitch, were the oldest artifacts of that stone to have been recovered.

Among implements unearthed with mummy bundles were long, crooked digging sticks and fending staves, spear throwers (atlatls) and darts, snares and nets.

As excavations gnawed into the pruinose talus, architectural remains were encountered. Working upward at a forty-five-degree angle along the loose slope face, the men cut through cribbings of dry laid stone and horizontal pine logs braced by transverse cedar, piñon, and cottonwood poles built by the inhabitants to hold the blanket of refuse in place and so increase the area of livability on the cave floor. Above them it was seen that there had been erected upon a deposit of hard-packed sand, roof sloughage, and thin debris a conglomeration of storage cists made of sandstone slabs set on edge and mudded over. These were roughly circular, ranging from two to six feet in diameter. Some such storage places with sandstone-slab disks as covers still contained caches of vegetal materials such as gourds, or, in one case, seven hundred ears of corn. Dwellings amid the granaries were erected along the vaguely circular plan of the storage chambers and were surprisingly large, twelve to twenty-five feet in diameter. Small posts had been placed vertically about a scooped-out, slab-lined pit rim, usually not more than six inches apart. These were slanted inward at a seventy-degree angle and were plastered over with thick mud. Next a mass of reeds had been put in horizontal layers about the pole framework, this in turn covered by vertical sticks and a second horizontal layer. The two sets of poles and reeds were lashed together to form a firm meshwork which was daubed with three inches of mud reinforced with vegetal substances or coarse sand. The whole affair presumably had been roofed with poles and brush, often having burned and fallen to the floor. Occasional floor features, cists or basins, were present.

Although exploration that first season was confined to the earlier remains which underlay the deteriorating house blanketed in solidified layers of trash, Ann undertook to reproduce in color the painted frieze which was to be seen around a kiva bench. It consisted of a pattern of white geometric designs on a wide, red, encircling band outlined in white. Earl had observed that bit of aboriginal art during the Bernheimer reconnaissance and had shoveled dirt up over it to conceal it from the casual visitor who might have had an impulse to add his initials to the motif. Ann discovered to her satisfaction that she had a flair for that sort of work. Besides, it got her away from the gagging clouds of dust raised by Earl and Oley.

Not having respirators of a type employed by cave diggers of a later day, those two shovelers wrung water through handkerchiefs and tied them over their faces, stopping work every so often to rinse away the deposits which collected with each breath. To ignore this precaution was to flirt with trouble because the mixture of residues of human excrement, animal dung, and household sweepings could be poisonous and bring about fever, chills, pneumonia, and even death.

The high pitch of excitement which had gripped Earl the day he first rode into the indrawn recess of del Muerto did not fade with the summer heat. He resented nightfall, which brought a halt to excavation, but he used the time to catalogue, mend, and ponder. Sundays were considered days of rest. After the necessary washing had been done, Earl and Ann swung cameras and shovels over their shoulders, tucked a mutton sandwich or two into pockets, and took off on exploring trips. One of these brought them to the cool ampitheater of Tseahatso, a mammoth overhang three miles down canyon.

Superficially this seemed a relatively sterile place in which to dig, although potholes left by the Days showed that they had tested the fill. There were several small Pueblo structures poking up around the floor of the high vaulted but open arch, otherwise the surface gave no indication of occupation. A dune and a double-spired fin of rock partially concealed the breadth of the opening and protected the silty deposits from being blown away. This, and the lack of sizeable houses, had caused Earl earlier to overlook the cave's potentialities. With no particular plan, he selected a drift and began to turn the soft, pulverized soil. As he worked down through layers of sand and deposits of corn husks, grass, and roots he encountered a burial, and then another, and another. That empty cave, pitted and given up as unworthy of attention by the trader pothunters, had been the greatest Basket Maker graveyard yet found and was rich in cultural as well as physical specimens.

Even Earl tired of a steady stream of artifacts. On that first Sunday at Tseahatso, after having hiked to the cave and dug steadily all afternoon, he was weary and as the evening fell, he turned to leave. Then something prompted him to walk to a far recess hitherto untouched and shove his shovel blade into the dirt. He hit wood and with the natural acoustics the sound was amplified. On his knees, quickly removing the fine covering of corn chaff, turkey droppings, and sand with his whiskbroom, he exhumed a sixteen-inch, hollow cylinder of wood. Gently lifting it from its resting place, he found that a yucca cord had been lashed around the specimen twenty-one times, holding in place a piece of cloth over a slit opening along the top. Upon Ann's eager urging, he removed the cord and looked inside the tube. There lay an unbelievable assortment of colored feathers and bird skins which had successfully defied the centuries. This represented a treasure which had been cached away by a thief or by some suspicious person in the most unlikely of all places, the turkey pen! Who could explain the unseen hand of fate which led Earl to shovel into that particular spot, when further pitting showed the ground all around to have been nothing but an enclosure for squawking poultry?

Earl had stratigraphy in Mummy Cave but he could not interpret it unequivocally. The fault lay with the aborigines and not himself. The shelter unquestionably had been home to a group of Basket Makers, apparently for a long time judging by the accumulations of their discards. Because of the high stage of evolution of sandals and baskets, the residents might have been less ancient than those uncovered in other caves to the north and west of del Muerto. Earl could not be sure with only one session of excavation whether he had Basket Maker II, III, something intermediate, or all three. At least all levels of the talus were distinctly nonceramic and all had been so mixed by these early people and by the Pueblo who moved in later and leveled off the cave floor in order to put up their stone houses that cake-layer stratigraphy was too highly mixed. Kidder, discoverer of the Kayenta Basket Makers, thought that if Earl went to hardpan, he would encounter jug-shaped cists, long-headed mummies, and fringed-toe sandals characteristic of Basket Maker sites elsewhere.[8] To Wissler, Earl reported, "The culture sequence is here just as I was convinced upon my first visit, but the proof is somewhat more elusive than I anticipated. The superimposition of masonry over slab structures is beautifully clear in Mummy Cave and every other ruin I have visited. It is plain enough that both early and the late Pre Pueblos peoples erected slab houses, and in my mind there is no doubt that they were the homes of the Basket Makers also. The proof of the latter is what has not as yet been obtained."[9]

As far as Wissler could see, Earl would never have the chance of straightening out the tangle because, in order to earn more money to provide for his new wife, he had resigned from the museum to join the Carnegie Institution on December 15, though he would continue to be on summer assignments for the American Museum for a few more years. Wissler advised Earl to keep his finds quiet so that looters would not move in when he moved out. But the finds were too spectacular to remain unknown for long.

In New York, when the collection from del Muerto was unpacked and prepared for photographing and exhibition, Earl became a celebrity. Over morning cups of coffee the public learned of the stubborn breed of Indians who once inhabited the sunlit canyons of the San Juan, and they studied photographs of Earl and Oley and rows of vacant-eyed skulls and grimmacing mummies. At the twenty-second annual meeting of the American Anthropological Association, then in session in New York City, Earl was put on a three-man committee, along with Judd and Kidder, to recommend ways of curtailing vandalism to the reservation sites.

In the fall of 1924 Earl returned to del Muerto in order to make repairs on the deteriorating foundations of the House of the Tower in Mummy Cave and to gather museum specimens for the University of Colorado. Armed with sketchy knowledge of the exceedingly difficult and guttural Navajo language, Earl drove down canyon to various hogans where he bargained for the hod-carrier services of six men. These gathered fallen building stones spotted along the slope by the east house and dumped them beside the white masons who had sunk a precarious scaffolding into the steep talus so that they might have a level base from which to work. Earl and Oley cleared the old foundation walls and swept the dust from the tilted bedrock or chipped it to give secure bedding. Earl had planned to use thin, rich cement as he had done in previous restoration work. It was going to be expensive since materials would have to be freighted in by wagon from Gallup and then reshipped up canyon. When he discovered a deposit of adobe clay at the arroyo's edge, tough and stubborn as any cement when not exposed to moisture, he felt that mud mortar would be just as satisfactory and far less obvious. The Indians mixed the mud in a well sunk in the bed of the wash and carried it in pails up the trail to the foundation walls. In an effort to expedite the operation, which found the masons spending most of their time waiting for the next express from the arroyo-side factory, Earl offered to pay each man twenty cents a pail, with a bonus of a can of peaches and a box of crackers to the one carrying the largest number of loads. This was a revolutionary economic idea to the Navajo and called for a long counsel. Finally they agreed to try the new scheme, and at day's end were delighted to see that they had in this way earned more than the two dollars fifty cents daily wage for which they had contracted. And the masons had a more constant supply of mortar.

After five days Oscar, Oley, and Earl had dismantled and rebuilt twenty-six-and-a-half feet of wall for an average height of four-and-one-half feet of varying thickness depending upon the space available. Buttresses had been constructed beneath and enclosing the large blocks under the west end of the Tower and under the undermined portion. A new retaining wall had been joined with the remnant of the old one at the brink of the ledge and the space behind had been filled to form a platform. The House of the Tower was safe for another year.

This project at Mummy Cave was the beginning of a happy relationship for Earl with the modern Indian occupants of the canyon systems of de Chelly-del Muerto. They recognized him as Natani, the boss, and came to him in increasing numbers with their illnesses and problems. Earl, as Natani, tried to render the services expected of him. When necessary he pulled teeth with a pair of pliers, loaned money, prescribed aspirin, and persuaded Mac, the camp cook, to dish up beans and bacon to Indians who seemed to make a point of being on hand at meal time. Often Earl's exodus from the canyon country coincided with the Navajo withdrawal to their winter hogans on the rimlines of the deep breaks gashing westward from the mountains, and he loaded them down with cast-off field clothing and unused supplies. Once he paid for a nine-day curing ceremony which with some alarm he saw grow from several neighborhood families to include two hundred Navajos from a large part of the reservation.

Earl occasionally risked Navajo anger which could have brought severe consequences had he been discovered. From under piles of boulders or deep in dark recesses along the cliff walls where Navajo bodies had been stuffed in hasty deposits, he exhumed an old blanket or two which he judged to be a century old, buffalo skins, and a few skulls. No obvious burial cists were violated. The skulls he shipped to Bernheimer who in turn gave them to his dentist for a study of American Indian tooth structure.

One Navajo find by Oley was particularly unusual. It consisted of several ten-foot spears stuck into a crack across the canyon from where the party was camped. As neither Earl nor the other men had ever seen the Indians using such an implement, they did not at first consider them Navajo articles. Oley took the spears home as souvenirs. Some years later Jesse Nusbaum, as Director of the Laboratory of Anthropology, sent Earl an old photograph from the eleven hundred negative collection made by a pioneer photographer, Ben Wittick, and presented to the archives of that institution. It was desired that Earl try to identify the log cabin in the background. It was the nucleus of Cozy McSparron's trading post as it had appeared in the 1890's when operated by Sam Day and in the foreground stood a group of Navajo men armed with long spears. Earl immediately purchased the del Muerto spears from his helper and turned them over to the Laboratory.

Excavations in Mummy Cave in 1924 did little to positively unravel the sequential status of the Basket Maker strain present. Contrary to Kidder's prediction, no jug-shaped cists had been sunk into the bottom of the cave. The slab cists known from earlier digging had been sealed with mud onto rock. Earl felt sure they had been both storage chambers and domiciles. As these had become crammed with trash, other storage cists and homes had been erected above them. The process had been repeated continually until later the masonry house completely overrode the earlier strata. There were certain technological differences between this Mummy Cave Basket Maker culture and that considered standard (only because of its prior discovery) which implied an elaboration of a basic Basket Maker horizon—the utilization of several colors in textiles and basketry and the intricacy of sandal construction. It appeared that some fringed-toe sandals of an earlier day were retained and some robes of later times were used. So what might have been overlaps and retentions complicated the picture. But Earl wondered if in reality minor disparities in cultural content between del Muerto and the Kayenta might be areal rather than temporal. "It is debatable whether the graves should be listed as straight Basket Maker III, because the sandals found in them were slightly scallop-toed instead of square, and lacked the fringe so typical of Basket Maker II footgear from Grand Gulch and the Kayenta country."[10] It was puzzling to observe, too, that many of the skulls were brachycephalic rather than dolichocephalic and were undeformed. The lack of homogeneity of the Basket Maker physical stock would become increasingly apparent as work progressed.

There was little question that the pottery-free talus slope at Mummy Cave had been built by the Basket Makers. The cists and the few fragments of fired pottery found above the slope were considered early Pre Pueblo. In a few more seasons the latter stage would be called Basket Maker III. There was additional material which represented late Pre Pueblo in Earl's terminology, or Pueblo II in the 1927 Pecos classification. It was noted that most of this horizon seemed to be located in the open bottomlands rather than the caves. The masonry houses which had been erected on sloping bedrock and rubbish and reached to the cave ceiling were Full Pueblo in age, the Tower having definite Mesa Verde qualities. Nowhere in the canyons did Pueblo occupation seem extensive although Mummy Cave showed a larger settlement of classic periods than much of the rest of the area. Earl thought it likely that there had been present in del Muerto a very small Pueblo population which for unknown reasons withdrew from the gorges for long periods of time.

Back in Tseahatso, burial ground of Basket Makers of undetermined affiliation, it was learned that the entire one thousand feet of its length was a complex maze of slab cists and the bases of pole-and-mud dwellings of Basket Maker times but as usual there had been Pueblo occupation in one area and scattered Navajo deposition. The impressive amount of early rebuilding seemed to indicate a small population which inhabited the cave for considerable time, long enough to have passed from Basket Makers who knew nothing of ceramics to Basket Makers who made and used plain gray pottery. More burials of the sort recovered in 1923, and thought to be contemporaneous with the jacal houses, were encountered below refuse dumps and turkey dung with their padding of shredded bark excelsior and wizened occupants surrounded by fragile products of their hands.

A particularly rich burial Earl called The Chief's Grave. It consisted of a deep cist in which was found the skeleton of an aged man who had been clothed in finely tanned buckskin and wrapped in a feather robe. Also in the grave were shell bracelets, an abalone shell pendant, a stone pipe, atlatls and darts, and flutes. A great mass of shredded juniper bark, which Earl estimated as sufficient to fill a wagon bed, had covered the body and for some unexplained reason had partly burned.

The biggest mystery of the season concerned The Burial of the Hands. In a cist were found the lower arms and hands of an adult, laid palms upward upon a bed of grass. They were accompanied by shell rings and pendants and, surprisingly, a pair of exceptionally fine sandals. The fate of the unfortunate individual whose limbs were so buried could not be determined.

As he was working for two institutions on this particular field trip, Earl was determined to make a fair division of the artifacts obtained in accord with the amount of funds allotted by each. In the name of Charles L. Bernheimer he forwarded to the American Museum of Natural History all material removed from two caves in Trail Canyon and a cave near Massacre Cave where he had made a survey at the end of the season. To the University of Colorado he shipped the specimens taken from Tseahatso (including those from The Chief's Grave and The Burial of the Hands), one cave in Trail Canyon, and Pictograph Cave. Through his efforts those two organizations, one a metropolitan institution with researchers dispatched to all parts of the globe and the other a small college museum with collections crowded into two rooms of Hale Building, became leading repositories for perishables of some of North America's earliest inhabitants. A few Tseahatso specimens from Boulder eventually were traded to the Museum of New Mexico where the curator was thwarted in his desire to create a Basket Maker display by the disbelief of Director Hewett in the reliability of that cultural designation.

The collection placed at Boulder aroused much interest. Impressed, museum curator Henderson asked, "Is all of this material supposed to be prehistoric? It looks so very fresh."[11] Earl felt great concern because of the lack of protection against fire. All his previous collections made for the University of Colorado Museum had been nonperishable pottery and stone. From the time of the 1924 expedition to del Muerto until a new fire-proof museum became a reality in 1937, Earl continued to worry.

The fascinating finds made in the canyons of de Chelly and del Muerto had excited tremendous public interest in Southwestern archaeology. Earl's angling for subsidization by the interested wealthy had brought pleasing results. Patrons of the American Museum, spearheaded by Bernheimer and Ogden Mills, legislator from New York and later Secretary of the Treasury, subscribed over three thousand dollars and asked that it be earmarked for further canyon exploration. Ironically, Wissler felt that Earl, with reports on the La Plata and Aztec past due, was in no position to undertake any additional enterprises. He sought the aid of Ted Kidder, rather than Earl. It was planned that Kidder devote at least a month of the fall of 1925 to survey and study of what was left to be done in de Chelly during the next several years. Kidder thoughtfully included Earl in the project.

The Kidder entourage drove from Gallup to Chinle in two Ford touring cars from Pecos known as "Pink" and "Blue" and a museum Dodge truck turned over to the project by Pliny Earle Goddard who had been in New Mexico doing ethnological fieldwork. Mr. and Mrs. William Claflin, Jr. and Mr. and Mrs. Raymond Emerson, Boston friends of the Peabody Museum, were on hand. Monroe Amsden was in from Chaco to serve as cook until George MacClellan, Earl's cook of the previous summer, could finish his current task at Judd's camp. George Vaillant, Harvard student assistant at Pecos and later the most outstanding specialist on the Aztecs of Mexico, and Erich Schmidt of New York also accompanied Kidder. When the caravan topped the rim of de Chelly, the prospects for driving to Mummy Cave looked unpromising. Water spread out over the sands down below in a wide arc. Well seasoned Southwestern travelers as Kidder and Amsden were, they reasoned that the cars were apt to sink out of sight the moment they chugged into the canyon bottom. The group made camp near the trading post and began to wonder when Earl, Ann, and Oscar would arrive.

It was not until the next noon that the Morris's car limped into view. It had broken down on top of the mountain, and Earl had replaced a burned-out bearing with a durable bacon rind from the grub box.

The next morning the canyon which hitherto had been breached only by the Morris Ford was to succumb to the onslaught of four determined vehicles. Because of his acquaintance with the hazards offered by the area and his earned reputation for getting through, everyone looked to Earl for leadership in the strenuous task ahead. Equipped with two hundred feet of three-quarter inch rope and a double block and tackle which could be hooked between a stuck car and boulders or a buried "dead-man" weight, and accompanied by many stout-hearted drivers who enjoyed excavation—even of cars—the group made its way in three-and-a-half hours to the camp at the base of Mummy Cave.

Earl and Kidder probed the rubbish which had accumulated above the retaining walls of the ruin. Emerson, a surveyor by profession, set about to map the ruins. Ann and Mrs. Claflin catalogued. And when opportunity arose, everyone explored, Earl often leading the way up cliffs like a mountain goat, depending upon friction of shoe soles and finger tips to present slipping. Old hand-and-toe-holds were used where present. Also there were to be found notched logs which the Days had placed horizontally across slick areas to enable them to gain entrance to half-stranded caves. There were so many grottos in the fingering cuts of the canyon system, some choked with rock slides and dense growth, that there seemed always to be the possibility of discovery. Navajo burials and sweat houses spotted among the remains of the Anasazi were noted. In Massacre Cave, to which various winded expedition members scrambled, were picked up a child's skull crushed perhaps by a rifle butt, a spherical bullet, fragments of squaw dresses and blankets, and sherds of old Hopi and Zuñi pots, mute remains of an 1804 slaughter of local Indians by a punitive expedition from the New Mexican settlements.

With the arrival of October, fall showers began to roll red clouds from the mountains. Camp was shifted down to the cornfields below Tseahatso. Work in that cave uncovered more of the same kind of things found in the past by Earl and his diggers. While the others busied themselves there, Earl and Oscar returned to Mummy Cave to place tie rods in the high Tower to hold that structure to the cliff behind. No scaffolding had been erected to raise a workman to the appropriate level. It was necessary to strap a rope over the end of a projecting roof timber and on it swing out and around to the front of the Tower and with almost breathless care tighten up the screws. Never one to allow others to take risks for him, Earl cinched up the rope, swung himself into position, and dangling a hundred feet above a jagged mass of boulders and buffeted by a cold breeze that penetrated his thin jacket and stiffened his fingers, he accomplished what he set out to do.

The best known ruin in the canyon network was the one to which Earl, in his quest for undisturbed deposits, had paid least attention. A split-level house, Casa Blanca, as it was called in early literature, had been so named because of a coating of whitewash which set off several rooms of the cave section of the ruin like a performer under a bright spotlight. Above it towered a colossal face of shimmering red cliff discolored with black water-streaks from the ragged canyon rim, and below lay a fan of unsoiled white sand. Being in the lower, more accessible reaches of the declivity and in view from a trail hugging the rim opposite, the old house had been thoroughly ransacked long before Judd's 1920 trip first had brought Earl there. Some unknown persons, probably Navajos in search of fire and building wood in this nearly treeless canyon, had stripped every beam from the roofs. The Days, prospecting for loot, had been there. Victor Mindeleff, during his study of the antiquities of the region, had added his name to the roster on a plastered wall which also contained incised pictographs. Earl too had gained entrance by climbing a rope looped over a projecting beam.

As the expedition members viewed the scene from their camp, the house in the cliff seemed completely distinct from the house located on the floor of the canyon directly beneath it. A thirty-five foot, vertical cliff wall separated the two with the authority of a fortress moat. From stains upon the rocks it could be seen that in times past the two levels of occupation had been linked by a five-story section on the bottom house, now slumped and washed away. The only ready means of access was a homemade elevator which Kidder described in his field notes. "After breakfast with Earl, Ann, George, and Oscar to White House. Tied a couple of ¾ inch bolts to a length of binder twine and threw them over the beam set across the narrow entry to the upper house. The difficulty was to get them to roll off the little flat platform below the beam and fall down again. Finally, by twitching the cord we edged them off and got them down carrying the cord with them. Then hauled up a ⅜-inch rope and with that a ¾-inch, up which Earl climbed. He added an oak pole to the beam as a strengthener, attached a block to the paired sticks and we hauled each other up."[12]

During this exploration it was agreed that White House study and protection would be a valuable piece of work for the following season.

Although it was not likely that anything new and startling would turn up, what material was left should be taken into scientific custody. The lower house which was blotting up water from the arroyo like a sponge would be a total loss in a very few years if preservative measures were not taken.

Kidder lingered on at White House a few days after the others had departed to do some testing. That was his last excavation in the area since he had decided to withdraw completely in favor of Earl. In *Natural History* he appraised his friend's contribution, "I can only point out, as Mr. Morris in his excessive modesty will certainly not do, that the work was admirably conceived and most admirably executed."[13]

After brief diggings at Camp Verde, Arizona, and in the Mimbres area of southwestern New Mexico, the next summer Earl returned to de Chelly to finish the work proposed for White House. His first task was to divert the arroyo waters which already had devoured a sizeable chunk of the bottom unit of the ruin, after which he did some testing of the structure and arroyo bank. The usual sequence of cultures from Basket Maker III through Pueblo III were amply represented. White House itself was Pueblo III. It had been a crossroads metropolis with pottery indicating trade radiating into the canyon from Chaco to the west, the Little Colorado to the south, Mesa Verde to the north. There were some burials within the village rooms, but many more were beneath the refuse dump to the east.

In 1927 at the very time when the first Pecos Conference was pointing up the need to learn of the ancestors of the Basket Makers, an indication of an earlier cultural horizon was being uncovered. Near Folsom, New Mexico, flint points fashioned by men were encountered twelve feet below the present land surface in positive association with the bones of extinct bison. A number of archaeologists went to the excavations to personally judge the merit of the finds. Kidder was one who made this pilgrimage and upon his return wrote to Earl, "Went over to Raton at Roberts' request and looked at bison and points. Damned interesting. Association is certain. Question now is, is the deposit Pleistocene?"[14] The geologist who made the first study of the data, Harold J. Cook, thought it was.

In all, nineteen similar projectile points and twenty-three bison of an extinct subspecies were recovered at Folsom. As publicity was given the find, reports began to trickle into museums of the same kind of points being picked up from Alaska to Mexico. Widely dispersed as the points were, throughout the next decade nothing more was learned of the men who had created them. About all that could be said was that from the numbers of such points recovered, it could be inferred that the Folsom people had been big game hunters who had followed their meat supply out into the great intracontinental tablelands. There was absolutely no evidence to tie them to the nether end of the Basket Maker-Pueblo cultural sequence.

That gap which lay beyond the Basket Makers was to be searched with surprising results during the course of the next twenty years. Many dry mountain caves scattered over New Mexico, Arizona, Nevada, and Utah yielded evidences of human utilization long before man had learned of the miracle of corn or the possibility of sedentary existence. Few, however, were discovered in the center of what was to become the stronghold of the Basket Maker, perhaps because aridity and elevation of the plateau did not attract hordes of game. Furthermore, it seemed that not all men had been hunters in that far-off day because some deposits (with their abundance of milling stones) implied dependence upon the gathering of wild seeds and berries and the foraging for small animals. Occasional bits of baskets, snares, and traps revealed a knowledge of rudimentary weaving. On the other hand, as the plains of eastern Colorado and west Texas blew themselves away in clouds of dust, further finds of lithic industries were made, each to shed another ray of light upon an exceedingly complex problem. An extensive Folsom camp near Fort Collins, Colorado, was dug meticulously by Frank Roberts. For the first time tools other than points could be attributed to the Folsom complex as gravers, drills, choppers, smoothing stones, and bone awls were taken from the edges of a weathered gully. Seldom were two places identical either in stone assemblage, geological deposition, or associated faunal remains. Yet there was a demonstrable cultural relationship.

To distinguish between early and late phases of the aboriginal cultural spectrum with which he personally was most concerned, at that date not considered continuous, Earl felt one might contrast the Basket Makers with the Pottery Makers. Each group had produced articles of the other's specialty craft but not with the same degree of excellence. Basket Makers made pottery of a rough surfaced, crudely decorated sort and Pueblos wove baskets and sandals with far less skill and variation than their predecessors. This was not a completely accurate statement, however, because there was a time in Basket Maker history when pottery was totally absent. Archaeologists, therefore, were interested in the origin of the ceramics which became so fundamental to Pueblo culture.

Although a fragment or two of mud vessels had been recovered at Tsegi caves and at Du Pont Cave in Utah, it was not until work at del Muerto produced pieces of ninety-five such containers that Earl became certain that herein lay the first steps toward true ceramics. From lower talus deposits the unfired mud dishes composed the entire ceramic find. From upper cists, originally called Pre Pueblo but by 1927 termed Basket Maker III, came both mud pots and fired pottery. Thus the old lingered on some time after the discovery of the new, and to Earl there was conclusive cross-tying of techniques and form to make the family tree of pottery an almost established fact. Gradually, as pottery became dominant, both mud vessels and baskets declined in popularity.

In consideration of the process leading to true pottery, Earl suggested that after observation of a vessel form of hardened adobe in a mortar basket left unemptied by a careless mason, some inventive person must have applied a definite coating of mud to the interiors of other baskets to create containers. These vessels would have been formed of daubs of mud pressed inside wide-mouthed baskets. After the inevitable shrinkage produced by drying, the vessel in a basket would have been successfully freed from its mold. At once it would have been found that unless foreign substances like shredded bark or sand from the arroyo were added to the mud as a binder, the vessels would not be tough enough to remain whole. This was no innovation to the Basket Makers because reinforcement of the mud used in storage cists and house walls was common practice; and if the original pot had indeed been accidentally hardened mortar mud, it would have incorporated such material. The mud container thus produced would have been useful to the Basket Maker household for storage of dry materials only as, of course, liquids would have dissolved the vessel walls. Still it could have been made with considerably less effort and time than a basket.

Mud and pottery seemed a long way apart, but Earl reasoned that perhaps they were separated only by a fire which swept a cave home and accidentally transformed the mud vessel into something more permanent and useful. Once the Indians observed that a burned vessel was durable and impervious to liquids, they were ready to become potters.

Earl was confident that his studies of del Muerto material, together with ceramic data gathered east of the Lukachukais and on the La

Plata, enabled him to say, "In the San Juan area pottery making has been traced back to and almost beyond its beginnings with a definiteness which has not been paralleled or even approached anywhere else on the continent."[15] It was a neat lucid explanation.

For many of Earl's colleagues it was too pat. Some scholars were not ready to endow the human mind with the degree of inventiveness and originality Earl suggested, being more inclined to cling to the older hypothesis, still unproven, that maize agriculture and pottery traveled parallel diffusion routes from Middle America into the Southwest. Local invention of the mud vessels they could accept, but they were quick to point out that some Southwestern seed-gathering peoples were accustomed to parch the wild edibles in basket trays which, interestingly enough, were lined with mud to prevent scorching. The fact that every Basket Maker cave had its cists partially filled with various kinds of wild seeds of grasses, sunflowers, or piñon nuts would seem to strengthen the idea that the mud vessels were not dishes at all but were tray liners.

In 1929 Bernheimer again invited Earl to be his guest on another field trip. The target for the upcoming season was to be the inhospitable canyon and mesa country west of Blanding, Utah, a region which in the 1920's was seldom visited. As Earl thought of the Grand Gulch and Graham Canyon in that sector, he felt a mounting eagerness to do his own exploration there which a trip with Bernheimer would make feasible. It was his particular desire to find some dry protected settlements which could be definitely limited to Basket Maker III times with no chance of admixture of either later or earlier material. In that way he could positively determine just what was initial and what was terminal in the Basket Maker cycle. In accomplishing that, he could place the churned deposits of del Muerto into their proper relative positions. So it was for such towns that he planned to search as he met the party at Monticello, Utah, in early June.

The same men who had ridden together on past Bernheimer Expeditions were present with a single addition. Barnum Brown was going into the pathless wastes of southeast Utah to try to recover some reported dinosaur remains. He was the American Museum representative; Earl was acting as the agent of the Carnegie Institution. It was the archaeological rather than the paleontological discoveries which were to merit the headlines.

Moving down indistinct trails with forty-four animals and the necessary twenty-five hundred pounds of oats to feed them, the men wound around canyon heads and down escarpments in a loop which took them through parts of West Canyon, Cottonwood Wash, Butler Wash, Comb Wash, and Arch Canyon, eventually to the forested slopes of Elk Mountain and then to Kane Canyon, Grand Gulch, and down to the junction of the San Juan and the Colorado. From there they made their way north along the Colorado River, up White Canyon to Natural Bridges. This was home ground to Zeke Johnson, who delighted Bernheimer with a running account of early Mormon ventures into the region which in the time of their pioneering was a nest of hostile Utes and renegades. It was John Wetherill, however, who stirred up in the New Yorker hopes of crossing the trail of the ancients as he described that bitter winter of '93 when he and his brothers, Richard and Al, had spent four months exploring Grand Gulch and Cottonwood Wash and bringing to light the first evidences of the Basket Makers, specimens which Bernheimer had viewed at the American Museum.

Earl devoted his time to criss-crossing the path of the caravan in order to inspect a wide swath of terrain lying on both sides of the trail. As he walked over mounds along the rolling knolls or tongues of land leading to the washes, through rock shelters along steep canyon walls, and around canyon head sites, he was revisiting portions of areas already traversed by two old friends, Nels Nelson and Neil Judd. The general conclusions Earl reached were: "West of Grand Gulch the country is so utterly worthless that the old people let it pretty much alone. From the beginning of aboriginal occupation hunting parties have worked through the region, and sometimes they took shelter in the caves, but as a whole, the district is markedly barren of remains. In one of the lower eastern tributaries of the Colorado we found a small cliff house and some burials with Kayenta pottery. In Moki Canyon, both Basket Makers and Pueblo resided, but only in small numbers. In Comb Wash I found one tiny site with typical Posty sherds, and several large ones of pre-Pueblo age. The best part of Grand Gulch I missed, namely Graham Canyon where the bulk of the Wetherill and McLoud and Graham collections were secured. And I did not get to see the lower reaches of the canyon. However, in the part we traversed, by diligent search I found one small open site which yielded a half dozen Posty sherds. Not another trace of this period did I see until we reached the Caroline Bridge in White Canyon, at one end of which there are two mud rooms in good condition. Then elsewhere in the same canyon I saw several sites of the same age. I anticipate that were one to work along the south foot of Elk Mountain, some Posty sites would come to light, but not enough to indicate more than a very transitory occupation. Thus it would seem that the whole triangle between the San Juan and the Colorado was practically untenanted during the period in question. It seems not unnatural that such should have been the case in view of the utter barrenness and general worthlessness of the country. The more I see the more I believe that del Muerto and de Chelly were a veritable breeding ground for the Southwestern cultures, and I believe we will learn more from them than from any other district."[16]

When there was time, Earl dug. Burials were sought in refuse dumps; trenches were drifted into mounds. Nothing of much significance was uncovered until at the turning-back point in Moki Canyon in the soft dirt floor of a north-wall cave a few feet above the canyon bottom to which Wetherill had guided Judd in 1923, Earl came upon two Basket Maker burials in the only open area of the recess, the remainder of the fill having been covered by a huge block scaled from the roof.

In one of the burial pits, which lay under a bed of small sandstone slabs, was an elderly female who had had her hands tied in front with four wraps of yucca cord and had her head covered with an inverted basket. Laid over the body was a cedar-bark blanket. In the second pit was a young woman on an oval frame rather like a huge cradle board. Her legs had been tied at the ankles with a cord of fine human hair. She wore a yucca-fiber apron, a human hair belt, and a bracelet and necklace composed of two hundred fifty beads of stone and seeds. Covering the entire body were sections of fine twined bags with red and black transverse stripes. Baskets which had accompanied the burial were decayed beyond recovery. The most interesting thing about this woman was that buried with her had been a small child and a foetus. At the conclusion of the trip most of these specimens were donated to the Mesa Verde National Park museum; the remainder were deposited at the American Museum.

Already having handled scores of similar interments, Earl at the time did not consider these of special interest except that one old woman had been wrapped in a cedar bark blanket instead of the fur or feather robe most often used in del Muerto. In retrospect he came to consider them extraordinarily crude, perhaps representative of the oldest Basket Maker strain, as he wrote: "in the eastern tributaries of the Colorado north of the San Juan where the Basket Maker II remains impress me as the most primitive I have seen."[17]

Bernheimer, who spent his normal days enmeshed in the intricacies of the cotton market, could not feel casual about the mummies, especially since the deposit above them also yielded a cotton boll and a tatter of cotton cloth, the first evidence of human modesty in the form of a lady's gee-string he told the reporters in New York. The *New York Post* of July 30, 1929 stated: "In the fore-mentioned caves the party found a cotton boll with seed and lint, and their findings cause them to believe that the Basket Makers, oldest known race of North America, living possibly 10,000 years ago, and dying out before David founded the royal Judean dynasty at Jerusalem, both spun and wove cotton."

A second article which excited Bernheimer was a curved club with a pitched handle and four linear grooves down its face. This sort of implement, not unusual in Basket Maker debris, was considered by some archaeologists to have been a stick used in rabbit hunts such as is employed by modern Hopi. Earl preferred to think of them as fending weapons. "The representatives of the type (club) recovered by Guernsey and Kidder were all found in association with either atlatls or adjuncts of the atlatl, indicating some close connection between the two. This was exactly as it should be, for I think there can be no doubt that the two composed the normal armament of each fighting man. The atlatl with its darts was the offensive, and the club the defensive, component."[18] Fending weapon or not, to Bernheimer the crooked form suggested a boomerang, although he realized it would not always swerve back to its original place of thrust. Using the club as a springboard, he wondered in the newspapers if the Basket Makers had been Mongolian at all, if there might not have been some shadowy connection with ancient Australia rather than ancient Siberia. So fascinated was he with the "boomerang" that while on a trip abroad he presented a replica of it to a museum in Paris.

Earl diplomatically kept silent about the publicity. He felt that as the cotton had come from nearer the surface of the cave probably it had been dropped by a Pueblo who had dwelt in the small house in its warm shelter. That find, however, continued to lurk in his thoughts and must have been behind a later statement that he had never decided positively that the Basket Maker did not know of cotton.[19] He felt that the Australian aborigines and Southwestern Indians most likely had never had the slightest relationship. And in 1929, with the tree-ring calendar about to be announced, he certainly would have thought that ten thousand years was too remote a date for the Basket Makers who seemed to have run, not walked, to the cultural exit leading toward the Pueblos. Rather than having reached their zenith before the time of David, they might have lived and died as contemporaries of Jesus Christ.

Not having found north of the San Juan the sort of Basket Maker III sites he wanted, Earl returned to del Muerto for what was to be his final five weeks of excavation there. Work in the canyon had been interrupted for several years by an Arizona statute prohibiting removal of antiquities from the state's confines, even from federally controlled lands. The only trip to the area had been for the purpose of collecting beam specimens from Mummy Cave and White House which Douglass hoped would bind together the tree-ring calendar, Antelope House beams having been bored by the First Beam Expedition. As usual, on Earl's trip without even digging he made another find weathering from the soil, this one of a burial beneath the tower quarter of Mummy Cave which contained carrying baskets and oval bowl-shaped baskets unlike any found previously in the canyon. An expense account would indicate the usual travel problems as entries read: "October 30, to Indian for fence posts and wire used in getting car out of quicksand—$1.50; November 2, to Indians for help getting car out of quicksand—$1.25." When it was shown that the state of Arizona had no authority over government lands, work was to be resumed.

For the first time, the crew of excavators arrived in midsummer. Earl knew it was a mistake the moment he halted his caravan of vehicles in the muddy yard of McSparron's store. The canyon sands beyond glistened with the moisture of many rains. Fighting devouring quicksand and adobe mud with its flypaper adhesiveness, forward cars pulling out the rear guard, he finally slithered to a halt at a camping spot near Antelope House. Tents were pitched beside a heap of peach pits left from a Navajo orchard which provided a convenient source of fuel for the cook stove. From there, on foot, most of the lower del Muerto sites were tested but plans for intended reconnaissance of side canyons had to be abandoned.

Across the canyon from Antelope House in the south wall of del Muerto was a large overhang some five hundred feet in length which appeared similar to Tseahatso because the commodious expanse contained only one small, eight-room, masonry, cliff house. When Earl had first visited the cave in 1923, he had observed fragments of a blackened olla and a decorated jar scattered over the surface near the house as well as human bones thrown out of a trench cut in early times by the exploring Day family. He had failed to note that the building had been erected over the wreckage of Basket Maker III slab rooms. Now with the experience of four seasons behind him, Earl felt the undisturbed fill in the east third of the shallow cave might produce materials pertaining to an early horizon.

He was correct. Into a water-laid adobe deposit almost as hard as stone had been dug cists of bizarre forms, some large mouthed, others bottle necked, many times ramified beyond a circular depression and connected. Cist contents were without doubt uncontaminated Basket Maker II with not a trace of pottery. It was the skeletonized disarticulated human bones which gave the diggings a special flavor. Nearly all showed evidence of great violence. Faces had been smashed in, jaws cracked, skulls crushed like egg shells. One poor old lady had gone to her death with the murder weapon still embedded above a rib, and in approved theatrical fashion, it was the slender foreshaft of an arrow still containing a stone point. The Basket Maker did not use the bow and arrow but unquestionably an enemy people did, with indisputable effectiveness. Because of the obvious massacre to which the dead testified, the site was named Battle Cave.

While Earl, Oscar, and Oscar's son Omer dug, Ann painted. From her meeting with Bernheimer had grown a project to copy in full color and accurate detail as many of the hundreds of pictographs along the canyon's gallery walls as possible. Daily she set up studio at the base of the cliffs and tried to recapture with her brush the spirit and style of both Anasazi and Navajo artists. At summer's end she had copied the pictograph murals at Antelope House, Pictograph Cave, and Standing Cow Ruin. The paintings were exhibited at the second Pecos Conference and subsequently were hung at the American Museum.

The archaeology of the 1929 season had many highlights, but it was other events which would be the ones longest remembered. Oscar, at the age of seventy-seven, recalled one of these. "On a Friday Earl and Ann departed in the Packard to meet Dr. Merriam and party at Gallup. Dr. Merriam was at the head of Carnegie Institution at that time. They were to go to Mesa Verde, then to the Aztec Ruin, and return to del Muerto on Monday. On Saturday afternoon a plane made a few trips up and down the canyon. On the last trip down and soon after passing from our view, we heard the engine stop. We knew of no place within many miles where a plane could land so felt quite uneasy about the safety of the passengers. As it began to get dark, I noticed someone crossing the stream that I thought to be a Navajo carrying a bundle of wood, but later I could see that it was a man and a woman and definitely not Navajo, so I walked out to meet them and welcome them to our camp. The man said, "My name is Lindbergh and this is my wife, Anne."[20]

Charles Lindbergh, still America's hero two years after his historic transatlantic flight, had breezed unannounced into one of the land's most isolated corners. The party learned that the day previously the Lindberghs had spent at Pecos. From there they had flown over parts of New Mexico and Arizona, making the first aerial photographic survey of many Southwestern ruins. Upon Ted Kidder's suggestion they had brought the first (and last!) air mail letters direct from Pecos to del Muerto. After a day's exploring up and down the canyon, they climbed up to the mesa-top landing strip and soared away, with Navajos and white excavators watching in open-mouthed wonderment. Back at Pecos they were welcomed gleefully because when they failed to return the day before, fears were being felt for their well-being.

No sooner had the Lindberghs departed del Muerto than the heavens opened up. By morning the meandering stream in the canyon bottom was bulging out of its channel and creeping relentlessly toward camp. Soon the tents were marooned on an island with swirling, silt-clouded water cutting off escape by car or by foot. Omer, serving as cook, had cut deeply into food supplies in order to serve the distinguished guests as he thought proper. Now, with del Muerto in flood, there was little chance of replenishment of stocks at the trading post. By Friday night when Earl and his party finally were able to make their way up canyon, happily loaded with groceries, the crew was staring at its last bit of food—one can of saurkraut and one pound of salt.

Few visitors to the canyon could resist the temptation to attempt to climb the sheer rock walls. Lured on by the mirage of untouched Indian treasures, guests and workers alike scrambled over talus slopes and narrow sills of rock and sometimes brushed with death. One particularly dangerous incident of this sort occurred when Earl and Omer had to rescue a young lad named Bud Weyer who had worked himself out to a point of no return on a slick cliff face.[21]

Homeward bound at the end of the season, Earl and Oscar had put in a long discouraging day packing two hundred specimens, unsuccessfully trying to make them conform to the available space. Meanwhile Omer had folded up the tents preparatory to departure only to discover that two of the vehicles balked at starting. By late afternoon much of several engines lay as a pile of nuts, bolts, and pieces while overhead thunder-heads were gathering. Doubts of early departure began to cross many minds. Oscar, whom Earl described as "silent and indefatigable, my stand-by in any situation"[22] took up a shovel and went across canyon to the shallow rock shelter of Battle Cave to work off a few tensions.

For twenty years Oscar, a neighbor at Aztec, had dug alongside Earl, and in the apprenticeship he mastered not only tremendous skill in excavation and acquired a store of archaeological knowledge, but had become sensitized to specimens. Seldom did he err in his judgment of where artifacts ought to be. This day he went straight to an open space near the masonry house and as though guided by a divining rod dug directly into the bark layer covering a tomb.

This was no ordinary tomb. It had been so carefully sealed by five ceilings of alternating poles, stiffened rush matting, the shredded bark of Utah juniper, and earth that no grain of dirt had trickled into its cavity. A vacuum-packed burial, that much the men learned in the first moments of clearing away the drift of sand and dessicated corn husks because Earl, who had caught the scent of a find like a bloodhound, had lifted up one corner and peered into the crypt below. Seeing a dark mass of what he took to be a buffalo robe surrounding a human form, Earl said they had struck a Navajo burial and would go no further. Oscar, shovel laid aside and crouching on his heels, stole a peek for himself and pronounced the robe to be bear skin. As it was then twilight, they would have to wait until the next day to resolve their differences of opinion.

Next morning all the diggers in the party were at the edge of the burial pit being photographed by Ann's movie camera. The roof elements removed, it could be seen that that robe was composed of feathers, still so soft and fluffy they appeared as fur in the half-light of the previous afternoon. Knowing then that the individual on whom attention centered was no Navajo, exploration continued.

The mummy, that of a large man, lay on its left side on a reed mat patterned with black stripes. Its head was propped on a hard wooden pillow which by dendrochronological determinations would furnish an interment date. Across the bundle lay a digging stick and stout bow, which with human error had proved too long for the pit and had been snapped in two. By their side was a single arrow, its wooden tip hardened by fire. Scattered over all were the large sharp-edged fragments of an enormous water jar broken at time of burial. "The larger sherds were put with the body, but the smaller ones were scattered about over the paved area. A tiny one was noticed near the brink of the pit which led to a removal of the paving, and the sifting of all the dust to the lower level of grave excavation. There resulted the recovery of all but three small sherds of the vessel."[23] Three other pottery bowls were quickly identified as from the hands of potters adhering to the Mesa Verde ceramic customs. Five baskets, some containing foodstuffs for the afterlife, were stacked about the body.

The item from the burial which was most unusual, aside from the splendid shroud, was made of thick skeins of fine and coarse cotton cord graded for size suitable for warp and weft which wrapped about the bundle and through its edges. Ann calculated its length as approximately *two miles,* and that spun entirely by means of a spindle whorl on a stick. From these skeins and a spindl whorl the individual was judged to have been a weaver.

"A rumor spread among the Navajo that we had a great bundle done up in buffalo skin, and great was the surprise of those who came to view it, that it was a dead man in a robe of 'turkey hair'."[24] But this was no ordinary proletarian turkey feather robe. The feathers employed were those of the golden eagle, *Aquila chrysaetos,* befitting for high priests or civilian leaders of the community. Only the downy proximal portions were used, dyed to a deep brown color. When one considered that the eagle population probably never had been large, it could be appreciated what an enormous amount of time had been involved in collecting a sufficient number of feathers to make the garment.

The bundle itself was so well preserved and unusual it would make an excellent unopened exhibit. Curiosity being the motive of archaeologists, Earl could not resist doing a little peeking. His hands slid down inside the robe around the greasy body to learn that two blankets had wrapped the corpse and between them on the breast had been laid a single ear of corn.

As Earl compromised with his good intentions and turned back the wrappings from the head, Ann wished he had not done so. This person who must have commanded high status in life was in death one of the ugliest creatures she had ever seen. "It is difficult to imagine a more gruesome spectacle than that presented by the head. It is extremely large, tremendously broad, and very much flattened at the back. The hair, faintly shot with grey, is loose over the forward part of the head. That from the back is caught in a thick knob and tied with a spiral wrapping below the nape of the neck. A few hairs droop from the extremities of the upper lip, and on the chin is a short scanty beard. The tip of the nose settled to the left, partly because of the tightness of the wrappings. These pressed the lower lip inward until it appears as if fused with the slightly protruding tongue."[25]

All of the burial accoutrements marked the man as a Pueblo of the Mesa Verde period in the canyons. The nearest town of that age lay half a mile distant. It could be assumed that with suitable ceremony the old fellow had been carried from there on the shoulders of his mourners.

Twenty years after the find of The Tomb of the Weaver had been made, Earl wrote of it for *Natural History*. The editor who accepted the article for publication, calling it one of the most excellent pieces of scientific writing for the layman,[26] was the man whose life Earl had saved upon the red cliffs of del Muerto.

An interesting parallelism existed in the two branches of Earl's research as it developed in the 1920's. In the same year, 1923, he had taken on del Muerto and Maya problems, the latter a result of his association with the Carnegie Institute. In one he dealt with the origins of a civilization, in the other with a renaissance. The gross aspects of Basket Maker culture were simple and unsophisticated; the material rewards gathered had no value in the monetary markets of the modern world. It was vastly different with the Maya of Yucatan who, stimulated by the infusion of peoples from the Mexican highlands, had created an elaborate society of great complexity and left behind for the archaeologists impressive treasures of architecture, sculpture, mural paintings, personal ornamentation of semiprecious stones and, in the murky waters of the Sacred Cenote at the site Earl worked, a fabulous collection of gold leaf, alabaster, jade, and pearls. Both fields of endeavor brought Earl academic and social rewards beyond the average and gave him an opportunity to tread the paths of the unusual, the rare, and the colorful. But even a person such as Earl, with unlimited enthusiasm for study of man's cultural heredity, could not do full justice to two lines of study, either one of which would have usurped the entire time of most individuals. From the beginning it was inevitable that a choice would have to be made. With mounting personal frictions in Yucatan and a homesickness which dogged his waking hours, Earl returned permanently to the Southwest, "bred in the bone" with him, he had written his confidant.

It was no easy decision. For several years Earl had cast about for some position which would permit him to devote full efforts to the archaeological questions of the San Juan. Jobs were discouragingly few and poorly salaried. Then in 1927, when frustrations and worry seemed to be robbing him of life's pleasures, a stroke of good fortune came which was to open a new door. Kidder resigned his post with the National Science Council to become Chairman of the Historical Division of the Carnegie Institution of Washington and Earl's superior.

With his powers of discernment and long acquaintance, Kidder understood Earl. More than most men he appreciated the engrossing attraction of the Southwestern area and its prehistory. When the opportunity arose at the completion of the excavation of the Temple of the Warriors at Chichén Itzá, where Earl had worked for five winter seasons, he saw to it that Earl was allowed to withdraw and come home. The Carnegie Institution, with Earl and Kidder as representatives, was to enter the Southwest. Morley, in charge of the Yucatan project, complimented Earl on a job well done, "It is no exaggeration to say that the rare combination of archaeological knowledge and engineering ability demanded by this delicate work could hardly have been found in any other man."[27]

Before the work undertaken in Yucatan could be considered completed, there were reports to be written. Work during the next several winters in Aztec and Washington produced a two-volume technical study in which Ann and well-known artist Jean Charlot coauthored sections devoted to the murals of two temples which they had copied. In that work Ann proved herself an artist of some stature. She went on to demonstrate talents in another direction when she wrote a sprightly account of a wife's trials and tribulations on a Yucatan dig, a humorous and at times exciting tale which must have prompted many a coed into anthropology. Not to be outdone, Earl published a layman's version of *The Temple of the Warriors*. Educational and entertaining, book reviewers joined in praising it as one of the best archaeo-travelogues of the time. "A correspondence course in archaeology, and it is delightful reading in the bargain," said Mason in *The New York Times* for January 10, 1932. As both books came out at the height of the Depression, they failed to make money for their authors. By 1954 with only eighteen copies left in the publisher's hands, *The Temple of the Warriors* had grossed less than nine hundred dollars.

Nonetheless, there were other satisfactions, for what is more enjoyable than recognition in one's home town? "It was therefore with great pleasure that a tribute from a librarian in a New York City library last week in a letter to Farmington, included a tribute to the literary ability and attainments of a man who was born and raised in Farmington and who is probably remembered here best as a young man who had more of a mania for running about the hills hunting old prehistoric ruins and digging up bones and pots than a desire to do the things that a community at that time expected of its youth. Now that he has developed into a nationally known scientist and writer, his old home town life of course becomes of greater interest."[28]

At the same time the University of Colorado wished to honor Earl. At the 1931 alumni day banquet it bestowed upon Earl, class of 1914, the Norlin Medal for outstanding work in his chosen field, the local newspaper ironically listing his work in Mexico but overlooking that accomplished within the state.

Begun together, the diverse research projects ended together. The final season of del Muerto excavation was also concluded in 1929. Many of the ambitions Earl had felt when he laid his original plans for the canyons had been fulfilled. The del Muerto archaeological archives had been more extensive than he had dared hope. There were the odd and bizarre discoveries which gave flight to the imagination and resulted in three popular articles by Earl, one in *National Geographic Magazine* and two in *Natural History*, organ of the American Museum of Natural History, and a second book by Ann which was selected as a book of the month by the Junior Literary Guild and the Scientific Book Club. There were the usual discards of man's occupation which in their volume became commonplace. From both, the unusual and the ordinary, could be drawn a composite of life within the canyon walls. Naturally questions remained. But in his attempt to understand by whatever means at his command, Earl was doing service toward inviting the cultural and spiritual unity of all mankind at any time in any place.

By 1929 Earl was without a challenger, other than Sam Guernsey, in range of experience and working knowledge of the San Juan Basket Makers, although less intensive research in that field had been carried on by a number of men. By no means was he finished with their study. Information gained from the canyons was incorporated into three technical papers, one on pottery, one on basketry, and a brief one on prayer sticks found embedded in walls of the Mummy Cave Tower. A fourth dealing with sandals, those of del Muerto comprising a large part of the bulk of a tremendous collection, lay unfinished on his desk at time of death. Unfortunately, no site report on the del Muerto work was ever written, a delay at first probably due to the lack of time and later a procrastination arising from dissatisfaction with the less precise excavation methods employed in that period of Southwestern archaeology.

Before leaving Mummy Cave, Earl had one more job to do, not one which involved the Basket Makers but one which again focused upon the Tower. In 1931, with consent of the Navajo Tribal Council, President Herbert Hoover had proclaimed the magnificent gorge system of de Chelly and del Muerto a National Monument. It thus became the second cluster of antiquities which Earl's work had spotlighted sufficiently to demand governmental protection. The antiquities as yet unexcavated would be guarded from curiosity seekers, and the large houses of which that in Mummy Cave was an outstanding example would be preserved for posterity. As part of the process of setting aside these remains for the American people, certain stabilization measures would have to be undertaken in order to insure them from further collapse. After an inspection trip made in the company of Horace M. Albright, Director of the National Park Service, and Frank Pinkley, Superintendent of Southwestern Monuments, Earl suggested that the missing corner of the Tower wall be rebuilt to join the sides and front together as a single unit and some absent poles of the ceilings be replaced to defy the destructive conspiracy of gravity, gales, and rodents. With the approval of the Carnegie Institution, he offered his services. As at Aztec Ruins and Mesa Verde, his final labors were to be in the field of restoration. Again he was to be aided by his "Three O" crew—Omer, Oscar, and Oley—plus Willard from Boulder and Gustav from Yucatan.

At Mummy Cave of first necessity were long, stout timbers for scaffolding and to be used to replace ceiling beams torn out by the ancients and others. Because the area had been occupied by numberless generations of fuel-consuming Indians, seasoned wood was hard to find in the canyon. After much scouring, several long logs were seen along the crests of the talus slopes and others were spotted where they had fallen into concealing thickets. It was a back breaking job for the men to lower the unwieldly timbers down rock slides with ropes half-hitched around standing trees and then snake them to the ruin. Some at more distance were lashed diagonally on top of the truck and were hauled to the site in that way.

Between the west wall of the Tower and the cliff Oley made an interesting discovery of a prayer stick and several calling cards. One was a note with the names "M.D., Jer Sullivan and Alex M. Stepen, A.M." It was dated forty-seven years previously, September 2, 1885. A postscript by I. K. Westbrook had been appended in 1915. Later, as Earl was taking down the high corner of the Tower above the second floor, he found a series of variously shaped prayer sticks aligned in the hearting of the wall. These were slender rods approximately one foot long with one end blunt and the other roughly carved into a serpent head. The arrangement in the wall consisted of groupings of pairs of prayer sticks bound together at the head by twigs shaped like miniature bows.

Earl had always considered the Tower as a structure erected by Mesa Verde immigrants because of pottery found in the building and because of the style of architecture and the block-type, dimpled surfaced masonry. In the unusual prayer stick arrangement he had mute evidence that Mesa Verde architects had built and occupied the Tower, but at the time he did not know it. Two years later, while stabilization work was under way at Mesa Verde under Earl's direction, prayer sticks were found embedded in the corners of some portions of Cliff Palace and Balcony House, both cliff dwellings of the classic Pueblo period.

It was imperative to get a photographic record of the prayer sticks *in situ,* a job both difficult and dangerous. "The two scaffold verticals offered the only points to which a camera could be fastened far enough distant from the sticks to permit getting them all on one plate. I tried first the south one, but it was too close to give a good view. The north one was eighteen inches farther away. I passed a heavy rope under my armpits so that I could lean far backward from the vertical, my feet resting on a coffee box placed on top of the scaffold. Gustav lashed it fast and I tied the coil of it with a shoestring passed from back to front over one shoulder so it could not slip down if I lightened my pressure by leaning forward. We took one leg of the tripod, lashed the extremity of one of the remaining pair to the upright, so that it stood nearly vertically, and passed the other in a horizontal plane to the top of one of the ceiling timbers where it was tied fast. By wedging under one side of it, and wedging between it and the upright where they crossed, we finally got the tripod head in a horizontal plane and at the same time swung it far enough to one side to permit the lens to shoot past the upright . . . The whole proceeding was an aggravating job, but worth while if the picture is a success. A cold gale blew constantly. I became so chilled that I was afraid to try to climb down the rope to solid ground. At 11:30 the sun struck the outer corner of the scaffold and by noon enough strength had returned to my hands to enable me to hold onto the rope."[29]

Kidder expressed the relief of everyone that the aerial feats were over when he said, "I am more than delighted that you got off that Tower safely. It is just like you to have taken all the risks yourself."[30]

When the Tower stood braced, proudly erect like a fortress, the corners rebuilt and bonded, some ceiling vigas back in place and the upper story partially replaced, the wounds of reconstruction healed so successfully that few visitors would realize the modern efforts which had been expended upon the old house. Numerous photographs and flash pictures were made from all angles with Gustav inventing an ingenious device to enable the simultaneous firing of three bulbs connected to a three-cell flashlight, using tin wash basins as reflectors.

On a crisp October morning in 1932, Earl's partnership with Mummy Cave and del Muerto was terminated. He recorded his exit as follows, "Going down canyon perfect. Easiest trip I have ever made except once when canyon was frozen solid."[31]

The experiences and knowledge gained in the decade of his work in the Canyon of Death would mold Earl's thinking about the Old People and provide pleasurable reminiscence for his remaining lifetime. This feeling was stated to Weyer, "Like yourself homesickness for the canyon country at times assails me. It would be good to go back again. But if I never do, memories of things that happened there remain a treasure that I shall revel in to the very end."[32]

Red Rocks

"I firmly believe that in these canons where conditions for the preservation of perishable materials would be operative, the transition from the Basket Makers to the first pottery makers is to be found. This would be the most important discovery one could hope for, since it would fill the only apparent gap in the chronological table for this region."[33]

The scene of Earl's drama with the Basket Makers shifted to the northeast where a crescent-shaped bowl lying between the massifs of Lukachukai to the south and Carriso to the north was to receive considerable attention. Situated some twenty miles south of the Arizona-Utah boundary, this was the Red Rocks Valley, largely bypassed by white settlers except those bent on making a financial profit through Navajo trade or a spiritual gain through conversion. Once the home of a large segment of the Navajo tribe, in the present day it was relatively empty of human life. Only a few octagonal hogans clung to its margins, with stunted rows of summertime corn planted in the more protected portions of the valley bottom.

With instinct sired by experience, upon his first view of the area Earl knew at once that here was a spot for investigation. "In the summer of 1928 a piece of high-grade gold ore sold to a trader by a Navajo who gave a false statement as to its source led me on a trip abortive, as far as gold was concerned, to the Carriso Mountains. It was a fortunate venture, however, because from the crest of the mountain I looked across the lower country between the Carrisos and the northwestern end of the Lukachukais and saw in the fissured red sandstone of the mesa the dark mouths of caves similar to those in Canyons del Muerto and de Chelly. It was this glimpse that impelled me to connive with John Wetherill to lead the Bernheimer Expedition of 1930 through the country between the two mountain masses."[34]

Characteristically, Earl turned to prospecting for ruins and artifacts. "On the prospecting trip Jack Lavery, Leo Hampton, and I, in order to cover our tracks, approached the Carrisos from the south by way of the Red Rock Post. For several miles north from the latter the most direct track toward the mountain parallels the eastern side of the Red Wash. Finally it crosses the wash and about a quarter of a mile farther on passes the west end of an isolated sheer-walled mesa. On the slope between the wash and the foot of the mesa there are many small ruins dating all the way from Basket Maker III to early Pueblo III. For the most part they are nearly washed and blown away. The one nearest the road is the largest and best preserved. It consists of a long string of rooms, apparently only one tier in width, running from east to west. It is of early Pueblo III age, as shown by the potsherds scattered over the meager refuse deposit on the brink of the declivity to the southward. In wandering over this area I saw the knees of an adult skeleton protruding where wind had swept the sand from under the edge of a small bush. The skeleton lay on its back, with knees elevated, head to the north."[35]

For many years Earl had ridden through and around that Lukachukai mountain chain importantly silhouetted on his western horizon. He had dug all along its eastern slopes in the early 20's when his reservation finds were making headlines. As early as 1922 to Bernheimer he had proposed its exploration in the belief that it might have the secret of the relationship between late Basket Maker and early Pueblo. The following summer he had looped across its northern flank in the Bernheimer trip to de Chelly-del Muerto. Many times he had traveled into the mountains with a Catholic priest in search of the locally famous Lost City of the Lukachukais.

That legend of the San Juan stemmed from early in the century when, on a mission to the Navajo, Fathers Fintan and Anseln of an establishment in Farmington had chanced to see off in the distance a beautiful silent ruin half hidden in the deep shadows of an arched recess. To the travelers it appeared larger and more lovely than the cliff dwellings of Mesa Verde which had just been proclaimed a national park. Having neither time nor energy at the moment to break trail through the rugged mountains in order to reach the site, they rode on. But when in later days they sought to return to the ruin, it could not be found. Earl was compelled to check out the tale firsthand, but without the luck of discovery. An old Navajo to whom he once talked said that indeed such a city had been there but that the entire roof of its cave had fallen in upon the walls, burying them forever beyond the reach of the modern world.

It was astonishing to Earl, then, that with all his tracking through the region, he had never before happened upon Atahonez. Even had he done so, it was likely that without the experience of del Muerto, where the most unprepossessing surfaces yielded the greatest returns in remains of the oldest strata of human occupation, he would have remained unimpressed. Others who knew of the valley had paid little heed to its large overhangs because the Pueblos, seeming to have avoided the region, had never erected the multi-roomed masonry towns which would have attracted looters and visitors. To the west Emil Haury, then of Gila Pueblo, had dug Vandal Cave in the Hospitibito drainage, and W. S. Fulton, of the Amerind Foundation, had worked Painted Cave still farther to the west. Atahonez in the Red Rocks Valley, however, remained the dream of every field man—before him, archaeologically unknown and untouched.

The Eighth Bernheimer Expedition took that field in late May of 1930, using the trading post of Bruce Barnard of Shiprock as headquarters. This time it was accompanied by a movie cameraman direct from Hollywood who in the course of three weeks exposed hundreds of feet of film of Bernheimer garbed in a white Stetson, immaculate riding breeches, and polished leather leggings.

Securing the guide services of an Indian who lived along the western side of Red Rocks Valley, an expressionless chap who had an incongruous moniker of "Jimmie the Boatman," the men made their way to the caves Earl had seen two years before from a mountain summit. Leaving the horses hobbled near a patch of grass and a scum-covered pool of water, they scrambled high up a steep slope to reach a shelter which, because of a monolith guarding the canyon below, Bernheimer named Obelisk Cave. They found themselves in a recess two hundred feet long and some thirty feet deep at its widest point whose floor was covered with a large mass of small rock which had fallen from the roof. One Navajo cache and some long ears of mottled blue corn indicated a little modern utilization but the archaeological stuff which lay in the shallow refuse was strictly Basket Maker.

Several large slab rooms were in view, but as usual it was the trash which proved exciting for pothole exploration. A few hours' digging unearthed many of the same items Earl had recovered by the wagonload in the canyons running toward Chinle.

As he studied over the articles which had to be carried back to camp, Earl came to the realization that here was the sort of site for which he often had wished. It certainly had little, if any, later Pueblo activity to confuse the deposition, and the finding of pottery chips and arrow fragments would place most of the occupation in the Basket Maker III horizon. Although the open ridges nearby gave surface indications of a similar occupation, it was the promise of the caves that appealed most strongly. Perhaps by working in Red Rocks, Earl could answer the problems of del Muerto.

The second overhang to be explored was called Owl's Head Cave by Bernheimer, later renamed Broken Flute by the women of Earl's digging party because one of the first articles recovered was a fragment of such a musical instrument. Situated at the head of Dirty Wash, Broken Flute Cave was several hundred feet above the valley floor. It was a deep, horseshoe-shaped shelter with a living expanse at the center of the curve being some sixty feet across, all protected by the cliff projection above. In the western third of the arc there were small masonry cists rising above the general level of the surface deposits of sandstone slabs fallen from the roof. Another wall seemed to have been part of a bench of a Great Kiva, the floor level of the structure having been at ground level. Depressions resulting from the grinding of axes and a few indistinct pictographs were the only obvious signs of human frequentation.

Superficial scratching of the surface produced specimens. Earl found a baby's mummy covered with fur cloth resting on an oval frame of wood; Wetherill discovered a conical basket filled with turkey feathers and a bundle of eagle feathers neatly bound together; and Johnson unearthed a clay pipe.

During the ensuing time in the field the men divided into small parties and scouted along the drainages of the Prayer Rock district, so called because of a red sandstone pinnacle projecting from the center of a ridge said to be sacred to the Navajo, hoping to find other caves as promising as the two first visited. Many shelters were seen to be wet or clogged with roof sloughage. Other times they were discovered to have been rifled by ancient vandals.

Again and again, discouraged with other sites, Earl and Wetherill returned to Broken Flute and Obelisk. There they cleared several cists and recovered more artifacts, including a feather box identical to the one Earl had taken from the Tseahatso turkey pen, a scoop of mountain sheep horn, bone whistles, pottery, aprons, baskets, and to Bernheimer's noticeable joy another "boomerang." Of particular interest to Earl was a runged ladder of hardwood well polished by use, of Basket Maker III age and identical to the Pueblo III one he had found in a room fill at Aztec.

Loaded down with two hundred fifty specimens and tree-ring samples for Douglass, the expedition rode over a divide into Tsegi-ho-chong, where one ruin of Pueblo age housed a square kiva in as perfect condition as the day it had been vacated, and down into Hospitibito where a cliff wall had been converted into the most used art gallery of the Anasazi empire. In this western portion of the general Red Rocks district was observed more frequentation by the Pueblos, with pottery of both Mesa Verde and Kayenta style being present.

In Red Rocks, Earl had found his Basket Maker III, strongly allied to those he had known in del Muerto but in no sense laggards or provincials. The absence of the Pueblo from the valley puzzled him for, to a white observer, it would have seemed to have offered all the Old People could have desired.[36] In other sectors they had lived with less advantage. Their scorn of Red Rocks was to the inestimable benefit of the researcher, and Earl would capitalize upon that fact during the next summer.

This valley being deep in the Navajo Reservation, Earl needed the Indians' permission to penetrate their preserve. He had a governmental permit which gave him necessary authorization to dig, but a slip of paper despite all its official looking seals, could not insure Indian pleasure at his presence. Through the good offices of the trader at the Red Rocks store, he laid his problem before the Navajo men. It was of prime importance to construct a road into the Atahonez over which supplies could be brought and specimens taken out. If they would grant such a privilege, many of them would be employed on the project.

The principal objection, besides traditional reluctance to welcome intruders, was that this had been a year of little grass. Earl did not quite understand what grass had to do with cars as he reassured the Indians that his "chuggies" (Navajo term for automobiles) did not eat the blades of grass needed by their sheep and goats. In the end, the desired permission was obtained, and fourteen men took eight days to put through a rough, high-centered road to the camp; access to the outside world remained so difficult that for the four-month session mail and supplies were secured from the trading post only every two weeks.

The crew was recruited from the La Plata diggers of the previous summer. Young Morrow, Rodgers Johnson, and Marjorie Trumbull returned from the East. Deric O'Bryan and Williard Fraser represented the West. The stand-by diggers, Oley and Oscar, were on hand as was George MacClellan, the reliable cook. The Kidders and Gladys Reichard, an ethnologist who was concentrating on the Navajo, were visitors. Earl reported that there were seldom less than twenty persons in camp.

Work commenced at the huge arc named Broken Flute. Here systematic digging stirred up the familiar choking clouds of dust but more importantly revealed that the broad cave floor once had housed a sizeable Basket Maker community. Portions of circular slab, pole-and-mud structures which had sat nearest the brink of talus had crashed down the slope. Presumably burials which might have been placed in that sloping drift of refuse also had eroded down into Dirty Wash at the canyon bottom and had been tumbled to ruin. In the matter of mummies the excavations were not nearly as productive as those in del Muerto. But houses and storage cists were in abundance, in most of their features similar to Basket Maker III habitations at Mummy Cave in Canyon del Muerto and Shabik'eshchee Village in Chaco Canyon. No Basket Maker II jug-shaped cists had been sunk beneath the living surface to which the houses pertained, although there were a few indications that those people might have visited the caves before their successors had claimed them.

As with other Basket Makers, those at Red Rocks showed their greatest technical skill in the field of textiles. The fabulous baskets demonstrated advancement over those of earlier days in profuse black-and-red-colored ornamentation of intricate composition and delicate execution. The twilled ring-basket made of yucca leaves trimmed to uniform size common in later Pueblo horizons in the Red Rocks district made its appearance in Basket Maker III. Seamless twined bags were obtained in both colored and plain styles. Waist bands of menstrual aprons and garters (?) were elaborately decorated. It was in the sandals, however, that the Basket Makers had reached their highest attainments in textile art.

The rarest woven specimens were recovered just a week before a Pecos Conference was to meet. Earl had been asked to prepare an exhibit of his finds but felt he had nothing new to show. Then his phenomenal luck burgeoned again as it had so many times in the past.

For several weeks Marjorie Trumbull had worked by herself in one section of Obelisk Cave. The others enjoyed kidding her about being a sandhog secessionist until she inspired considerable envy through the discovery of two complete mud vessels in a cist she was clearing. Earl and Oscar then moved in on her plot hoping that with the mud dishes there would be more specimens. There were, and Marjorie had the pleasure of finding them right beside the pits of Earl and Oscar, a feat which Kidder commemorated with a cartoon ballad entitled "Marjorie Trumbull, Cinderella of Obelisk Cave." From a bark-lined cache Marjorie removed a roll of a half dozen exquisitely made sashes. Two were white, two were brown and white, and two were brown, and all were fresh and softly pliable as if they had just come from the cleaners. They were very well made by a finger weaving technique, one and a half to three inches in width and six to nine feet in length, with square braided fringes strung with olivella shell beads. Subsequently two more sashes of lesser quality were taken from beneath the floor of a pit-house in Broken Flute. Few scholars could have distinguished any of them from sashes produced by Pueblo hands, another bit of evidence for the unbroken cultural continuum from Basket Maker through Pueblo. Of particular interest was the fact that the white fiber later was identified by David E. Johnson, of the Smithsonian Institution, as dog hair; the brown was thought to be either jack rabbit or beaver but it too later proved to be of canine origin.

Beans were abundant in the refuse. Beans had been recovered from cists and in refuse of the mixed deposits of del Muerto and in caves of the Tsegi. They also had been distributed through early levels of Mesa Verde caves but often they were of strictly modern varieties and owed their presence to the beans the Wetherills had used for poker chips during evening games at their camps in the cliffs. Earl thought his Red Rocks beans, which would prove to be the oldest dated examples in the San Juan, were of a single species, *Phaseolus vulgaris* (the common bean), which botanists considered a native of Mexico. He also felt that the bean first appeared in the northern Southwest in Basket Maker III times, long after corn had become an intregal part of the diet. Later research would show that *vulgaris* in three or four varieties rather than one had been grown by the Basket Makers, indicating either a long cultivation or agricultural influences from several sources. However, there had been a considerable period of time when corn and squash had been grown and beans had not. *Vulgaris,* a highland plant, would not grow in the hot regions of southern Arizona where the Indians had domesticated an indigenous plant, *Phaseolus acutifolius* (the tepary). That species received only secondary cultivation by the aborigines on the Colorado Plateau.

Another common item found in the accumulations of trash showed that gum chewing was not unique to modern American youth. These were knotted quids of fiber with a lump of rosin in their centers. The balls, some with teeth impressions retained as in a dental mold, must have been either Basket Maker chewing gum or lozenge. Because they were never found stored away in caches of ceremonial objects, there was small likelihood they had been wads of incense or perfume. Nor, because of their gummy unclean condition, did it seem plausible that they had been prepared balls of fibers to be stored for future use. Hanks or twists of prepared fibers were uncovered, but these were clean with the individual strands separate.

In the works of clay and mud Earl saw what he felt was further substantiation of his theory of the origin of San Juan pottery. Smashed upon the house floors were many fragments of mud vessels. These were so characterless—other than a surface color which ran from soot black to salmon pink—that their reassembly into vessels was a most exacting task which later absorbed Earl most of one winter. Some of the mud vessels had remained unfired, hence were friable and quick to soften with the presence of moisture. These Earl restored using a thick mixture of adobe and ambroid which when dry was hard as stone. Other of the mud containers seemed to have been accidentally baked in household fires. Since their fate had made them impervious to liquids, their repair was accomplished with normal techniques using plaster of paris patches. Ultimately a collection of twenty-five mud vessels stood upon museum shelves. Several very interesting observations could then be made.

As at del Muerto most of the mud vessels were of the flattish tray shape obviously made within a basket, with a wide rim added free above the basket and downraking solid lugs placed either near the free standing portion or over basket coils after removal from the mold. If the containers of that shape had been intended as mere liners for baskets used in the parching of wild seeds, it would be difficult to explain those lugs.

However, all mud vessels were not of the tray type. Some did in fact duplicate pottery forms. There were miniature bowls, jars, and dippers. Such diminutive utensils were known through the total course of Pueblo history. Most often archaeologists attributed them to the hands of children who attempted in a bungling way to copy adult craft. Among large vessels there were bowl shapes, some quite steep sided like the tub vessels of the northern San Juan and there were seed-jar or squash-pot shapes. Both of these forms were typical of the earliest pottery. Usually the unfired examples had been begun in a basket but above that base were put together by concentric strips of kneaded clay poorly bound together. Several of these unfired pottery forms were bark tempered but at least one was sand tempered as was the contemporaneous pottery. Maybe, as his critics said, through the Red Rocks mud vessels Earl could not demonstrate each step in the evolution of true ceramics, but these morphological duplications between mud and clay containers could not be ignored. The explanation which occurred to him was that at Red Rocks the idea of ceramics was demonstrated but without the knowledge of the methods of manufacture.

Another use of clay evident at Red Rocks was intriguing because of its implications with the spiritual aspects of the culture. These were twenty-three clay figurines all of a few inches in size and all with emphasis upon the breast and bulging hips of the female form. They were elongated slabs of unfired clay with pinched up nodules forming nose and breast features. A crotch cleft was very apparent. Punctated designs about the neck gave the impression of necklaces.

From the beginning of work among Basket Maker III remains, it was thought that figurines had considerable importance in that culture. Guernsey had recovered six figurines in the Tsegi, and Earl had taken five from del Muerto. The collection of figurines (twenty-three in clay and four in wood) from Red Rocks was the largest and most diversified made at any Basket Maker site. Because they were female figures, Earl thought they might have had something to do with a fertility cult. This would not have been unusual for an agricultural society which found its prosperity tied to productivity of the soil and benignity of the weather. Undoubtedly there were other uses as revealed by some figures which had been stuck with thorns or cactus spines as if for magical practices wherein one sought to destroy an enemy by wrecking an image.

Whatever its meaning, the figurine complex seemed to have arrived in the northern Southwest at about the same time as pottery first appeared. Many scholars felt that in both could be seen Mexican influence. Pottery increased in vogue and underwent extensive evolution, but figurines seemed to have passed from popularity as the Anasazi shifted from semisubterranean or cave homes into the open. Or perhaps more correctly stated, the vulnerability of unbaked figurines in unprotected locales had precluded their having been recovered.

The caves of Atahonez were more than satisfactory in yield of data and rubbish specimens discarded long before Columbus. The two thousand articles obtained from seventeen caves and open sites, particularly from the cache of textiles at Obelisk Cave, once more threw the public spotlight upon Earl. This time it was at Santa Fe at the joint meeting called for the third Pecos Conference and the opening of the Laboratory of Anthropology.

The Laboratory was the direct result of a broken pot. Two persons keenly interested in the ancient and modern native crafts of the Southwest, H. P. Mera and Elizabeth Shepley Sargent, unhappy over the fate of a lovely but shattered Zuñi jar, hit upon the notion of establishing a fund through private donations to buy examples of the artistic heritage peculiar to the Southwest before the arts were lost forever. The resultant Indian Arts Fund interested John D. Rockefeller, Jr., in founding an institution not only to house the collections but to provide facilities in which scholars might study regional cultural problems. So convinced was Rockefeller of the value of such a workshop that he provided two hundred thousand dollars with which to construct a headquarters and agreed to match operational funds obtained from other sources up to seventy thousand dollars for a period of five years. Fifty acres of land upon which to build the Laboratory were donated by local citizens. Shortly thereafter an adobe structure of Franciscan mission style stood on a mesa above town, and within its vaults was the nucleus of the most complete archives of native pottery, silver, and textiles ever assembled.*

The evening of the opening ceremonies saw a throng of four to seven hundred local people and visiting dignitaries, plus a large number of archaeologists direct from their widely scattered camps, pour into the massive *luminaria* outlined building. Governor Arthur Seligman and Senator Bronson Cutting spoke briefly to an audience in the Auditorium. Wissler and Kidder addressed the gathering. But standing quietly in the rear of the hall, puttees well polished and khaki field outfit spotless, was the man of the hour. A Santa Fe paper reported, "Easily the center of interest in the whole building were the belts and sashes of wool from the mountain sheep and some other unknown animal, cunningly woven about the second century of the Christian Era, preserved in dry earth with no other covering for seventeen centuries so perfectly that they could have been fashioned and laundered yesterday. The Exhibition fresh from the Morris excavations filled a large case, hundreds of articles, exquisite arrow points, yucca fiber sandals and medi-

* Incorporators of the new Laboratory of Anthropology were drawn from the ranks of leading anthropologists of the day: K. M. Chapman of the Indian Arts Fund, R. B. Dixon of Harvard, F. W. Hodge of the Museum of the American Indian, N. M. Judd of the Smithsonian Institution, A. V. Kidder of Phillips Academy, S. G. Morley of Carnegie Institution of Washington, and Clark Wissler of the American Museum of Natural History. Earl was elected to serve on the thirty man Board of Trustees composed of scholars from America's foremost scientific institutions, under the chairmanship of A. V. Kidder. Jesse L. Nusbaum was appointed the first Director.

cine bags, flutes, red corn grown in the time of the Caesars looking as if fresh from the stalk; pottery primitive as a child would make from mud today; other handcraft made and ornamented with finished art."[37]

However, it was not to be the exquisite dog-hair sashes nor the pointed-bottom burden baskets nor the crudely fashioned mud bowls which would bring to Red Rocks lasting archaeological fame. The charred remains of pine and spruce roof supports and wall timbers, fresh because of their mud encasement, would have more far-reaching significance to all regional scholars of the past because they would be found to extend the year record back another seven centuries to its earliest date thus far read and would permit the coupling of several floating chronologies and, in turn, their connection to the historic beam calendar.

At the time the invaluable tree-ring specimens from Red Rocks arrived at Douglass's laboratory attempts were being made to anchor three early but unassigned chronologies. It was uncertain which series came first and whether any preceded A.D. 700, the terminal readable date on the Christian chronology, although archaeological deduction would place the sites from which the wood came as culturally earlier than any ruins yet dated. Two months later Douglass wired Earl that wood from Obelisk Cave, which from the beginning Earl had considered earliest of the two principal sites, yielded a splendid two-hundred-fifty-year record identical to some rings from del Muerto; wood from Broken Flute, culturally more advanced, matched others.[38]

Another year passed before Earl heard more of the progress in dating these early cultures. He knew that Douglass was trying to tie in some specimens from Shabik'eshchee Village of Chaco Canyon submitted by Roberts and from Mesa Verde Step House sent by Paul Franke, Park Naturalist, both sets of specimens Basket Maker III. Then came an involved announcement from Douglass that the seemingly impossible had been accomplished. Through a particularly fine series of configurations in a specimen from Red Rocks two chronologies could be matched and hooked together with a slight overlap. In a most offhand manner Douglass handed Earl a bombshell, "Obelisk Cave had some very fine beams that gave us the complete first century A.D., that is beginning near 10 A.D."[39]

It seemed incredible to Earl that now, a mere fourteen years after Douglass had first explained his research to him at Aztec through examination of annual rings laid upon a tree, man might reach beyond the Christian Era. Largely through his own untiring efforts at supplying materials upon which to work, the small corps of dendrochronologists had made one of the most remarkable contributions to the world of archaeology. "It is truly astonishing that you have been able to piece together nature's record for so great a span of years. I had not even surmised from your previous letters that the sequence might extend as far back as the year 10 A.D.," was his pleased response to his old friend.[40]

The new date from Douglass was adding substance to what Earl had written earlier. Of his three hundred specimens of wood from Red Rocks he had said, "While this will not connect with the nether limit of Dr. Douglass' present historic series which reaches back to 740 A.D. further excavation will eventually provide timbers to bridge the gap, thus extending the positive year for year chronology for the aboriginal cultures of the northern Southwest very near to, if not beyond, the beginning of the Christian Era."[41]

This A.D. 10 date, later modified to A.D. 11, did not mean that Obelisk Cave had been occupied at that time. It did show, however, that one beam used in house construction had begun its life in that year, probably on a windswept mesa top near to the mother mountain. Utilization of the cave as a home for a group bearing a rather primitive type of Basket Maker culture had occurred in the late fifth century. All the dates at which structural timbers had been cut clustered from A.D. 470 to A.D. 489. However, it was never determined that these might not have represented beams originally haggled by the earlier Basket Maker II in the region. Broken Flute, scene of a larger, more elaborate settlement, had been used by man for four hundred years from A.D. 354 to A.D. 730, the heaviest concentration of dates indicating the largest population about A.D. 625. Culture represented probably was Basket Maker II in the beginning progressing through the full cycle of Basket Maker III.

Archaeological conclusions resulting from these dates were provocative. "The culture in question seems to have remained surprisingly static during that interval. There would appear to have been a slight increase in size and somewhat greater stability in house construction; the addition of two types of pottery, rock tempered decorated and polished red, with a considerable amplification of the range of vessel form; otherwise little change."[42] Why, for two hundred years, did the Red Rocks Anasazi coast when at other periods they raced toward change, if not advancement? Here again, the much earlier dating of Obelisk Basket Maker III was open to suspicion.

As expected, Mummy Cave, with its deep deposits of potteryless trash, produced dates ranging a century earlier than those at Obelisk.

To Earl's amazement, a beam from the talus room had a cutting date of A.D. 348, but the same structure had seen further remodeling at A.D. 485, thus making it contemporaneous to the Red Rocks cave to the east. Furthermore, the A.D. 348 beam was not a part of a structure when found so its place in the scheme of things would remain uncertain. The cribbing which had held back the refuse blankets to create residential areas had been erected and repaired for over three hundred years beginning with the first inhabitants of the fourth century. The cists, also begun in the fourth century, had been reworked and reused into the eighth century. The span of Mummy Cave dates, from A.D. 348 in the talus to A.D. 1284 in the Tower, made that shelter the longest consecutively occupied dwelling spot in North America.[43]

With the cementing together of the various chronologies, other Basket Maker III sites assumed their rightful positions in the historic scheme. The structure of that period in Step House Cave on the Mesa Verde was erected in A.D. 610. Pithouses later dug there also were of that general period. Shabik'eshchee Village southward in Chaco Canyon at this time remained undated because the wood obtained during excavation was unusable for dendrochronological purposes, but through later work by Gladwin's staff at Gila Pueblo it was seen to have been constructed during the middle 700's. Thus the fifth, sixth, and seventh centuries belonged to the Basket Maker III, with a tenuous beginning possible in some areas in the fourth century and an ending in outposts dragging on into the eighth century.

For some time there remained what Douglass considered a weak transition from the early chronologies to the modern one at the year A.D. 700. Specimens of suitable age which would permit further cross checks were scarce in the eastern and northern San Juan. For some reason there appeared to have been an interruption of occupation in some districts at that time, a period which also coincided with the gradual emergence of the so-called Pueblo culture. To attempt to get more borings or charcoal with which to work, in 1934, accompanied by Earl, Douglass made a trip to Red Rocks and del Muerto, seeing for himself the localities from which came his oldest readings. No timbers of the needed sort were found. However, just at this time work by John McGregor, of the Museum of Northern Arizona, on timbers secured from ruins along the western portions of the San Juan provided the necessary reinforcement for the weak juncture. The bridge from the Basket Maker centuries into those of the Pueblos was made firm.

Just as there was no time gap left between Basket Maker and Pueblo, so there remained no doubt that the cultural continuity had been unbroken. Basket Maker merged into Pueblo with such slight perceptibility that were it not for the gradual dominance of a round-headed physical stock and the acquisition of several new cultural items no distinction between the two could be made at all. Anasazi they were from beginning to end, with varying emphasis giving individual color to the two components. Actually more differences were seen to have existed between Basket Maker II and Basket Maker III than between Basket Maker III and Pueblo I.

The three centuries A.D. 400 to A.D. 700—the time of the Basket Maker III—had been the most important years of man's evolution in the Southwest. During that time he had acquired at least in rudimentary form every basic concept and technique which he would carry with him throughout the remainder of his people's history. Perhaps most of the foundation stones of his civilization had been passed to him from some source outside of the San Juan, although Earl was not of that opinion in 1931. Agriculture, house type, weapons, ornamentation, and crafts may not have been the products of the Basket Maker's own mind, but he had the innate intelligence to make them his.

Regarding the shriveled-up men of the caves and all their kinsmen who chose to dwell across the Colorado Plateau as the most outstanding of the aboriginal parade of human life in the Southwest, Earl saluted them. "All that one can grant to the periods after Basket Maker III is the development and, in certain cases, the improvement of the component traits of material culture that had long before been brought together into a virile and progressive ensemble. It is easy to take that which is found existent and to carry it to further development. But to invent, to innovate, is another matter, demanding creative ability, that rarest of mental qualities, which put upon its possessors the true stamp of genius."[44]

From the Red Rocks research grew a technical paper on basketry, a short article on the figurines, and a brief statement to be used as background for a report on the dates. A complete site report was never finished by Earl. Many of his findings underlay the ideas expressed in the La Plata monograph.

After Earl's death the artifacts recovered from this excavation were given to the Arizona State Museum by the Carnegie Institution. There they were restudied as part of a doctoral dissertation by his eldest daughter.

FALLS CREEK

"There seems to be something peculiar about the Durango district. This stuff appears to vary in certain respects from the standard run of Basket Maker II material."[45]

For the first ten years of their marriage the Morrises did not have a home. They lived out of a duffle bag at one archaeological camp and then another, content to pour their full energies into pursuit of the Old People. In any review of their dwelling spots one would have thought of the tents in del Muerto which often collapsed to the ground in the face of wild winds, of the hacienda at Chichén Itzá where walls felt eternally damp, of the little Pueblo-style house set at the side of Aztec Ruins. None of these was a home. In 1933, knowing that whether they really enjoyed it or not a prolonged stint of study, analysis, and writing lay ahead, Earl and Ann bought a house in Boulder near to the collections in the university museum.

It was a barny old place perched upon a hillside above town with the shadow of the Rockies at the back door and the immensity of the Colorado plains sweeping out in front. Earl with his hammer and Ann with her paintbrush turned the drab building into a house of great charm. Lifetime collections of pots and artifacts sat on lengthy shelves beside an extensive library. Handwoven rugs of Navajo origin lay across gleaming floors. Oil paintings of the Southwest hung on the walls. Most importantly for Earl, on the ground level was a large workroom in which he could at last look forward to the anchoring influence of laboratory research.

The anchor for Ann was a new daughter, Elizabeth Ann, born in Omaha the year before. She was joined in another year by a second girl, Sarah Lane.

So two aspects of adult life—home and family—overtook the archaeological nomads simultaneously and drastically altered their manner of living. Earl went off on occasion to some task like realigning Quirigua stelae toppled by a Guatemala earthquake, taking Emil Haury through the Red Rocks district to secure beam samples, or visiting Gila Pueblo with Kidder. But mostly his days were consumed with the unglamorous routine of preparing manuscripts for publication. The La Plata report covering seventeen years' excavation, work upon the Gobernador pottery secured in 1915 and Red Rocks mud vessels gathered in 1931, and meticulous analysis of the examples of basketry he had unearthed conspired to sap his energy. "As to my writing, I, like the rest, prefer the digging. I have sat at a desk until I feel like a hibernating toad. But no matter what it does to me physically, I am determined to leave a record of at least the most important work I have done before I hit the long trail", were his comments to a companion of many another trail, John Wetherill.[46]

Already a legend in the small college town, a quickly distinguishable figure because of the leather leggings, khaki pants, and stiff-brimmed Stetson hat he always wore, Earl was called upon frequently for lectures about his favorite subject, the Indians of the Southwest. He gave freely of his time to address noon gatherings of the Rotary, to speak to school assemblies, to patiently answer the serious and often inane questions of youngsters who came to his door with a recently found arrowhead or bone. In 1937 he had the satisfying pleasure of realizing a dream conceived in his undergraduate days, to participate in the dedication of a new university museum building which housed archaeological treasures of his own gathering during the course of twenty years. Unquestionably the fragile nature of many of the irreplaceable specimens was a strong factor in the decision to erect the edifice.

Ann enjoyed some triumphs. She was honored by her alma mater with an honorary degree. Her books were greeted with acclaim. But a troubled state of mind was increasingly apparent. Restless without deep absorption in Earl's technical problems, inquiring but without a needed goal, she began to drift. She found frustration in the restrictions inherent in motherhood. She experienced prolonged periods of depression. She sought answers to her problems through conversion to a new religion. In the pull of despair or boredom or loneliness, her illness closed in upon her.

Personal unhappiness dominated the house on the hillside. Always reserved, Earl retreated further into himself. He shared his problems with no one but continued to make a brave showing of tranquility. His letters of the period only hint at Ann's failing health and his mounting responsibilities with the young daughters for whom, in the agony of his concern for Ann, he developed a fierce attachment. A further worry arose with his mother who had become an arthritic invalid. She was moved from her cottage in Aztec to a nursing home in Boulder where at the age of eighty-eight she found release from her suffering.

Seven distressed years passed before the Basket Makers lured Earl back to the field. This time he headed for Durango, a seat of early white occupation in the region and apparently also a seat of early Indian inhabitation as well. He ran right into trouble.

The decade of the 30's witnessed one of the most virulent epidemics of pothunting ever to sweep any sector of the San Juan. The center of the outbreak was concentrated in the upper Animas valley of southern Colorado. Here signs of the ancient ones were not spectacular. Yet from the first thrust of white penetration into the region in the 1870's occasional finds of Indian relics had been made. They were so rare and generally without individuality that they excited little interest in a public impressed only by the biggest or the oldest, one of which lay unknown at the town's limits.

With a growing awareness of the tremendously rich archaeological finds coming to light elsewhere in the San Juan basin, local weekend collectors formed a society where enthusiasm and knowledge could be pooled. They were met with unexpected success as reports of more and more ruins were made, and collections of artifacts grew to sizeable proportions. "Evidently all these years I have walked past a veritable BM III stronghold in the vicinity of Durango, Colorado. Literally thousands of vessels have been exhumed in the last three years and most of the sites pretty badly wrecked," was Earl's remark to his superior.[47]

Archaeologists, lacking the strengthening rod of law, sought to stem the tide of potting by preaching. Too often their manner was either condescending or threatening. The reaction in the collector ranks was defiance and hostility, resulting in fortified determination to continue the Sunday hobby regardless of antipathy in certain quarters. Many pursued the avocation because of the love of the quest. Others were genuinely interested in the study of the Indians. A few, mistakingly believing that oldness meant remunerative value, saw what was hoped to be a chance to pick up some extra cash. These were the ones inadvertently encouraged in their digging for relics by the professionals themselves who bought collections rather than see them dispersed into a dozen channels.

One of the principal leaders of the Durango amateur clique was I. F. (Zeke) Flora, a watch repairman and owner of a combination curio store and pool hall. He introduced himself to the best-known archaeological authority on the area, Earl, who helped him sell to Harold Gladwin of Gila Pueblo a good collection of more than a hundred locally acquired pots, most of Basket Maker III age. The upshot of this transaction was the employment of Zeke by Gladwin to make an archaeological survey of the upper Animas valley and the subsequent opportunity to study Gladwin's dendrochronological method. Earl's own interest in Zeke stemmed from an excited letter about a new discovery.[48]

After having been informed by a fellow society member of numerous, small, rudimentary and almost weather-obliterated paintings in red, yellow, black, white and green pigment upon a cliff wall, Zeke had found his way to the escarpment, located six miles up canyon from Durango in a narrow valley fingering off the Animas. In a crack along the shelter face, where neither rain nor snow had penetrated, he had uncovered a remarkable mass of human bodies, all naturally dried into a state of preservation and all accompanied by clothing and offerings. One fine specimen Zeke named Esther.

The dessicated female known as Esther was no beauty. She had been a girl of twenty years when she had met an unexplained death. Her bony legs were bent up under her shriveled thighs making it appear as though she were standing on her knees. Her arms were crossed over her groin, partially covered by a fibrous apron, above which was the sunken hollow of the abdomen. Her skull was long and undeformed. Her eyes, one partially sealed shut and the other wide open, stared blindly at her viewers. Her leathery skin hugging the skeletal frame was complete, with only two small patches just below the knees having disappeared. Her cropped black hair, lashes, and even fingernails were preserved. All her attributes notwithstanding, Esther greeted the world with an ugly grimace caused by lips retracted and a tongue swelling out between her teeth and curving up over her upper incisors. But beauty or not, this young lady was the finest specimen of her kind ever to have been found. Knowing the rapid decay caused by moisture, Earl must have shuddered for her well-being as he read Zeke's comment, "In attempting to give her a much needed bath with garden hose and scrub brush, I was surprised to find the skin soften, could move the lips and tongue, adjust features, and open the eyes and see the pupil of the eye on intact eyeballs."[49]

Wasting no time, Earl put a few necessities into his car and drove to Durango. When he arrived, he discovered that because the Flora house was under quarantine, he could only view the finds through a window. Because of the noticeable lack of pottery and the presence of standard objects of the culture, Earl felt there could be little doubt that Esther and her friends were Basket Maker II, making them the most eastern of that strain yet found. Wryly he recalled his prolonged efforts to find in the north country locations which might yield perishables attributable to the early cultures, only at Durango in his old haunts to be outdone by another. The fact that the door was opened by someone else did not dampen his own desire to get to a new task.

"Maybe I exaggerate its importance, but no comparable lot of material has been found as far east in the San Juan country, either north or south of the river. Moreover, there seems to be something peculiar about the Durango district. This stuff appears to vary in certain respects from the standard run of Basket Maker III material and later there seems to be contemporaneity of Basket Maker III and Pueblo I, with the latter going back considerably earlier than it is known to have done elsewhere", he wrote Kidder just ten days later.[50]

With a feeling of urgency, Earl suggested that the Carnegie Institution buy the complete array, retaining it as a unit to be studied and published upon, a plan to which Zeke agreed. Thus the withered occupants of the Durango rock shelter, together with their worldly goods, were brought to the Morris home in Boulder.

Although the mummies were a sensational find, it was mainly the hope that some kind of associated Basket Maker II architecture might also be found in the Durango area that prompted Earl and Bob Burgh, his laboratory assistant, to undertake three seasons of excavation there.

Both Durango shelters selected in 1938 for study were roofed by the massive La Plata sandstone formation commonly exposed in the area and both faced the east overlooking Falls Creek Valley from an elevation of six hundred feet. Without any wide expanse of livable area, they were jumbled with sand washed back from the vegetation covered drift of earth along the front of the cave and with great amounts of huge boulder overburden which, because of the danger of blasting, had to be crushed with back-breaking sledging. Beneath this covering the man-made deposits varied from a few inches on the three definable terraces to nine feet in depth in the talus slope.

Their excavation was not the productive sort of delving which turned up something new and exciting with each slice of the spade. In place of thrills, there were tedium and exertion with a day's labor producing only a handful of worked bone or stone. The reasons for the dearth of artifacts were obvious. In the first place, the occupants must have been poor in the tangible goods of civilization, their assemblage of articles of clothing and tools to carry on daily routine meager in the extreme. That fact was one even the most ardent collector could face. It was not so easy to accept the fact that because of moisture many of the things fashioned by Basket Maker hands had been snatched away from the grasp of the archaeologist. "The horizon is Basket Maker II without question. But unless there is a dry spot somewhere, the picture of the culture will be far from satisfactory", Earl lamented.[51] Daily it became more certain that Zeke had recovered all the perishables that were to be had.

Earl was disappointed but not discouraged. His principal aim had been to determine whether the Durango Basket Makers had had houses, and in this direction work was slowly revealing positive indications of floors. Within a week he noted, "It seems certain now that we have a Basket Maker II house type established." (Field journal, Durango, 1938, University of Colorado). But he spoke too soon. Smooth saucer-shaped floors there were, circular in outline, with a bowl-like fire pit dug into the earth and lined with clay and with both open stone-faced cists and others possessing waist-high clay superstructures. However, the style of construction of walls and roof remained a mystery. No skeleton of a pole framework could be found although bits of charcoal were frequent in the fill. The season ended with no solution to the wall-construction riddle, but with the presence of some kind of architecture in the Basket Maker II horizon being unquestionably demonstrated. To Kidder he reported, "I have not yet been able to prove that side walls or roofs ever existed. But in any event we have long occupied Basket Maker II living quarters."[52]

For five decades, beginning in the 1880's with the Wetherill discoveries in Grand Gulch a hundred miles to the west, Basket Maker II remains had been known and dug. Earl in 1938 was the first to be able to show that those early men had attained a degree of advancement which enabled them to provide themselves a protection from the elements without reliance upon those supplied by nature.

The two months stay at Falls Creek proved pleasant and did much to revive Earl's spirits. Aside from clouds of stinging mosquitos which made life miserable in early July, summertime showers which arrived with startling suddenness, and a hillside of high altitude which was alive with rattlesnakes, there were few discomforts. Sundays were spent at Electra Lake, mecca for fishermen within a wide radius. There the tensions of the years and the dilemma of the digging seemed to flow down the line to drown themselves in the obscure blackness of the lake bottom. The thought of the moment was confined to the securing of the legal limit.

Before work commenced the next season Esther had become a celebrity. She had made a triumphal entry into Washington where she was a star of a Southwestern display Earl had prepared for the annual exhibit of the Carnegie Institution. In June her guardian gave her in loan to the museum at Mesa Verde. The glass case in which she was housed became smudged with the fingerprints of the thousands of visitors who paused to pay their respects. Among the most curious viewers were the Navajos engaged in various jobs at the Park. Their traditional fear of the dead did not stop them from coming to her side, where many complained of dizzy spells, pains in the head, or loss of balance because of the "chindi" spirits.

The nineteen mummies, including Esther, had been found on Department of Agriculture lands where Zeke had no permit to work. After seven years of bitter controversy, he was divested of control over the collection by an order issued by the Acting Secretary of Agriculture, J. B. Hutson. Esther became a permanent occupant of the Mesa Verde museum.

During the 1939 digging season, in anticipation that wood from neighboring open sites of Basket Maker III affiliation would bridge back toward earlier charcoal samples recovered in North and South Shelters, Earl returned to the Durango area to continue his efforts to reveal the genesis of the Anasazi. The houses dug that summer were of the subterranean pit variety, and all contained pottery. Douglass dated them in the middle 700's.

The target for 1940 was a hillside slope near Trimball Springs in the Animas valley. At that place there appeared to be evidence of a nonceramic occupation which might be expected to have cultural contemporaniety with North and South shelters where house types and dates still had not been determined. All through the damp chill weather of an alpine May and into sultry June trenches drifted into the hillside continued to reveal a confused series of use-hardened mud floors and cists piled one above the other against the slope in a manner Earl likened to an offset stack of hot cakes. Each of the crew continued day after day in the attempt to trace out the various features encountered in his section of the site, clearing off skeletons found, and making note of numerous bone awls and stone tools which came to light. All were anxious to find something which would enable Earl to describe the elusive Basket Maker II house. But weeks rolled by when many obvious floors had been cleared and still there had not been found vertical wall posts or post holes. One day, June 4, he recorded, "No post holes in floor have been found." On June 18 he added, "Bob cleared away bank above the saucer rim of Room 2. Found trough for small horizontals, but not one trace of butts of lateral verticals." Two days later, "There are floors and more floors, cists dug through cists, animal burrows, and *chaos*." And the next day,

"Zeke and I worked in the area of Room 3. We cleaned out a filled slab cist that had had a domed top, developed floor levels, and by the end of the day were worse confused than at the start." Or, "The struggle to find floors weathered beyond recognition gets on everybody's nerves."[53] And so it went—many problems but answers not apparent.

Meanwhile Ann and the daughters had arrived from Boulder. The girls promptly underwent two of childhood's milestones, tonsillectomies and First Communions at the chapel in Farmington. After these ceremonies were past, they and their mother joined Earl at his camp headquarters. Not many days later Ann took to her cot, leaving Earl full responsibility for the welfare of his children in addition to that of his field party. Typically, he hid his anxiety from others by going to the dig each day and working on notes each evening. Ann seldom left her tent or made her presence known. Earl said nothing. But in his journal on July 10 he wrote, "Ann under again. What I am to do I don't know." Several days after that entry as he was preparing the girls' beds for the night one of them developed a serious nosebleed which could not be stopped for several hours. Earl was called upon to be an emergency nurse. "The combination of things is wearing me down," he stated. "I hope I can last."[54] Finally near the month's end, he took Ann to the Farmington hospital and turned the youngsters over to the daytime care of the wife of one of his workmen.

To further add to the gloom which hung over camp, all were concerned over a worsening world situation. On June 14 a notation read, "A dull, draggy day. News of the occupation of Paris this A.M. took the spirit out of all of us."

More than two months of hard digging and endless speculation passed before Earl at last found the answer to his problem of wall construction. One week before camp was to be closed, he was enabled to write, "Bob quit surveying about 10:30. Then set to work to ravel out the overlapping of the N edge of the Floor 3 area and the S edge of Floor 2. Soon he called me and we spent the rest of the day at the spot. At last we found an answer to the absence of vertical roof supports for the superstructures of the houses. Beneath the edge of Floor 3, there remained an arc of floor 2, wall some 15″ high and 5-6′ long that seemed conclusively to reveal the method of construction. Surmounting the first log, timbers of various sizes were laid horizontally, course upon course, and the interstices filled with mud. It is in effect a wood-and-mud masonry, strong as could be until the timbers rotted. A wall so constructed would have been amply strong to support the weight of a roof, with no mud for vertical supports . . . It is a relief to have the nightmare of lacking roof supports finally dispelled."[55]

One troublesome matter had been settled. Personal difficulties lingered. "It is well that the season is nearly over. Worry about Ann casts a constant shadow. And having the girls in camp adds to other complications. They are as good as youngsters could be. Thank heaven for Mrs. Bennett. When I have to be out on the job she looks after them like the gentle, gracious lady that she is."[56]

On August 6 Earl and his small daughters went home. A career of digging which had begun on the lower Animas in the latest ruins had come to an end on the upper reaches of that same drainage with work among the earliest remains of the San Juan. Earl never again engaged in archaeological excavation.

At fifty one, after forty seven years of almost continual digging or ruin repair, Earl laid down his excavation tools. Bowed by unhappiness and the burden of accumulated unfinished research, the man who had done so much to lead the way down the halls of Southwestern prehistory stepped aside for a new generation. Work did not cease for that was the essence of life itself. Instead, it took another tack.

With the technical aid of Bob Burgh, a definitive study of Anasazi basketry was published in 1941. Through that research, with the tedious dissecting of fragments, the tracing and even duplication of weaves, and the painstaking study of sherds of pottery vessels which retained coil impressions, Earl became the regional authority on a craft at which the earliest sedentary Southwesterners excelled. It pleased him to note that many of the most outstanding basketry specimens in at least four institutions had been unearthed under his own direction.

The next logical step to follow a technical paper on basketry in general was one to deal specifically with sandals. In this phase of weaving the Old People expended their most lavish care and achieved their finest workmanship. Aided by Jean Zeigler and Kisa Noguchi, two artist-draftsmen, work was started on a six hundred specimen collection of both worn out and little used Indian footgear, the Red Rocks material forming the core of the study. Before work had gone far, World War II took away both the girls and Burgh.

Meanwhile, because of his extensive knowledge of weaving, Earl was called upon to edit some sections of a manuscript by Burton Cosgrove, deceased excavator in southern New Mexico, dealing with caves where an impressive amount of perishable materials had been obtained.

In the wake of this assignment came the joint editorship with Kidder of a book upon the Basket Makers begun by Earl's fellow Farmingtonian, Charles Amsden, before his untimely death. In addition to helping with that manuscript, as a tribute to his friend Earl established the Amsden Memorial Collection at the Southwest Museum by presenting to that institution a valuable assortment of his own San Juan pots.

Even though he stubbornly kept himself at his ramified projects, Earl's spirits seldom rose above the low level to which they had sunk at the end of the Durango work. He became ever more introspective and dispirited, unable to believe he had made any contribution as a man or as a scholar. Even the receipt of an honorary degree from his university, handed to him by a classmate and later President of the University of Colorado Robert Stearns, did little to boost his morale as with humbleness he wrote, "I do not think I deserved it, but I do appreciate the consideration of those who saw fit to bestow it upon me."[57] Ann, periodically back in the hospital, was sinking rapidly, and the doctors charged with her welfare could not determine the causes of her physical breakdown. When for brief days she seemed improved, it was like the old days, with pleasant shop talk and banter with the girls. But as the months drew on, such times were less frequent. At last the house upstairs lay swathed in darkness, and the laboratory downstairs sat empty and covered with dust.

With the war raging around the world, it was impossible to secure the services of a cook, housekeeper, or baby sitter, which forced Earl to devote his hours toward the housekeeping duties. To Kidder he expressed some of his dilemma, "All along Ann had been too down to do anything herself. I have been, and am, about a fully occupied and as mentally efficient as a goat in a treadmill."[58]

Ann Axtell Morris died in the late spring of 1945 when she was forty-five years old. Into the life of Earl Morris she had injected a dash of romance and sparkle to counterbalance his own seriousness; in her passing there remained only loneliness and despair.

The numbness of long suffering clung to Earl as he struggled to pull together the threads of the old life he had known but would never recapture. A tonic for his grief was provided by the Paul Frankes who invited him and his daughters to spend the summer with them at Grand Teton National Park where they were stationed. There

Earl's loss gradually lessened. By fall he was able to return home ready to face a new kind of existence.

There was a letter from Ted Kidder waiting for him. "It is far too long a time since you have had a shovel in the ground," Kidder remarked,[59] knowing that the Earl of old would have responded faster to that treatment than to any other. But Earl was burdened with a sense of inadequacy and the care of two youngsters.

Both problems were to come under the healing hands of an old friend, Lucile Bowman. She was a sympathetic, forceful woman who had been principal of the elementary school which Elizabeth and Sarah attended. Lucile and Earl were married in 1946.

When the war ended, Earl was offered an opportunity to do special lecturing at the university, at last realizing an ambition once stated to Hewett long before graduation had become a reality. Encouraged by his contact with interested young people to whom Earl Morris was a famous name, confidence returned. Quietly in the background, Lucile with her pleasant gregariousness was guiding him back toward fulfillment. By the time Bob Burgh and the other helpers were home from war, the Durango specimens were unpacked and ready to be studied.

During the course of Earl's participation in Southwestern archaeology, the Basket Maker culture had been traced across wide stretches of the San Juan and neighboring drainages and wherever found, it had been shown to have been surprisingly uniform in content. A trait list tabulated for the Durango sites and the classic Basket Maker II finds elsewhere revealed a seventy-eight per cent correlation.[60] In general terms Durango Basket Maker culture was not greatly different from that of the Tsegi or del Muerto. There was, however, an important difference in emphasis.

The Durango sites were not just places of the dead with bark lined cists tightly crammed with bodies. They were homes, long in use and cluttered with household goods not normally placed as offerings with the departed. Thus the nonperishable finds from Falls Creek were of much greater significance to the scholar interested in finding more of the pieces of the Basket Maker jigsaw than was the unauthorized burial collection made by Flora.

Study of the material spread out in the Morris laboratory revealed that these early settlers in the trough of the Animas had been of mixed physical strains but all belonging to a genetic stream physical anthropologists called Southwestern Plateau, one of the basic breeding populations which peopled the New World. By the time of their arrival at Falls Creek they had already been touched by three of mankind's most potent molding forces—agriculture, architecture, and communal living. Were they then responsible for other peaks of culture beyond the confines of the Chaco, Mesa Verde, and Kayenta?

In the early periods of archaeological work in the Southwest it had been customary to think of the San Juan drainage, with its thousands of ruins obviously built over a considerable span of time, as being the nucleus to all aboriginal development which took place in the region. It was also fashionable to believe that very little influence had swept into the San Juan from adjacent regions, that somehow it was an island of aboriginal life hermetically sealed off from the rest of North America. Earl was one of those men behind the formulation of such a theory of culture evolution, and he tenaciously clung to that premise until the years brought forth a flood of contradictory evidence.

At the time of the first Pecos Conference in 1927 it was believed that all Southwestern cultures could be tailored into the Basket Maker-Pueblo framework, with deviations representing nothing more than distance from the San Juan hearth and consequent tardiness in being exposed to change. By the third Pecos Conference in 1931, however, when Earl had just shaken the soil from the well-publicized Red Rocks dog-hair belts, it had to be admitted that prehistoric affairs had been infinitely more complex than first supposed. As a consequence, another meeting convened, this one for the purpose of devising a separate chronological skeleton for the Gila Drainage of Arizona. After 1931 it was recognized that the Southwest had known two cultural patterns instead of one—the Basket Maker-Pueblo of the north (later termed Anasazi) and the Hohokam of the Arizona desert. Each development had been founded upon the raising of corn but there the similarity ended. House type, pottery construction and decoration, and method of burial differed, as did numerous lesser aspects of material culture. Nor did there appear to have been much exchange between the Hohokam dwellers of the desert and the Anasazi men of the plateau. How they related in time was uncertain because of the impossibility of dendrochronological determinations on the deciduous woods in the southern ruins.

In the middle 30's research was further complicated by the suggestion that still another basic stock might have been present aboriginally. As a result of excavation in west central New Mexico, Emil Haury postulated that a group he proposed to call the Mogollon deserved equal status with the old-line families of the Anasazi and Hohokam.

They were thought to have occupied the borderline areas along the New Mexico and Arizona boundary south of the San Juan and to have paralleled Anasazi development in some respects while remaining distinctive in others. Because of the meagerness of Haury's sample, the Mogollones were not well received by other archaeologists. However, in the fourteen years which elapsed between the finish of the Durango digging and the publication of a report, the validity of the separation of the Mogollon had become substantiated.

The question of whether there had been such a group as the Mogollon had particular significance to Earl because of one very important fact: they were much like his San Juan Basket Makers, particularly those of late periods who knew of ceramics. However, even though Mogollones made pottery before the Basket Maker, Earl remained reluctant to give them credit for its invention. To him and his colleagues it now seemed likely that the fundamental notion of pottery making must have filtered north from seats of higher civilization in Mexico. And further that one of the early stages of development which had been dependent upon the gathering of wild edible plants and seeds, such as the Cochise culture of southern Arizona and New Mexico, probably was parent to both Mogollon and Basket Maker.

With the suggestion that Basket Maker and Mogollon were later manifestations of a type of culture which had existed in the Southwest millenia before the time of Christ, Earl was joining with his colleagues in plugging the gap in cultural continuity which formerly had been presumed to have occurred. The mummies of Grand Gulch, del Muerto, or Durango no longer represented the base.

Late or not, the Durango Basket Makers promised to have the oldest date line in the San Juan. Earl stated this belief to Douglass. "There is the 1938 cave wood, which, if it be tied into the established chronology, might easily prove to be one of the most important lots ever exhumed, for certainly the cave culture was primitive far beyond anything that has been dated so far."[61] The actual counting and hooking together of rings which would transmute this suspicion into fact took more than a decade.

The honor of being the oldest dated site was taken away from Mummy Cave in 1941 when Sid Stallings, working for the Laboratory of Anthropology in Santa Fe, read a date of A.D. 217 in a single hunk of wood from Du Pont Cave in Utah. This had been a pure Basket Maker II site filled with body-packed cists excavated in 1920 by Jesse Nusbaum. At the time of work at Du Pont Cave tree-ring reading was taken about as seriously as tea-leaf reading. Nevertheless, Nusbaum with admirable foresight had cached away wood removed from the fill in anticipation of a day when it would prove invaluable. After the chain of dates had been stretched back to A.D. 11 through the help of a fragment at Obelisk Cave (though it will be recalled that this did not represent a cutting date which could be related to human utilization), Earl at every opportunity had urged his friend to secure that Du Pont wood for laboratory analysis, even offering to make the trip after it himself. Eventually the hoard was recovered, and duplicate specimens were mailed off to Douglass and Gladwin. Stallings, however, was the man who ultimately succeeded in dating it.

If Du Pont Basket Maker II had lived in the third century, there was every reason to hope that Durango Basket Maker II had also. Further, the large sample from the latter area offered the hope of something even earlier. By 1942, Douglass had read a cutting date of A.D. 325 in a log found on a floor in the North Shelter, with rings extending back through the 200's to about A.D. 175. Earl remained unsatisfied, his feeling fathered by the knowledge that there were several chronologies at the same site still unanchored.

It was not until 1949, after a wartime cancellation of tree-ring research, that a new date was announced for the Durango material, this one earlier by fourteen years than Du Pont Cave. With the achievement of this earliest authenticated date, Douglass retired from archaeological dating to concentrate full time upon his climatic studies. His disciple, Edmund Schulman, took over.

The key to the entire early sequence lay in a foot-long beam taken from a supporting wall in the west side of Mummy Cave by Deric O'Bryan at the same time that work was in progress at Durango. Gladwin had found that specimen to have an outside date of approximately A.D. 295 with over three hundred rings circling into a core which presumably would have begun life before the Christian Era. He had written Earl of that log back in 1940, but it did not assume personal importance until many years later when Gladwin presented a quarter section to Schulman. Jubilantly, Schulman discovered that the count made by Gladwin checked out, overlapping perfectly with MLK 211 from Obelisk Cave with the A.D. 11 signature. At once one of the floating chronologies from North Shelter moved on to the Christian calendar. On Valentine's Day, 1952, he sent Earl the best of all messages: one beam with bark attached had been felled A.D. 46! Furthermore that two-figured date was confirmed by specimens from at least two different trees. Another lump of black charcoal had an inner date of 59 B.C.

North Shelter had housed Basket Maker people for at least two hundred fourteen years. From more dated wood secured at Talus Village it was known that Basket Maker II culture continued up until at least A.D. 324 and probably lasted much later because the earliest Basket Maker III pithouses of the general area did not come into being until the late 400's. But what of that chronology that still drifted in time? Quite certainly it could be counted upon to push the men of the Animas even farther back in years. "If it is permissable to do so, it may be predicted that when the AFE series is dated—as it surely will be—it will confirm human frequentation of the shelter before the year 1 A.D.."[62] In his report he estimated that occupation to have begun a century or more before Christ.[63]

On this triumphant note Earl's contribution to the science of dendrochronology ended. He had systematically sought out beams and charcoal for each of the Pecos Classification stages of culture: Pueblo V on the Gobernador; Pueblo IV at Kawaikuh; Pueblo III at Aztec Ruins and del Muerto; Pueblo II and Pueblo I at del Muerto, Bennett's Peak, and on the La Plata; Basket Maker III at del Muerto, Red Rocks, and on the La Plata; and Basket Maker II at del Muerto and Durango. No man had done more toward supplying raw data and none was more gratified at the results. "Although I served only as a gatherer of material, I feel that what I did toward making the building of the chronology possible constitutes my most important contribution to Southwestern archaeology."[64]

The report upon the Durango mummies and their material culture was accomplished in spite of ill health which dogged Earl's remaining years. A ruptured vertebral disc put him in the hospital for several operations and long months in a cast, an injury which he attributed to work he had once done upon Morley's house in Yucatan. The vitality which bouyed him through years of brute labor and shattering tragedy suddenly dissolved. All at once he felt old and unaccountably weary as he wrote, "The last few months have been as unsatisfactory as any that I have lived through and with no basic reason on which I can put my finger. Some variety of mental disturbance all the time, very little accomplished in my work and a general lethargy that makes dragging one foot after the other seem a herculean task and constructive thoughts as hard to dredge as pearls. My mind goes back often to the lines "ere the evil days have come when thou shalt say, I find no pleasure in them."[65]

In spite of fits of depression, there came to Earl moments of satisfaction when he gave generously of his time to answer dozens of requests for advice from younger men of science in the university community, from youngsters eagerly searching for a profession, from collectors of antiquities or Navajo rugs or Pueblo pots, and from travelers who desired to visit out of the way spots in Indian country. Because of his well-known memory he was called upon to identify ruins, specimens, or photographs out of the past. His keen interest in the museum led him to serve for many years as advisor, unstinting of time or effort. He was invited to speak before student organizations, faculty audiences, church and civic groups. As long as he was able, he never turned away from these demands. He found further pleasures in the companionship of his second marriage and in watching his daughters mature. As there was time, travel was a favorite pastime when he attended several of the new-generation Pecos Conferences, took Lucile on Southwestern and Mexican tours to many of the places he had known in the past.

Awards had come his way during the multisided career but none meant more than that bestowed upon him by his peers, who selected him as an outstanding scholar who had contributed much to two fields of archaeological endeavor, that which dealt with Mexican antiquities and that devoted to the Southwest. Most important to Earl, the award was given in the name of his beloved friend, Alfred Vincent Kidder. As the second recipient of the coveted medal, Earl stood before an annual meeting of American anthropologists gathered at Tucson, Arizona, the Christmas season of 1953. A noisy buffet supper was in progress, and Earl being short and soft spoken could not gain the undivided attention of the group. Only those near the front could hear his eloquent simplicity or sense the waver in his voice. With genuine humility, yet aware that few men ever reach the towering goals erected in youth, he read his speech.

> To be the recipient of this award is the highest honor that ever has or ever will come my way. For me it has special significance because it is given in the name of the master archaeologist and splendid gentleman who for more than a generation I have been privileged to regard as friend. Long association, both personal and professional, has revealed the depth of his wisdom, the range of his foresight, the richness of his spirit and the warmth of his heart to the end that I hold toward him more respect, admiration and down right affection than I have ever felt toward any other man. Thus it is that the Kidder medal is a treasure that I value more than were it of gold and emeralds.

Delighted though I am to have the medal. I can not accept it with a conscience that is wholly clear. When I measure the little that I have accomplished against the goals that danced before me when I was young, I find myself more worthy of censure than of commendation. The years have sped and the long shelf that one day was to be filled with my writings remains largely empty. Meanwhile, others with the training in scientific methods of approach which was denied to me, have gone far toward raising Southwestern archaeology into the imposing historical edifice it is destined to become. The few roughly hewn blocks that I strove to shape for its foundation will be deeply buried and rightly forgotten. In short, at this moment I feel much as I did one morning long ago at Chichén Itzá. I looked down from the platform in front of the Temple of the Warriors to behold the local Inspector of Antiquities for the Mexican Government ascending the pyramid at a surprising pace. He gave me a bear-like *embrazo* and said "I congratulate you." Up to that moment he had picked flaws in every step of the excavation and reconstruction that I was directing. But one interpretation occurred to me. At last he had become convinced of the rightness of what I was doing. But suspicion lingered. To reassure myself, I asked. "Congratulated for what?" He answered, "Your countryman, Lindbergh, has made a solo flight across the Atlantic." The honor I receive tonight is little more deserved than were his congratulations then.[66]

Retirement came in 1955. The Historical Division of the Carnegie Institution—founded, nourished, and dismantled all within the span of his own association with it— almost simultaneously ended its archaeological projects. Even though he no longer remained officially employed, Earl continued to work with the sandal collection spread out upon his laboratory table, but he lacked the vigor to bring it to completion. The compulsion toward perfection which had characterized his work kept him from terminating the research.

Out in his rose garden one Sunday morning in the summer of 1956, Earl was seized with a heart attack. Rushed to the Boulder hospital, he died by nightfall. Gone was a person superior in the attributes which make a true scholar, magnificent in those which make a man. Ted Kidder, whom Earl always had hoped would write his obituary, paid him tribute. "His real greatness was of the spirit: gentleness, true humility, unfailing readiness to help, utter sincerity, innate appreciation of quality in people and things."[67]

On August 31, 1957, a memorial plaque designed by the National Park Service and donated by Earl's widow and daughters was installed in the portion of the Visitor Center at Aztec Ruins which had served as the Morris home. His kit of tools—whisk broom, dental pick, trowel, geologist pick, paintbrush—were placed on display. That same morning Earl's ashes were scattered within the ruin which more than any other stood close to his heart. The colorful pioneer era in Southwestern archaeology had come to an end.

V.

To Ring Down the Curtain

THE PIONEER PERIOD IN SOUTHWESTERN archaeology was devoted to the gathering of *things*, a direction uncommonly expressed in Earl's professional and private life. Only through assessment of these material objects was the succeeding theoretical phase possible. With hundreds of sites dug and museum chambers crammed, by mid-century scholars were ready to deal with broad syntheses of data concerning man in North America. In seminars they declared that the Southwest had by no means witnessed cultural evolution in total isolation but had received influences from all directions and further that the Southwestern sedentary developments had initiation in a so-called Desert Culture food-gathering society rather than in the paleo-Indian tradition exemplified by the Folsom finds.[1]

The earliest distinctive regional cultural manifestations in the San Juan were those of the Basketmaker. In his final report Earl suggested that this culture, about whose remains in the Durango area he was writing, might have evolved from a Cochise Desert Culture known to have existed six or seven thousand years ago along the modern Mexican border. His daughter, Elizabeth, in her doctoral dissertation—which deals with Red Rocks specifically and Basketmaker III in general—further elaborates that theme by postulating additional cultural influence moving at a later date from south to north along the elevated regions separating New Mexico and Arizona,[2] that is from Mogollon to

Anasazi, bringing into the San Juan at various times elements of agriculture, pottery making, and ceremonialism which were to induce radical change. Other scholars prefer to regard the San Juan Basketmakers as more directly related to Desert Culture groups who dwelt to the north and west of the drainage in the bleak fastnesses of the Great Basin. Caves along the ancient shores of Lake Bonneville, for example, contain numerous deposits attributable to the Desert Culture of the pre-Christian eras.[3] But in the same Great Basin some historic Indians like the Paiute and Shoshone continue Desert Culture marginal type of existence which finds them dependent for survival upon total consumption of all natural food resources, laboriously and endlessly sought. In operation one can observe the ways of the past being carried toward the future as some primitive men have failed to take the necessary steps toward technological advancement and cultural betterment.

Whether one would create the San Juan Basketmakers from Cochise or northern Desert Culture fabric, the fact remains that Basketmaker I, first postulated in the shadow of the Pecos mission the summer of 1927, has been found. With the recognition that Desert Culture and Basketmaker I are one and the same, the complete range of Anasazi prehistory is established. Thanks to the tireless efforts of men like Earl Morris whose only badges of office were the spades they swung, thousands of years of human history stand revealed.

Appendix

Participants of the First Pecos Conference, 1927

Present were the Amsden brothers of the Southwest Museum in Los Angeles—Monroe who had worked at Pueblo Bonito and Charles who had been in the Kayenta with Kidder and would be the author of a masterful book on Navajo weaving and another published posthumously upon the Basketmakers; Harold S. Colton at the University of Pennsylvania and soon to be founder of the Museum of Northern Arizona at Flagstaff and a leading figure in pottery studies; Bert and Hattie Cosgrove working in the Mimbres region of southern New Mexico for the Peabody Museum; A. L. Kroeber of the University of California who had made an early study of Zuñi; Byron Cummings from the University of Arizona, discoverer of Rainbow Bridge and a score of Arizona cliff ruins, a leading teacher of anthropology; Emil Haury of the University of Arizona, later of Gila Pueblo, still later chairman of the department of anthropology at Arizona, regarded by many as the most prominent archaeological figure in the region today; Odd Halseth, then of the Arizona Museum and later of the Pueblo Grande Museum in Phoenix; A. E. Douglass, the astronomer who would give to Southwestern archaeology its greatest gift—time; Clara Lee Frapp (Tanner) who would be a teacher of anthropology at the University of Arizona; Neil Judd of the United States National Museum, excavator of Pueblo Bonito; Walter Hough also of the National Museum, unearther of one of the first pithouse villages; Sylvanus Morley of the Carnegie Institution, a Maya specialist who had begun his career at Cannonball Ruin in southwest Colorado; Oliver Ricketson of the Carnegie Institution, had worked at Pueblo Bonito and was a member of the First Beam Expedition; Frank Roberts of the Bureau of American Ethnology, excavator of Shabik'-

eshchee, Village of the Great Kivas, sites in the Whitewater district and on the Piedra River, Lindenmeier, San Jon, and many other places; Lansing Bloom, K. M. Chapman, H. L. Mera, and Edgar Hewett of the Museum of New Mexico, students of the past and of modern Indians of the Rio Grande valley; Harry Shapiro of the American Museum, concerned with human skeletal development and at that time devoting attention to the Basketmaker strain; Leslie Spier then of the University of Oklahoma, creator of a chronology for sites in the Zuñi district, later director of the University of New Mexico field session in Chaco Canyon and a professor at that school; Jesse L. Nusbaum, then a newly appointed archaeologist for the United States National Park Service and for many years Superintendent of Mesa Verde National Park; Paul Martin then of the Colorado State Museum, later of the Field Museum in Chicago, future worker in the ruins of the Mesa Verde area and the Mogollon Rim; E. B. Renaud of the University of Denver, a student of the lithic complexes of the high plains; M. R. Harrington of the Museum of the American Indian; H. J. Spinden of the Peabody Museum; Erna Gunther later of the University of Washington; Robert Wauchope then of the University of South Carolina and later of Tulane University; T. T. Waterman of the University of Arizona; and Earl Morris and A. V. Kidder whose contributions are dealt with in this text.

Notes to Chapters

NOTES TO CHAPTER ONE

1. Introduction to Morris Memorial Collection.
2. Unpublished manuscript, University of Colorado.
3. Introduction to Morris Memorial Collection, University of Colorado.
4. Morris, 1931, 8.
5. Unpublished manuscript, University of Colorado.
6. Letter of July 15, 1915.
7. Kidder and Guernsey, 1919, 84.
8. Kidder, 1924, 18.

NOTES TO CHAPTER TWO

1. Prudden, 1903, 254.
2. Letter of April 30, 1916.
3. Nelson letter of April 8, 1916.
4. Moorehead, 1908, 256.
5. Letter of April 23, 1916, to Nelson.
6. Morris, 1924, 156.
7. Morris, 1915, 674.
8. Wissler letter of September 24, 1917.
9. July 17, 1918.
10. Report of 1918.
11. Morris, 1944.
12. Letter of September 23, 1918.
13. Letter of December 17, 1918.
14. Letter of April 20, 1921, to Wissler.
15. Wissler letter of April 26, 1921.
16. Letter of January 11, 1922, to Wissler.
17. Morris, 1924, 420.
18. Letter of September 7, 1920, to Wissler.
19. Nelson letter of May 3, 1919.

20. Letter of October 1, 1920.
21. Letter of November 21, 1920.
22. Letter of February 23, 1921, to Wissler.
23. Letter of June 23, 1921.
24. Morris, 1921, 115.
25. Letter of October 1, 1920, to Wissler.
26. Letter of May 16, 1922.
27. Wissler letter of October 16, 1920.
28. Letter of April 11, 1922, to Wissler.
29. Letter of October 27, 1940, to Harold S. Gladwin.

NOTES TO CHAPTER THREE

1. Letter of June 12, 1913, to Hewett.
2. Letter of June 12, 1913.
3. Prudden, 1903, 256.
4. Letter of June 27, 1913, to Hewett.
5. Letter of August 11, 1913, to Hewett.
6. Morris, 1919, 204.
7. Cummings, 1915, 274.
8. Letter of May 28, 1916.
9. Personal correspondence, Frank H. H. Roberts, Jr., February 18, 1960.
10. Report to George N. Pindar, public relations agent, American Museum of Natural History, 1920.
11. Report to Pindar, 1920.
12. Report to Wissler, November, 1921.
13. Letter of November 3, 1921, to Wissler.
14. Letter of December 24, 1922, to Wissler.
15. Shapiro, 1927, 268.
16. Guernsey, 1931.
17. Letter of December 29, 1920, to Kidder.
18. Letter of November 1, 1921.
19. Letter of September 17, 1922, to Henderson.
20. Letter of September 17, 1922.
21. Letter of April 19, 1923.
22. Roberts, 1929, 150.
23. Letter of August 6, 1927.
24. Morris, 1939, 75.
25. Morris, 1939, 26.
26. Judd, 1954.
27. Bryan, 1954.
28. Vivian, 1959.
29. Kidder letter of March 31, 1927.
30. Kidder, 1927, 489.
31. Kidder, 1927, 490.
32. Douglass, 1929.
33. Letter of October 28, 1928.
34. Letter of October 28, 1928.

35. Douglass's letter of July 16, 1929.
36. Douglass letter of September 19, 1929.
37. Letter of October 27, 1929, to Douglass.
38. Douglass letter of October 31, 1929.
39. Letter of October 27, 1929.
40. Letter of November 12, 1932.
41. E. A. Morris, 1959.
42. Letter of April 5, 1933, to Douglass.
43. Letter of February 22, 1930.
44. Letter of June 27, 1930, to Kidder.
45. Letter of April 19, 1930, to Kidder.
46. Brew, 1946, 190.
47. Morris, 1939, 143.
48. Letter of March 22, 1939, to Vannevar Bush, Head of Carnegie Institution.

NOTES TO CHAPTER FOUR

1. Letter of June 13, 1923, to Wissler.
2. Letter of July 26, 1922.
3. Morris, 1925, 129.
4. Letter of June 13, 1923.
5. Morris letter of June 25, 1923, to Wissler.
6. Letter of June 25, 1923.
7. Mindeleff, 1894-95, 116.
8. Kidder letter of February 12, 1924.
9. Letter of October 18, 1923.
10. Morris, 1939, 16.
11. Henderson letter of December 8, 1924.
12. Kidder notes, del Muerto, 1925, University of Colorado.
13. Kidder, 1927, 209.
14. Kidder letter of September 11, 1927.
15. Morris, 1927, 198.
16. Letter of June 24, 1929, to Kidder.
17. Morris, 1939, 18.
18. Morris, 1939, 14.
19. Morris, 1939, 28.
20. Personal correspondence, April 4, 1960.
21. Personal correspondence, March 23, 1960.
22. Morris, 1948, 66.
23. Field notes, del Muerto, 1929, University of Colorado.
24. Field notes, del Muerto, 1929, University of Colorado.
25. Field notes, del Muerto, 1929, University of Colorado.
26. Weyer letter of December 19, 1947.
27. Morley, 1931, 121.
28. Farmington *Times-Hustler*, August 4, 1933.
29. Field notes, del Muerto, 1932, University of Colorado.
30. Kidder letter of October 14, 1932.
31. Field notes, del Muerto, 1932, University of Colorado.

32. Letter of July 9, 1947.
33. Letter of December 10, 1921, to Clark Wissler.
34. Introduction to Morris Memorial Collection, University of Colorado.
35. Introduction to Morris Memorial Collection, University of Colorado.
36. Letter of June 27, 1930, to Kidder.
37. *Santa Fe New Mexican*, September 3, 1931.
38. Douglass telegram, January 7, 1932.
39. Douglass letter to April 10, 1933.
40. Letter of April 14, 1933, to Douglass.
41. Morris, 1932, 484.
42. Morris, 1936.
43. Morris, 1938, 138.
44. Morris, 1939, 43.
45. Letter of September 29, 1937, to A. V. Kidder.
46. Letter of March 11, 1938.
47. Letter of May 19, 1936, to Kidder.
48. Flora letter of September 19, 1937.
49. Flora letter of September 19, 1937.
50. Letter of September 29, 1937.
51. Field journal, Durango, 1938, University of Colorado.
52. Undated letter.
53. Field journal, Durango, 1940, University of Colorado.
54. Field journal, Durango, 1940, University of Colorado.
55. Field journal, Durango, 1940, University of Colorado.
56. Field journal, Durango, 1940, University of Colorado.
57. Letter of June 26, 1942, to Kidder.
58. Letter of May 20, 1944.
59. Kidder letter of September 26, 1945.
60. Morris and Burgh, 1954, 79.
61. Letter of April 15, 1940.
62. Morris, 1952.
63. Morris and Burgh, 1954, 49.
64. Letter of April 25, 1956, to Haury.
65. Letter of September 25, 1953, to Mrs. Harrison.
66. Unpublished manuscript, University of Colorado.
67. Kidder, 1957, 395.

NOTES TO CHAPTER FIVE

1. See Jennings, 1956.
2. E. A. Morris, n.d.
3. Jennings, 1955.

Bibliography

Published Materials Consulted

Amsden, Charles

1949a *Navaho Weaving.* University of New Mexico Press, Albuquerque.

1949b *Prehistoric Southwesterners from Basketmaker to Pueblo.* Southwest Museum, Los Angeles.

Bernheimer, Charles

1923 "Encircling Navajo Mountain with a Pack Train," *National Geographic Magazine,* v. 43, no. 2.

Brew, J. O.

1941 "Preliminary Report of the Peabody Museum Awatobi Expedition of 1939," *Plateau,* v. 13, no. 3.

1946 "Archaeology of Alkali Ridge, Southeastern Utah," *Papers,* Peabody Museum of American Archaeology and Ethnology, v. 21.

Bryan, Kirk

1954 The Geology of Chaco Canyon, New Mexico. *Smithsonian Miscellaneous Collections,* v. 122, no. 7.

Burgh, Robert F.

1957 Obituary, Earl H. Morris. *American Anthropologist,* v. 59, no. 3.

Carlson, Roy L.

1963 Basketmaker III Sites near Durango, Colorado. University of Colorado Studies, *Series in Anthropology,* no. 8. The Earl Morris Papers no. 1.

1965 Eighteenth Century Navajo Fortresses of the Gobernador District. University of Colorado Studies, *Series in Anthropology,* no. 10. The Earl Morris Papers no. 2.

Carnegie Institution

1930-56 *Annual Reports.*

Corbett, John M.

1963 Aztec Ruins National Monument, New Mexico. *National Park Service Historical Handbook Series,* no. 36.

Cummings, Byron
1910 The Ancient Inhabitants of the San Juan Valley. *Bulletin,* University of Utah, v. 3, no. 3, pt. 2.
1915 Kivas of the San Juan Drainage. *American Anthropologist,* v. 17.

De Harport, David L.
1951 An Archaeological Survey of Canyon de Chelly: Preliminary Report of the Field Sessions of 1948, 1949, and 1950. *El Palacio,* v. 58, no. 2.

Dittert, Alfred E.
1958a Salvage Archaeology and the Navajo Project: A Progress Report. *El Palacio,* v. 65, no. 2.
1958b Recent Developments in Navajo Project Salvage Archaeology. *El Palacio,* v. 65, no. 6.

Dittert, Alfred E., Jim J. Hester, and Frank W. Eddy
1961 An Archaeological Survey of the Navajo Reservoir District, Northwestern New Mexico. *Monograph,* School of American Research, no. 23.

Douglass, A. E.
1921 Dating our Prehistoric Ruins. *Natural History,* v. 21, no. 1.
1929 The Secret of the Southwest Solved by Talkative Tree Rings. *National Geographic Magazine,* v. 56, no. 6.
1935 Dating Pueblo Bonito and Other Ruins of the Southwest. National Geographic Society *Pueblo Bonito Series,* no. 1.
1937 Tree Rings and Chronology. *University of Arizona Bulletin,* v. 8, no. 4.

Fisher, Reginald
1947 Obituary, Edgar L. Hewett. *American Antiquity,* v. 13, no. 1.

Fowler, Don D.
1959 The Glen Canyon Archaeological Survey. *Anthropological Papers,* University of Utah, no. 39, Pt. 3.

Fowler, Don D., et al.
1959 The Glen Canyon Archaeological Survey. *Anthropological Papers,* University of Utah, no. 39, Pt. 2.

Gillmor, Frances and Louisa Wade Wetherill
1934 *Traders to the Navajo.* University of New Mexico Press, Albuquerque.

Gladwin, Harold S.
1957 *A History of the Ancient Southwest.* The Bond Wheelwright Company, Portland, Maine.

Guernsey, Sam
1931 Explorations in Northeastern Arizona. *Papers,* Peabody Museum of American Archaeology and Ethnology, v. 12, no. 1.

Guernsey, Sam and A. V. Kidder
1921 Basket Maker Caves of Northeastern Arizona. *Papers,* Peabody Museum of American Archaeology and Ethnology, v. 8, no. 2.

Hewett, Edgar L.
1936 *The Chaco Canyon and its Monuments.* University of New Mexico Press, Albuquerque.

Hooton, E. A.
1925 Obituary, Luis R. Sullivan. *American Anthropologist,* v. 27, no. 2.

Howe, Sherman
1947 *My Story of the Aztec Ruins.* Times Hustler Press, Farmington, New Mexico.

Jennings, Jesse D.
1957 Danger Cave. *Memoir,* Society for American Archaeology, no. 14.
1966 Glen Canyon: A Summary. *Anthropological Papers,* University of Utah, no. 81.

Jennings, Jesse D., editor
1956 The American Southwest: a Problem in Cultural Isolation. *Memoir,* Society for American Archaeology, no. 11.

Jones, V. H. and E. A. Morris
1960 A Seventh Century Record of Tobacco Utilization in Arizona. *El Palacio,* v. 67, no. 4.

Judd, Neil M.
1922 The Pueblo Bonito Expedition of the National Geographic Society. *National Geographic Magazine,* v. 41, no. 3.
1924a Beyond the Clay Hills. *National Geographic Magazine,* v. 45, no. 3.
1924b Two Chaco Canyon Pit Houses. *Annual Report,* Smithsonian Institution.
1930 The Excavation and Repair of Betatakin. *Proceedings,* U.S. National Museum, v. 77.
1940 Progress in the Southwest. Essays in History of Anthropology in North America. *Smithsonian Miscellaneous Collections,* v. 100.
1954 The Material Culture of Pueblo Bonito. *Smithsonian Miscellaneous Collections,* v. 124.
1959a Pueblo del Arroyo, Chaco Canyon, New Mexico. *Smithsonian Miscellaneous Collections,* v. 138, no. 1.
1959b The Braced-up Cliff at Pueblo Bonito. *Annual Report,* Smithsonian Institution.

Kidder, A. V.
1910 Explorations in Southwestern Utah in 1908. *Papers of the School of American Archaeology,* no. 15.
1920 Ruins of the Historic Period in the Upper San Juan Valley, New Mexico. *American Anthropologist,* v. 22.
1924 An Introduction to the Study of Southwestern Archaeology. *Papers,* Phillips Academy, Southwestern Expedition, no. 1.
1927a Southwestern Archaeological Conference. *Science,* v. 66.
1927b The Museum's Expeditions to Canon de Chelly and Canon del Muerto, Arizona. *Natural History,* v. 27, no. 3.
1957a Obituary, Earl H. Morris. *American Antiquity,* v. 22, no. 4, pt. 1.
1957b Reminiscences in Southwestern Archaeology: I. *The Kiva,* v. 25, no. 4.

Kidder, A. V. and Sam Guernsey
1919 Archaeological Explorations in Northeastern Arizona. *Bulletin,* Bureau of American Ethnology, v. 65.
1920 Review: Morris, 1919. *American Anthropologist,* v. 22.
1921 Peabody Museum Arizona Expedition, 1920. *Proceedings,* National Academy of Science, v. 7.

Lipe, William D.
1960 1958 Excavations, Glen Canyon Area. *Anthropological Papers,* University of Utah, no. 44.

Lipe, William D., et al.
1960 1959 Excavations, Glen Canyon Area. *Anthropological Papers,* University of Utah, no. 49.

Lister, Robert H.
1958 The Glen Canyon Survey in 1957. *Anthropological Papers,* University of Utah, no. 30.
1959a The Glen Canyon Right Bank Survey. In "The Glen Canyon Archeological Survey", Don D. Fowler et al. *Anthropological Papers,* University of Utah, no. 39, Pt. 1.
1959b The Waterpocket Fold. In "The Glen Canyon Archeological Survey", Don D. Fowler et al. *Anthropological Papers,* University of Utah, no. 39, Pt. 1.
1959c The Coombs Site. With Chapter, "Pottery" by Florence C. Lister. *Anthropological Papers,* University of Utah, no. 41, Pt. 1.
1961 Twenty Five Years of Archaeology in the Greater Southwest. *American Antiquity,* v. 27, no. 1.

Lister, Robert H., J. Richard Ambler, and Florence C. Lister
1960 The Coombs Site. *Anthropological Papers,* University of Utah, no. 41, Pt. II.

Lister, Robert H. and Florence C. Lister
1961 The Coombs Site. *Anthropological Papers,* University of Utah, no. 41, Pt. III.

Martin, Paul
1938 Archaeological Work in the Ackmen-Lowry Area, Southwestern Colorado, 1937. *Anthropological Series,* Field Museum of Natural History, v. 23, no. 2.
1939 Modified Basket Maker Sites, Ackmen-Lowry Area, Southwestern Colorado, 1938. *Anthropological Series,* Field Museum of Natural History, v. 23, no. 3.

Martin, Paul and John B. Rinaldo
1951 The Southwest Co-Tradition. *Southwestern Journal of Anthropology,* v. 7, no. 3.

McNitt, Frank
1957 *Richard Wetherill: Anasazi.* University of New Mexico Press, Albuquerque.

McWhirt, Jean
1939 Esther. *Mesa Verde Notes,* v. 9, no. 1.

Mindeleff, Cosmos
1894 The Cliff Ruins of Canyon de Chelly, Arizona. *Annual Report,* Bureau of American Ethnology, v. 16.

Moorehead, Warren K.
1908 Ruins at Aztec and on the Rio La Plata, New Mexico. *American Anthropologist,* v. 10, no. 2.

Morley, S. G.
1908 The Excavation of the Cannonball Ruin in Southwestern Colorado. *American Anthropologist,* v. 10, no. 3.
1931 Unearthing America's Ancient History. *National Geographic Magazine,* v. 60, no. 1.

Morris, Ann Axtell
1930 Rock Paintings and Petroglyphs of the American Indian. American Museum of Natural History.

1934 *Digging in the Southwest.* Doubleday, Doran, & Company, New York.

Morris, Elizabeth Ann

1958 A Possible Early Projectile Point from the Prayer Rock District, Arizona. *Southwestern Lore,* v. 24, no. 1.

1959 A Pueblo I Site near Bennett's Peak, Northwestern New Mexico. *El Palacio,* v. 66, no. 5.

n.d. Basketmaker Caves in the Prayer Rock District, Northeastern Arizona. Ph.D. dissertation, University of Arizona (1959).

Nelson, Ethelyn G.

1917 Camp Life in New Mexico. *American Museum Journal,* v. 17, no. 2.

Nelson, Nels C.

1916a Chronology of the Tano Ruins, New Mexico. *American Anthropologist,* v. 18, no. 2.

1916b New Mexico Field Work in 1915. *El Palacio,* v. 8, no. 2.

1917 Excavations of the Aztec Ruins. *American Museum Journal,* v. 18, no. 2.

1920 Notes on Pueblo Bonito, in Pueblo Bonito by George C. Pepper. *Anthropological Papers,* American Museum of Natural History, v. 27.

Nusbaum, Jesse L.

1922 A Basket Maker Cave in Kane County, Utah. *Indian Notes and Monographs,* Museum of American Indian.

Pepper, George C.

1902 The Ancient Basket Makers of Southeastern Utah. *American Museum Journal,* v. 2, no. 4.

1920 Pueblo Bonito. *Anthropological Papers,* American Museum of Natural History, v. 27.

Prudden, Theophil Mitchell

1899 An Elder Brother of the Cliff Dweller. *Harper's Monthly Magazine,* v. 95.

1903 The Prehistoric Ruins of the San Juan Watershed. *American Anthropologist,* v. 5.

1918 A Further Study of Prehistoric Small House Ruins in the San Juan Watershed. *Memoir,* American Anthropological Association, no. 5.

Roberts, Frank H. H.

1929 Shabik'eshchee Village, a late Basket Maker Site in Chaco Canyon, New Mexico. *Bulletin,* Bureau of American Ethnology, v. 92.

1930 Early Pueblo Ruins in the Piedra District, Southwestern Colorado. *Bulletin,* Bureau of American Ethnology, v. 96.

1931 The Ruins of Kiatuthlanna, Eastern Arizona. *Bulletin,* Bureau of American Ethnology, v. 100.

1932 The Village of the Great Kivas on the Zuni Reservation, New Mexico. *Bulletin,* Bureau of American Ethnology, v. 111.

1935 A Survey of Southwestern Archaeology. *American Anthropologist,* v. 37, no. 1.

1942 Review: Morris, 1939. *American Anthropologist,* v. 43, no. 3.

n.d. The Ceramic Sequence in Chaco Canyon and its Relationships to the Culture of the San Juan Basin. Ph.D. dissertation, Harvard University (1927).

Rodeck, Hugo G.

1956 Earl Morris and the University of Colorado Museum, an Appreciation. *Southwestern Lore,* v. 22, no. 3.

Schulman, Edmund

1952 Extension of the San Juan Chronology to B.C. Times. *Tree Ring Bulletin,* v. 18, no. 4.

Shapiro, H. L.

1927 Primitive Surgery, First Evidence of Trephining in the Southwest. *Natural History,* v. 27, no. 3.

Smiley, T. L.

1951 A Summary of Tree Ring Dates from Some Southwestern Archaeological Sites. University of Arizona Laboratory of Tree Ring Research, v. 5.

Steen, Charlie R.

1966 Excavations at Tse-Ta'a, Canyon de Chelly National Monument, Arizona. *Archeological Research Series,* no. 9. National Park Service.

Taylor, W. W.

1954 Southwestern Archaeology: Its History and Theory. *American Anthropologist,* v. 56, no. 4.

Vivian, R. Gordon

1959 The Hubbard Site. *Archeological Research Series,* National Park Service, v. 5.

Vivian, Gordon and Tom W. Mathews

1964 Kin Kletso, A Pueblo III Community in Chaco Canyon, New Mexico. *Technical Series,* Southwestern Monuments Association, v. 6, pt. 1.

Wendorf, Fred, Nancy Fox, and Orian L. Lewis, eds.

1956 Pipeline Archaeology. Laboratory of Anthropology and Museum of Northern Arizona.

Wheat, Joe Ben

1955 Mogollon Culture Prior to A.D. 1000. *Memoir,* Society for American Archaeology, no. 10.

Wissler, Clark

1921 Dating our Prehistoric Ruins. *Natural History,* v. 21, no. 1.

1927 The Aztec Ruin National Monument. *Natural History,* v. 27, no. 3.

1930 News note, *American Anthropologist,* v. 32.

NEWSPAPER ARTICLES CONSULTED

Aztec Ruins

Farmington *Times Hustler,* n.d., 1918

Rocky Mountain News, November 16, 1919

New York Tribune, n.d., 1922

New York American, March 26, 1922

New York Tribune, February 25, 1923

New York Telegram and Evening Mail, March 9, 1924

Durango

Durango *Herald Democrat,* October 1, 1945

Denver Post, October 2, 1945

Durango News, October 12, 1945

La Plata

Boulder Daily Camera, January 20, 1940

Moki Canyon

New York Post, July 30, 1929

Red Rocks

Santa Fe New Mexican, September 2, 1931

Rocky Mountain News, January 3, 1932

Yucatan

New York Times, January 10, 1932

Aztec Independent Review, August 4, 1933

Farmington Times Hustler, August 4, 1933

A BIBLIOGRAPHY OF EARL H. MORRIS

A BIBLIOGRAPHY OF EARL H. MORRIS

(Reprinted from *Southwestern Lore,* vol. XXII, No. 3, December 1956, through the courtesy of Elizabeth Ann Morris and the Colorado Archaeological Society)

1911 The Cliff Dwellers of the San Juan. *Colorado.* 2:7:27-30. Denver, Colorado.

1915 The Excavation of a Small Ruin near Aztec, San Juan County, New Mexico. *American Anthropologist,* n.s. 17:4:666-84. Lancaster, Pa.

1916 Explorations in New Mexico—Field Work in the La Plata Valley done by the American Museum-University of Colorado Expedition. 1916. Tribune Print. Farmington, New Mexico.

1917 The Place of Coiled Ware in Southwestern Pottery. *American Anthropologist,* n.s. 19:1:24-29. Lancaster, Pa.

1917a The Ruins at Aztec. *El Palacio,* 4:3:43-69. Santa Fe, N.M.

1917b Discoveries at the Aztec Ruin. *American Museum Journal,* 17:3:169-80. New York, N.Y.

1917c Explorations in New Mexico. *American Museum Journal,* 17:7:461-71. New York, N.Y.

1918 Further Discoveries at the Aztec Ruin. *American Museum Journal,* 18:7:602-10. New York, N.Y.

1919 Preliminary Account of the Antiquities of the Region between the Mancos and La Plata Rivers in Southwestern Colorado. *Thirty-Third Annual Report,* Bureau of American Ethnology. pp. 155-206. Washington, D.C.

1919a The Aztec Ruin. *Anthropological Papers,* American Museum of Natural History, 26:pt. 1. New York, N.Y.

1919b Further Discoveries at the Aztec Ruin. *El Palacio,* 6:17-23, 26. Santa Fe, New Mexico.

1921 Chronology of the San Juan Area. *Proceedings of the National Academy of Sciences,* 7:18-22.

1921a The House of the Great Kiva at the Aztec Ruin. *Anthropological Papers,* 26: pt. 2. American Museum of Natural History. New York, N.Y.

1922 An Unexplored Area of the Southwest. *American Museum Journal,* 22:498-515. New York, N.Y.

1924 Burials in the Aztec Ruin: the Aztec Ruin Annex. *Anthropological Papers,* 26: pts. 3 & 4. American Museum of Natural History, New York, N.Y.

1924a Report of E. H. Morris on the Excavations at Chichen Itza, Mexico. *Carnegie Institution of Washington Yearbook,* No. 23:211-213. Washington, D.C.

1925 Exploring in the Canyon of Death. *National Geographic Magazine,* 48:263-300. Washington, D.C.

1925a Report of E. H. Morris on the Temple of the Warriors (station 4). *Carnegie Institution of Washington Yearbook,* No. 24:252-59. Washington, D.C.

1925b Report of E. H. Morris on the mural paintings of the Temple of the Warriors (station 4). *Carnegie Institution of Washington Yearbook,* No. 24:260-62. Washington, D.C.

1925c Report of E. H. Morris on the temple on the northeast bank of the Xtoloc cenote (station 3). *Carnegie Institution of Washington Yearbook,* No. 24:263-65. Washington, D.C.

1926 Report of E. H. Morris on the Excavation of the Temple of the Warriors and the northwest colonnade, (Stations 4 and 10). *Carnegie Institution of Washington Yearbook,* No. 25:282-86. Washington, D.C.

1927 Report of E. H. Morris on the Temple of the Warriors and the northwest colonnade, (Stations 4 and 10). *Carnegie Institution of Washington Yearbook,* No. 26:240-46. Washington, D.C.

1927a The Beginnings of Pottery Making in the San Juan Area, Unfired Prototypes and the Wares of the Earliest Ceramic Period. *Anthropological Papers,* 28: pt. 2. American Museum of Natural History, New York, N.Y.

1928 Turquoise Plaque. *El Palacio,* 24:349-50. Santa Fe, N.M.

1928a Temple of Warriors Rebuilt. *El Palacio,* 25:425-26. Santa Fe, N.M.

1928b Report of E. H. Morris on the excavation and repair of the Temple of the Warriors (station 4). *Carnegie Institution of Washington Yearbook,* No. 27:293-97. Washington, D.C.

1928c Notes on Excavations in the Aztec Ruin. *Anthropological Papers,* 26: pt. 5. American Museum of Natural History, New York, N.Y.

1928d An Aboriginal Salt Mine at Camp Verde, Arizona. *Anthropological Papers,* 30: pt. 3. American Museum of Natural History, New York, N.Y.

1929 Archaeological field work in North America during 1928: Arizona. *American Anthropologist,* n.s. 31:339-40. Menasha, Wisconsin.

1929a Early Pueblos. *El Palacio,* 27:279-81. Santa Fe, N.M.

1931 Archaeological Research in southwestern United States: the San Juan Basin. *Carnegie Institution of Washington Yearbook,* No. 30:139-41. Washington, D.C.

1931a The Temple of the Warriors. *Art and Archaeology,* 31:298-305. Washington, D.C.

1931b El Templo de los Guerros. (In Los Mayas de la region central de America). *Carnegie Institution of Washington, Supplementary Publications,* No. 4:7-12. Washington, D.C.

1931c *The Temple of the Warriors.* Charles Scribner's Sons. New York, N.Y.

1931d *The Temple of the Warriors.* Part 2 in The Maya of Middle America. Carnegie Institution of Washington News Service Bulletin, School Edition. 2:17-21. Washington, D.C.

1931e Earl H. Morris, Jean Charlot, and A. A. Morris. *The Temple of the Warriors,* 2 vols. Carnegie Institution of Washington Pub. 406. Washington, D.C.

1934 E. H. Morris and G. Stromsvik. Quirigua. Annual Report of the Division of Historical Research—Section Aboriginal American History. *Yearbook,* No. 33:86-89. Carnegie Institution of Washington, Washington, D.C.

1934a Speaker Chief's House, *Mesa Verde Notes,* 5:1:4-6. Mesa Verde National Park, Colorado.

1935 *Adventure.* The Eleusis of Chi Omega. 37:4. George Banta Publishing Co. Menasha, Wisconsin.

1936 Archaeological Background of Dates in Early Arizona Chronology. *Tree-Ring Bulletin.* 2:4:34-6. Tucson, Arizona.

1937 Southwestern Research. Annual Report of the Division of Historical Research. *Yearbook* No. 36:17-18. Carnegie Institution of Washington, Washington, D.C.

1938 Mummy Cave. *Natural History,* 42:127-38. New York, N.Y.

1939 Archaeological Studies in the La Plata District. *Carnegie Institution of Washington,* Pub. 519. Washington, D.C.

1940 Southwestern Archaeology. Annual Report of the Chairman of the Division of Historical Research. *Yearbook* No. 39:274-75. Carnegie Institution of Washington, Washington, D.C.

1941 Southwestern Archaeology. Annual Report of the Chairman of the Division of Historical Research. *Yearbook* No. 40:304-5. Carnegie Institution of Washington, Washington, D.C.

1941a Prayer Sticks in Walls of Mummy Cave Tower, Canyon del Muerto. *American Antiquity,* 6:3:227-30. Menasha, Wisc.

1941b Earl H. Morris and R. F. Burgh. Anasazi Basketry-Basket Maker II through Pueblo III. Carnegie Institution of Washington Pub. 533. Washington, D.C.

1941c Book Review of Archaeological Work in the Ackmen-Lowry Area, Southwestern Colorado and of Modified Basket Maker Sites, Ackmen-Lowry Area, Southwestern Colorado. Paul S. Martin, Anthropological Series, Field Museum of Natural History, 23:2 & 3. Chicago, Ill. in *American Antiquity,* 6:4:378-382. Menasha, Wisc.

1942 Book Review of Excavations in the Forestdale Valley, East-Central Arizona. Emil W. Haury, University of Arizona Bulletin, No. 4, 1940. In *American Anthropologist,* 44:3:485-87. Menasha, Wisc.

1942a Southwestern United States. Annual Report of the Chairman of the Division of Historical Research. *Yearbook* No. 41:272-3. Carnegie Institution of Washington, Washington, D.C.

1943 Southwestern Archaeology. Annual Report of the Chairman of the Division of Historical Research. *Yearbook* No. 42:179-80. Carnegie Institution of Washington, Washington, D.C.

1944 Southwestern Archaeology. Annual Report of the Chairman of the Division of Historical Research. *Yearbook* No. 43:174-6. Carnegie Institution of Washington, Washington, D.C.

1944a Anasazi Sandals. Clearing House for Western Museums. *News Letters* 68/69: 239-41. Denver, Colorado.

1944b Adobe Bricks in a Pre-Spanish Wall Near Aztec, New Mexico. *American Antiquity,* 9:4:434-438. Menasha.

1946 Early Cultures of Southwestern United States. Annual Report of the Chairman of the Division of Historical Research. *Yearbook* 45:214-15. Carnegie Institution of Washington, Washington, D.C.

1947 Early Cultures of Southwestern United States. Annual Report of the Chairman of the Division of Historical Research. *Yearbook* No. 46:192-3. Carnegie Institution of Washington, Washington, D.C.

1948 Early Cultures of Southwestern United States. Annual Report of the Chairman of the Division of Historical Research. *Yearbook* No. 47:220-21. Carnegie Institution of Washington, Washington, D.C.

1948a Tomb of the Weaver. *Natural History,* 57:2:66-71. New York, N.Y.

1948b Book Review of Prehistoric Indians of the Southwest. Marie Wormington, Colorado Museum of Natural History, Pop. Series, No. 7, 1947. In *Southwestern Lore* 8:4:70. Colorado Archaeological Society. Gunnison, Colorado.

1949 Basket Maker II Dwellings near Durango, Colorado. *Tree-Ring Bulletin,* 15: 4:33-34. Tucson, Arizona.

1950 Journey to Copan. (in *Morleyana,* pp. 154-9) American School of Prehistoric Research and the Museum of New Mexico, Santa Fe, N.M.

1950a Southwestern Prehistory. Annual Report of the Chairman of the Division of Historical Research, *Yearbook* No. 49:205-6. Carnegie Institution of Washington, Washington, D.C.

1951 Basket Maker III Human Figurines from Northeastern Arizona. *American Antiquity,* 17:1:33-40. Menasha, Wisc.

1951a Book Review of Excavations in Mesa Verde National Park. Deric O'Bryan. In *American Antiquity,* 17:1:72-3. Menasha, Wisc.

1952 Note on the Durango Dates. *Tree-Ring Bulletin,* 18:4:36. Tucson, Arizona.

1952a Southwestern Prehistory. Annual Report of the Director of the Department of Archaeology. *Yearbook* 51:272. Carnegie Institution of Washington, Washington, D.C.

1953 Utilized Fiber Materials, in Wendorf, Fred, Archaeological Studies in the Petrified Forest National Monument, p. 154. Museum of Northern Arizona, *Bulletin* No. 27. Flagstaff, Arizona.

1953a Artifacts of Perishable Material from Te'ewi. Archaeological Institute of America. School of American Research, Monographs, 17:103. Santa Fe, N.M.

1954 Earl H. Morris and Robert F. Burgh, Basketmaker II Sites Near Durango, Colorado. Carnegie Institution of Washington Publication 604. Washington, D.C.

1955 Southwestern Prehistory. Annual Report of the Director of the Department of Archaeology. *Yearbook* 54:295-97. Carnegie Institution of Washington, Washington, D.C.

INDEX